SUNNYVILLE STORIES

VOLUME 1
BY MAX WEST

Published by
Different Mousetrap Press LLC
Greensboro, NC, United States

Printed in the United States of America

First Printing: July 2012
Second Printing: January 2013

This work is completely fictional. Any resemblance to actual persons, names (living or dead), places, and events is entirely coincidence.

This book collects episode 1-3 of Sunnyville Stories.

ISBN-10: 0-615-65392-8

ISBN-13: 978-0-615-65392-1

CONTENTS

Dedicated to
Benjamin Rodriguez,
who believed in me
when I did not

For Tom Motley, Tom Hart, Matt Madden, John Ruggieri,
Matthew Archambault, Sal Amendola, Josh Bayer,
Laura Weinstein, Nelson DeCastro, Stephen Gaffney,
and all the students of the School of Visual Arts Independent
Comics Seminar

For all the dedicated fans of Sunnyville Stories,
who enjoyed it from the very beginning

This book is dedicated to the memory of
Rusty Haller (1964-2009), who saw much
potential in me.

INTRODUCTION

Ladies and gentlemen, you hold in your hands
a cutting-edge work of over three years in the
making. Sunnyville Stories is a piece of
careful calculation while at the same time,
a revealing work that came from within.
Sunnyville is the genuine article, drawn from
my own solid experiences as well as from
the grace and charm of a bygone era.

It is that sense of nostalgia and that down-to-earth
feeling that makes the past come alive.

And that is what Sunnyville is all about.

\- Max West,
March 2012

Episode 1 - Beginnings

Written and Illustrated by
Max West

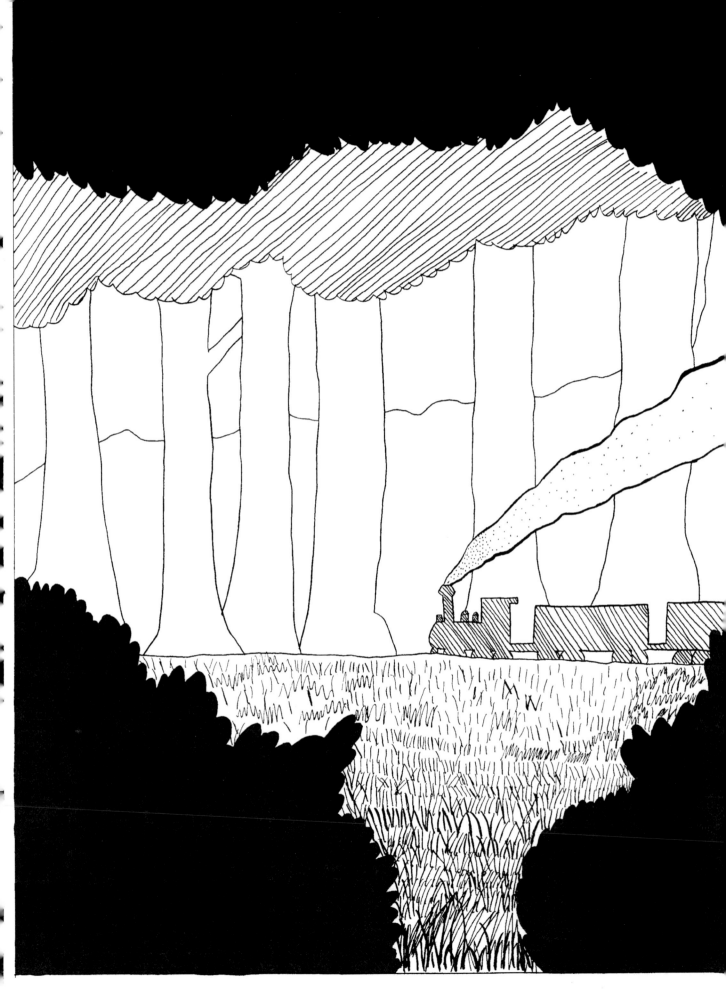

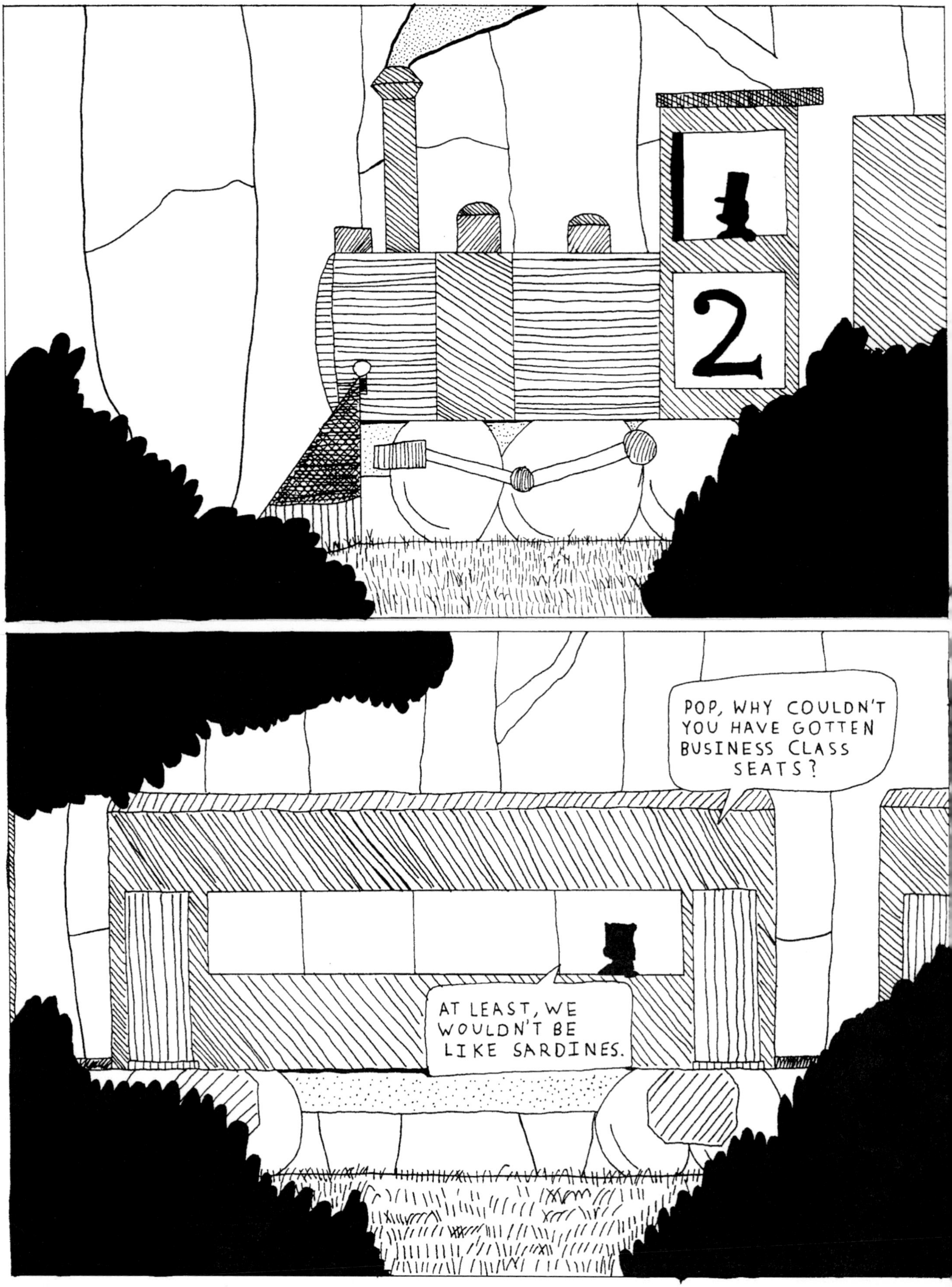
2
POP, WHY COULDN'T YOU HAVE GOTTEN BUSINESS CLASS SEATS?
AT LEAST, WE WOULDN'T BE LIKE SARDINES.

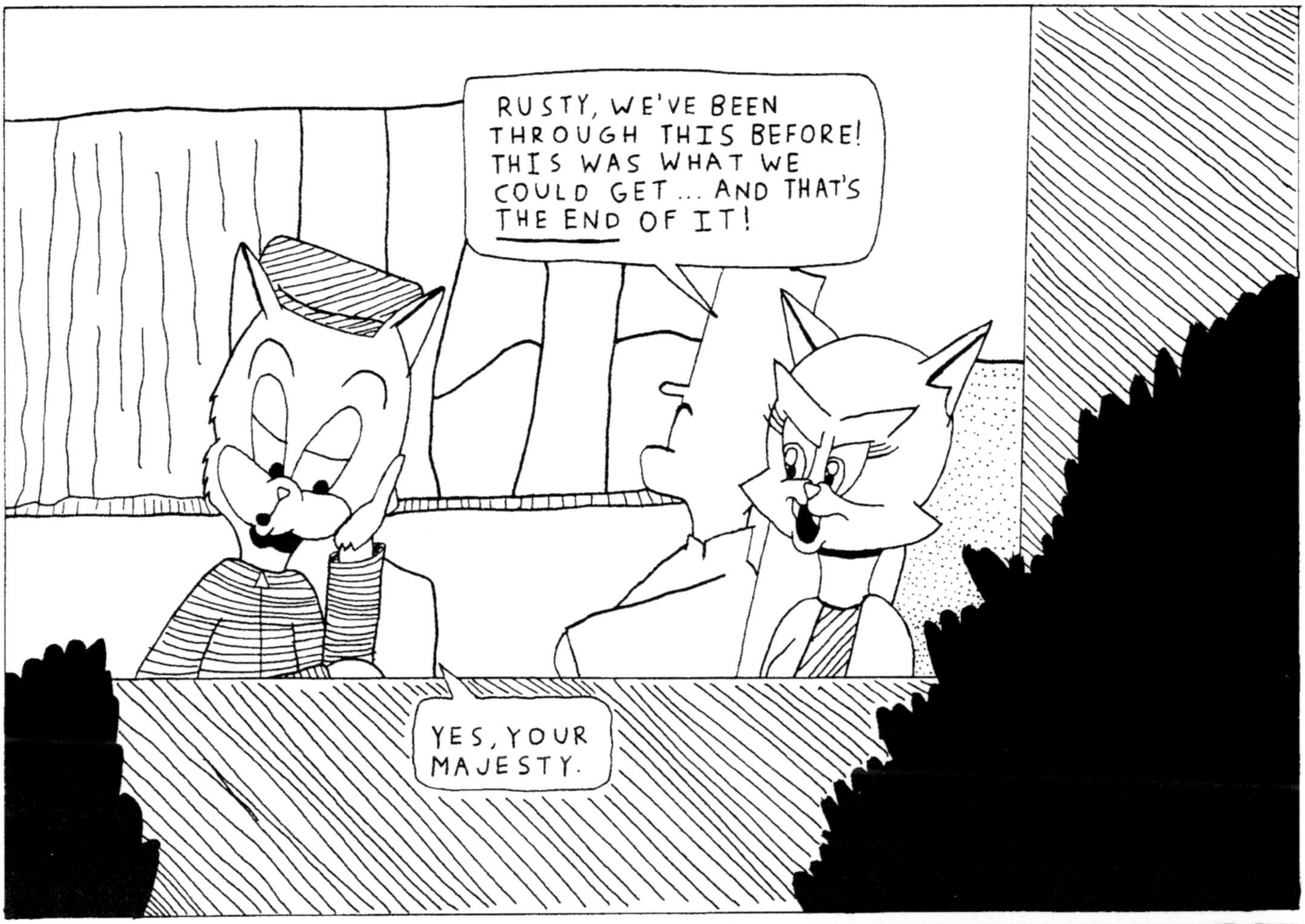
RUSTY, WE'VE BEEN THROUGH THIS BEFORE! THIS WAS WHAT WE COULD GET... AND THAT'S THE END OF IT!
YES, YOUR MAJESTY.
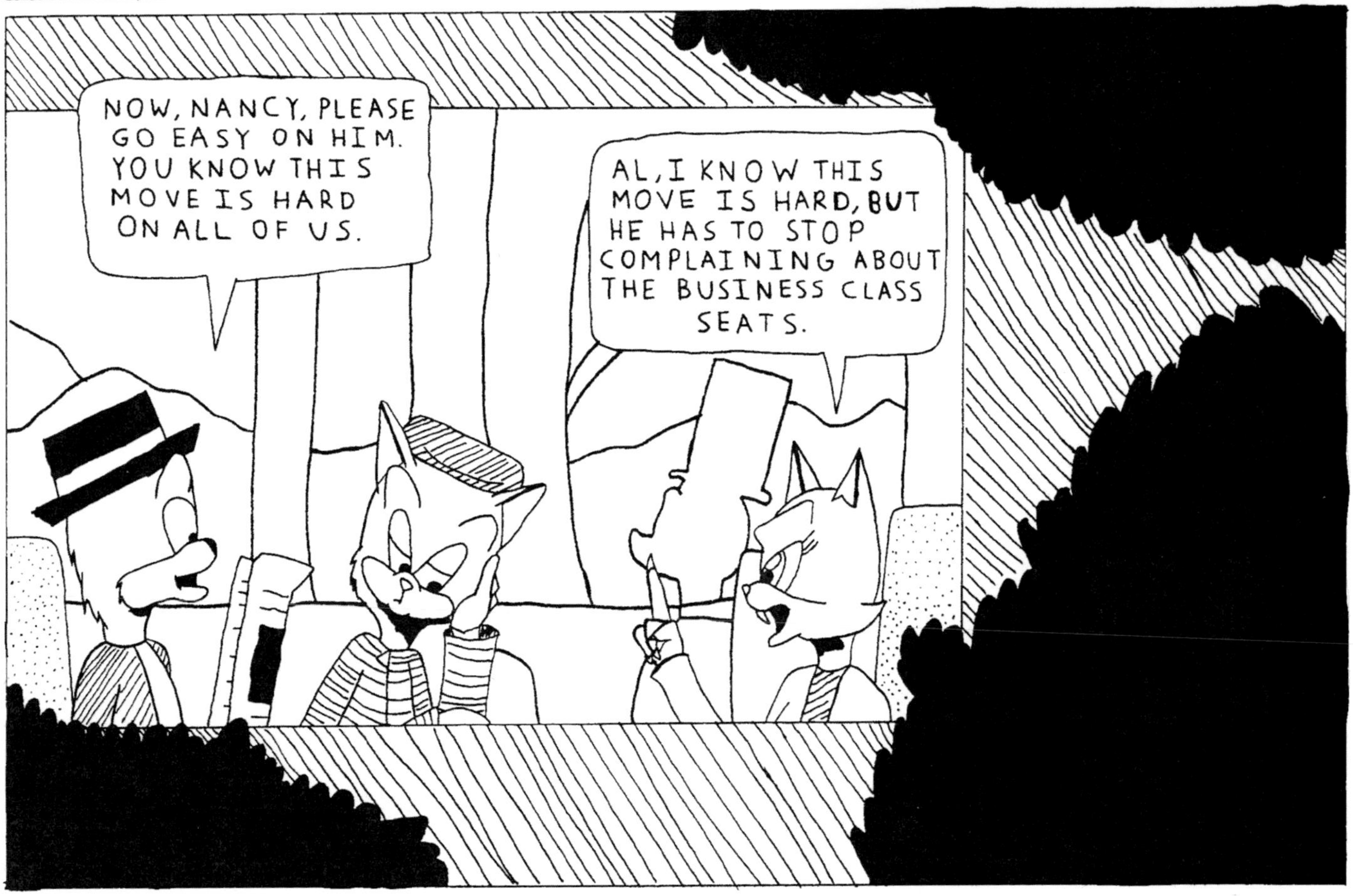
NOW, NANCY, PLEASE GO EASY ON HIM. YOU KNOW THIS MOVE IS HARD ON ALL OF US.
AL, I KNOW THIS MOVE IS HARD, BUT HE HAS TO STOP COMPLAINING ABOUT THE BUSINESS CLASS SEATS.

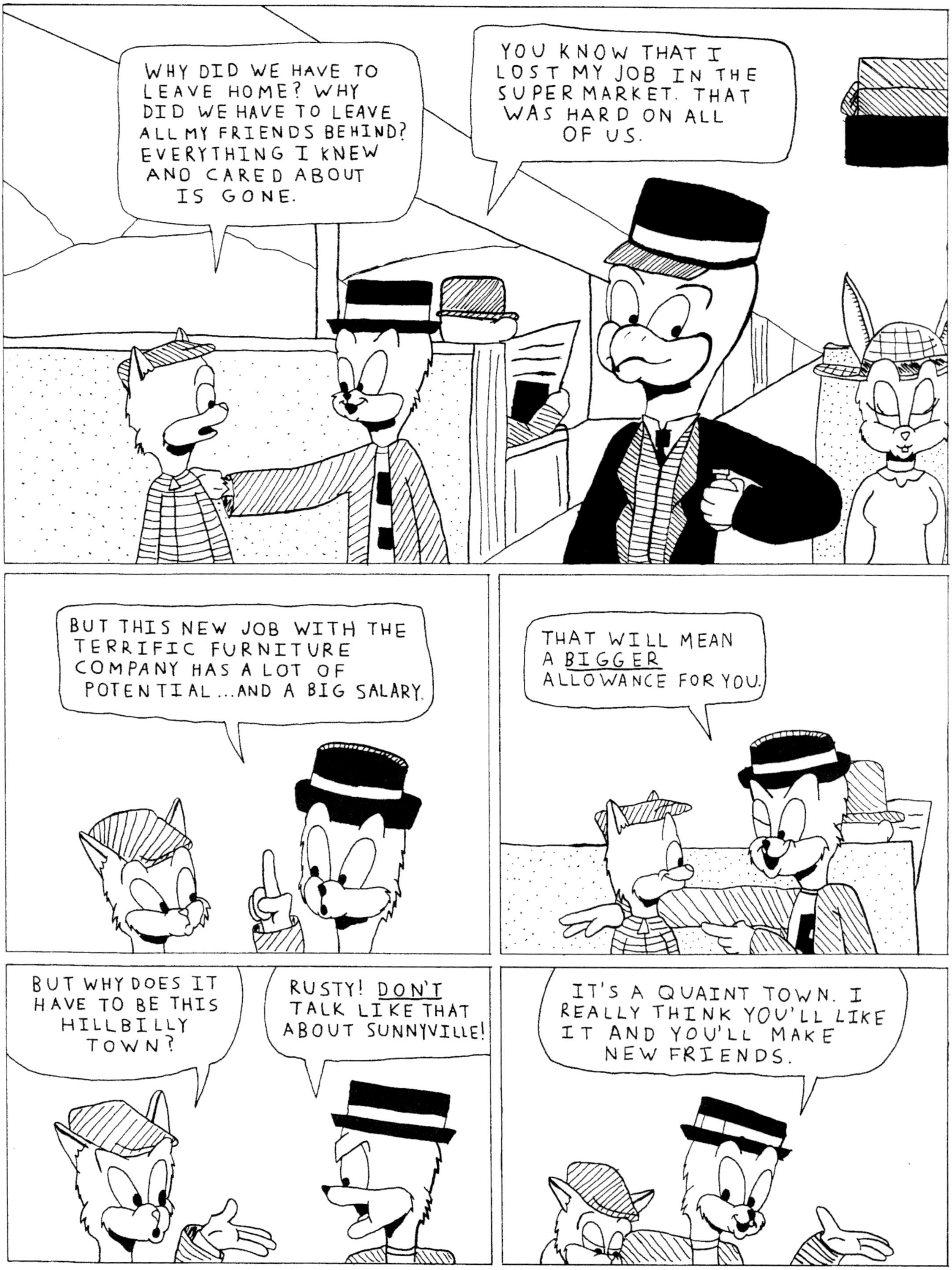

WHY DID WE HAVE TO LEAVE HOME? WHY DID WE HAVE TO LEAVE ALL MY FRIENDS BEHIND? EVERYTHING I KNEW AND CARED ABOUT IS GONE.
YOU KNOW THAT I LOST MY JOB IN THE SUPERMARKET. THAT WAS HARD ON ALL OF US.
BUT THIS NEW JOB WITH THE TERRIFIC FURNITURE COMPANY HAS A LOT OF POTENTIAL...AND A BIG SALARY.
THAT WILL MEAN A BIGGER ALLOWANCE FOR YOU.
BUT WHY DOES IT HAVE TO BE THIS HILLBILLY TOWN?
RUSTY! DON'T TALK LIKE THAT ABOUT SUNNYVILLE!
IT'S A QUAINT TOWN. I REALLY THINK YOU'LL LIKE IT AND YOU'LL MAKE NEW FRIENDS.

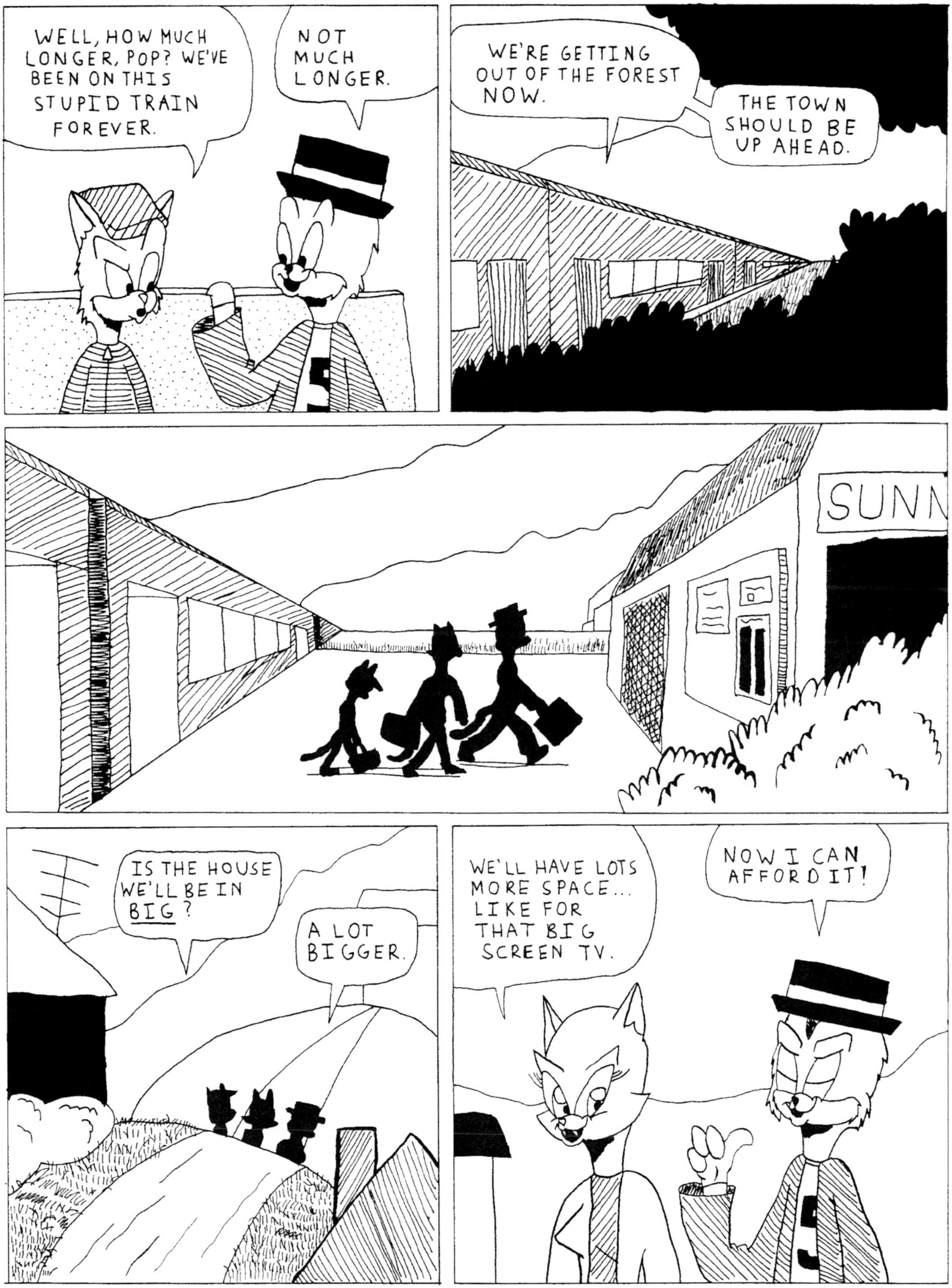
WELL, HOW MUCH LONGER, POP? WE'VE BEEN ON THIS STUPID TRAIN FOREVER.
NOT MUCH LONGER.
WE'RE GETTING OUT OF THE FOREST NOW.
THE TOWN SHOULD BE UP AHEAD.
SUNN
IS THE HOUSE WE'LL BE IN BIG?
A LOT BIGGER.
WE'LL HAVE LOTS MORE SPACE... LIKE FOR THAT BIG SCREEN TV.
NOW I CAN AFFORD IT!

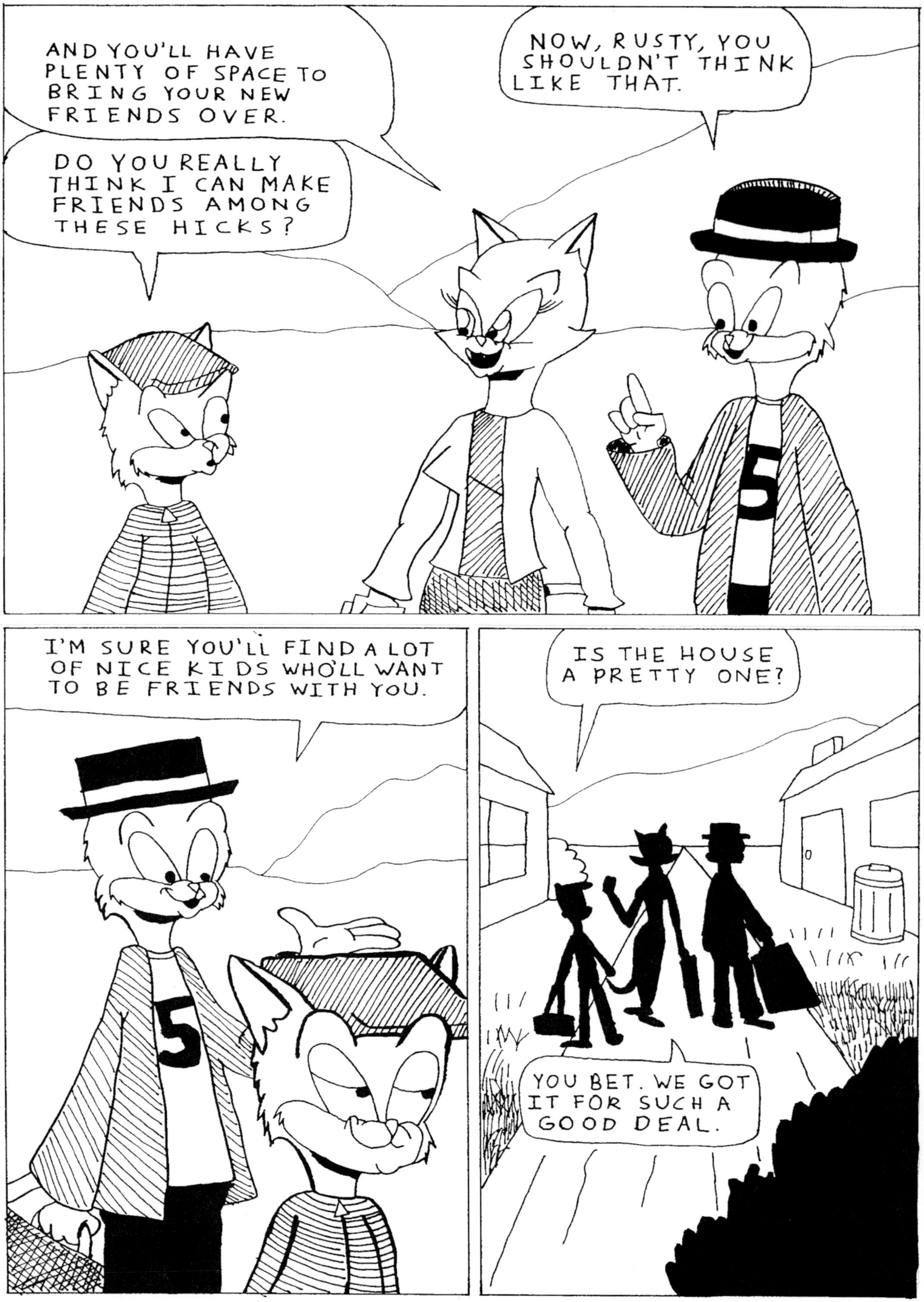
AND YOU'LL HAVE PLENTY OF SPACE TO BRING YOUR NEW FRIENDS OVER.
DO YOU REALLY THINK I CAN MAKE FRIENDS AMONG THESE HICKS?
NOW, RUSTY, YOU SHOULDN'T THINK LIKE THAT.
I'M SURE YOU'LL FIND A LOT OF NICE KIDS WHO'LL WANT TO BE FRIENDS WITH YOU.
IS THE HOUSE A PRETTY ONE?
YOU BET. WE GOT IT FOR SUCH A GOOD DEAL.

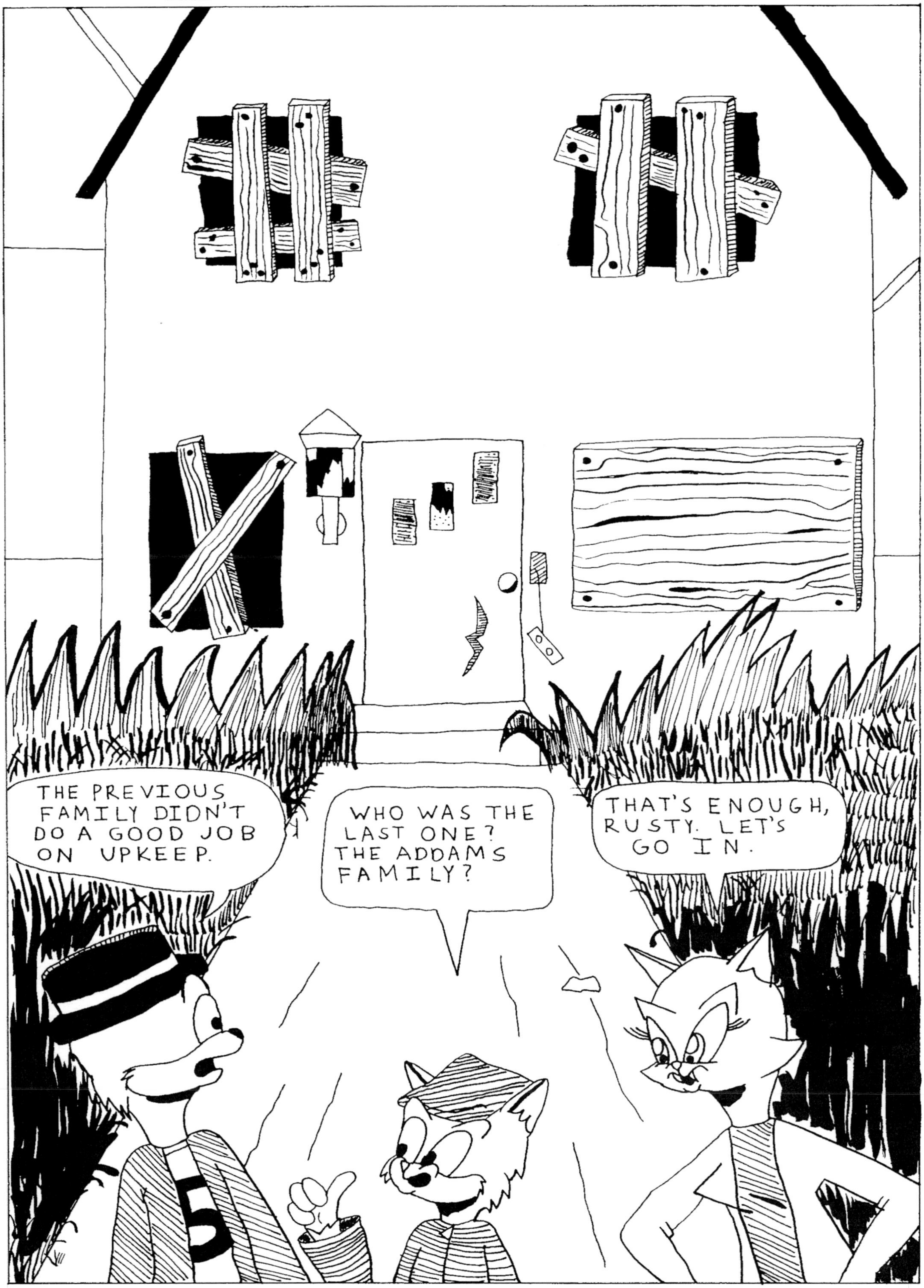
THE PREVIOUS FAMILY DIDN'T DO A GOOD JOB ON UPKEEP.
WHO WAS THE LAST ONE? THE ADDAMS FAMILY?
THAT'S ENOUGH, RUSTY. LET'S GO IN.

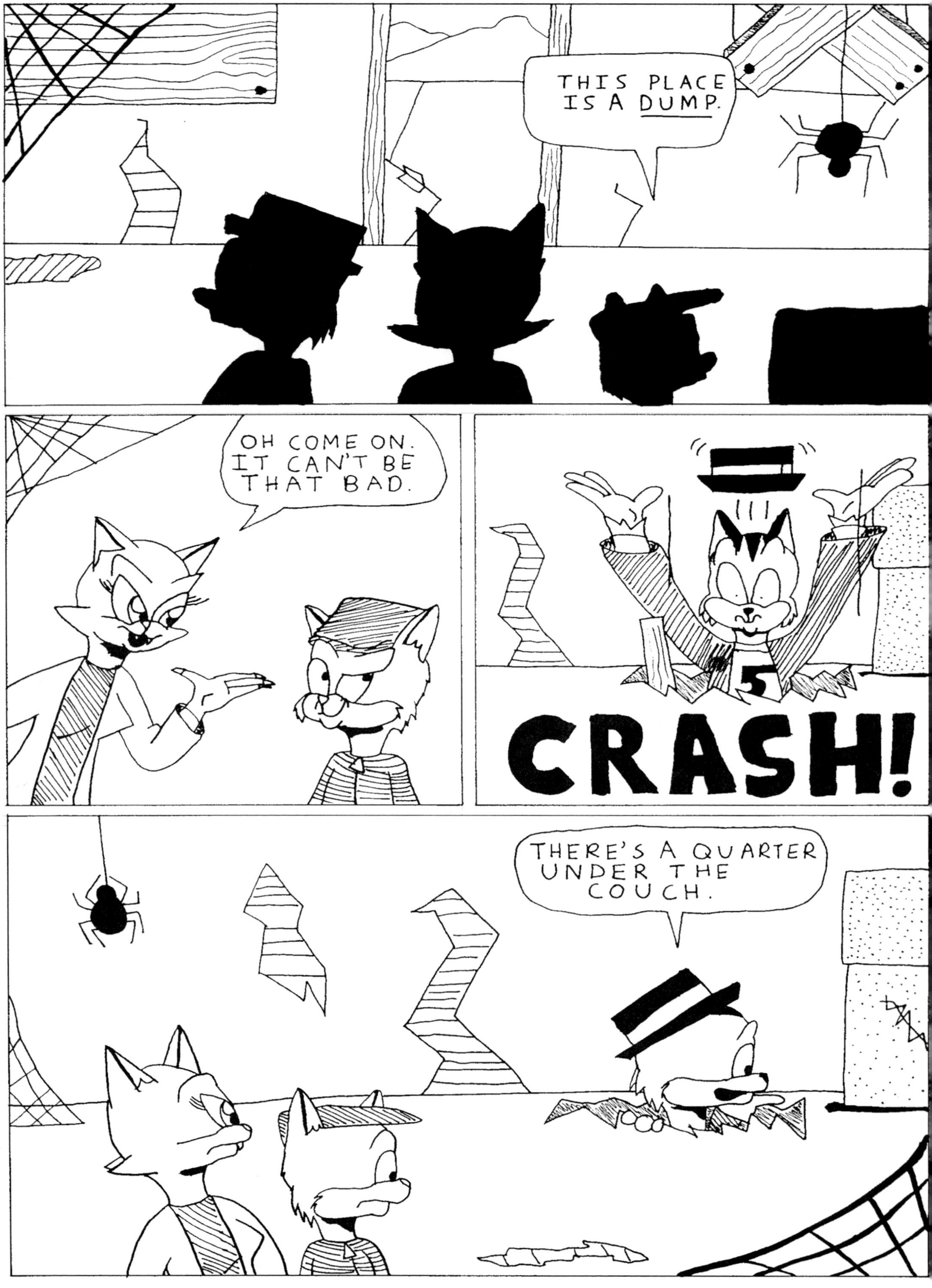
THIS PLACE IS A DUMP.
OH COME ON. IT CAN'T BE THAT BAD.
5
CRASH!
THERE'S A QUARTER UNDER THE COUCH.

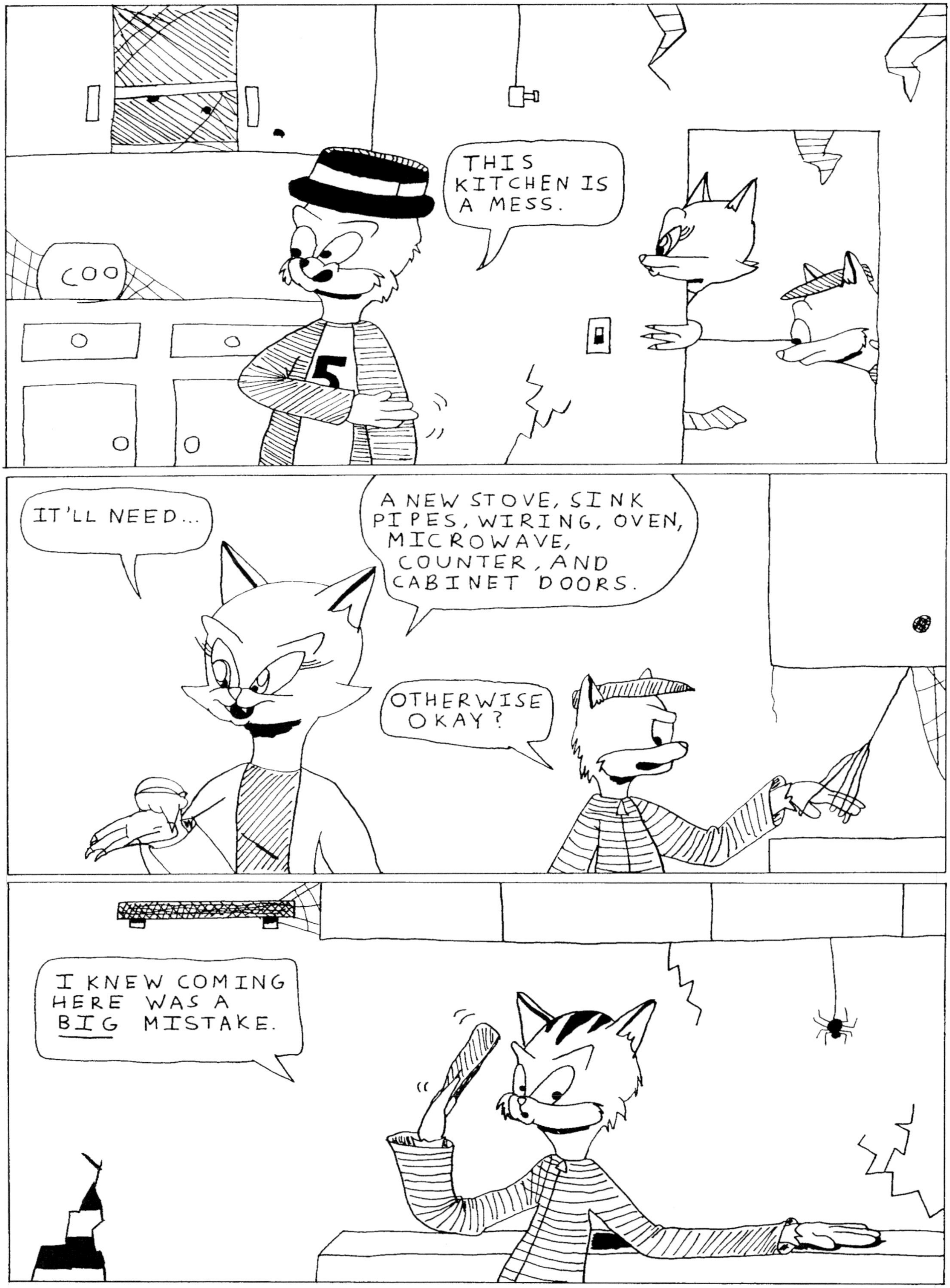
THIS KITCHEN IS A MESS.
COO
IT'LL NEED...
A NEW STOVE, SINK PIPES, WIRING, OVEN, MICROWAVE, COUNTER, AND CABINET DOORS.
OTHERWISE OKAY?
I KNEW COMING HERE WAS A BIG MISTAKE.

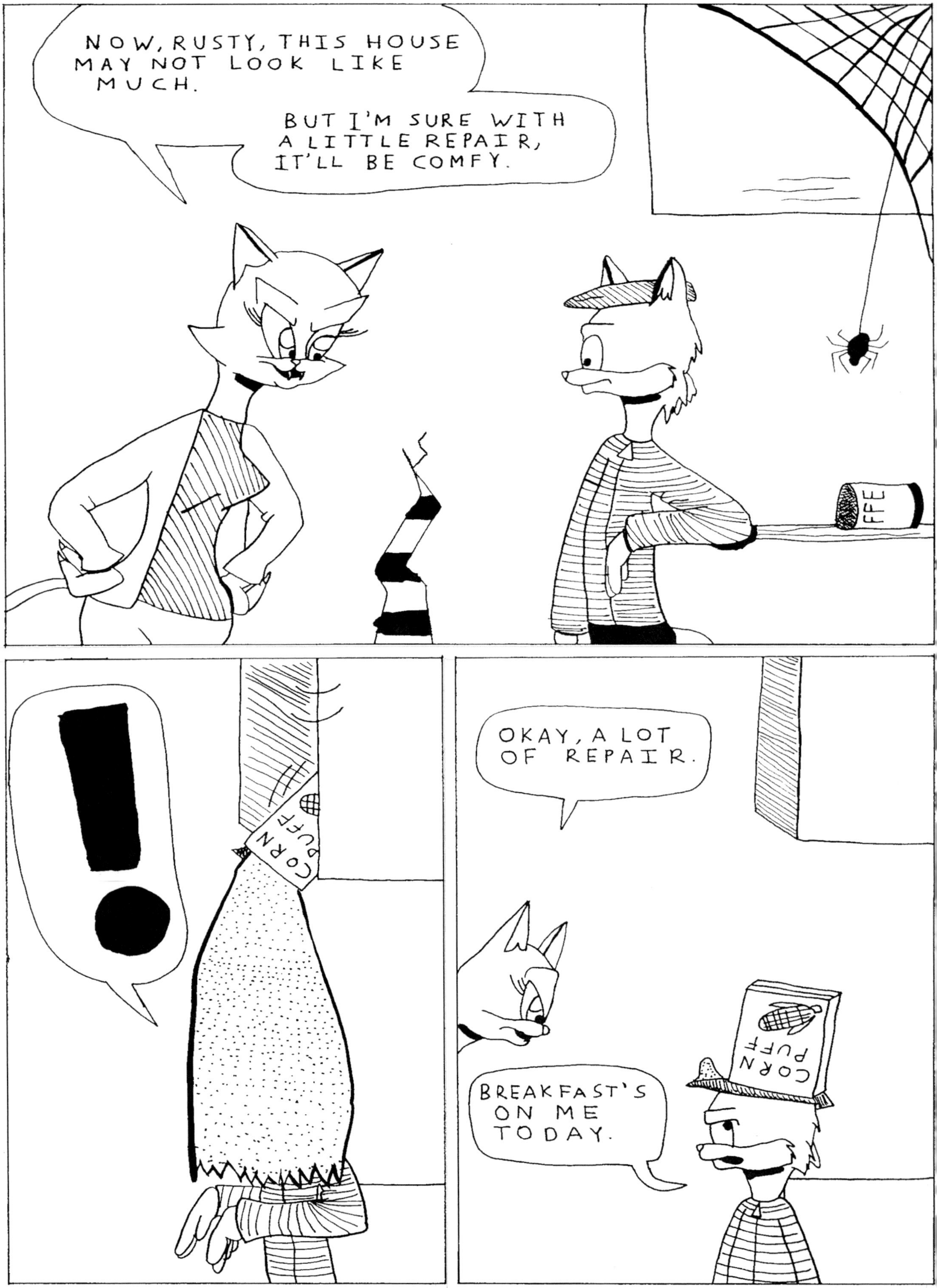
NOW, RUSTY, THIS HOUSE MAY NOT LOOK LIKE MUCH.
BUT I'M SURE WITH A LITTLE REPAIR, IT'LL BE COMFY.
FFE
!
CORN PUFF
OKAY, A LOT OF REPAIR.
CORN PUFF
BREAKFAST'S ON ME TODAY.

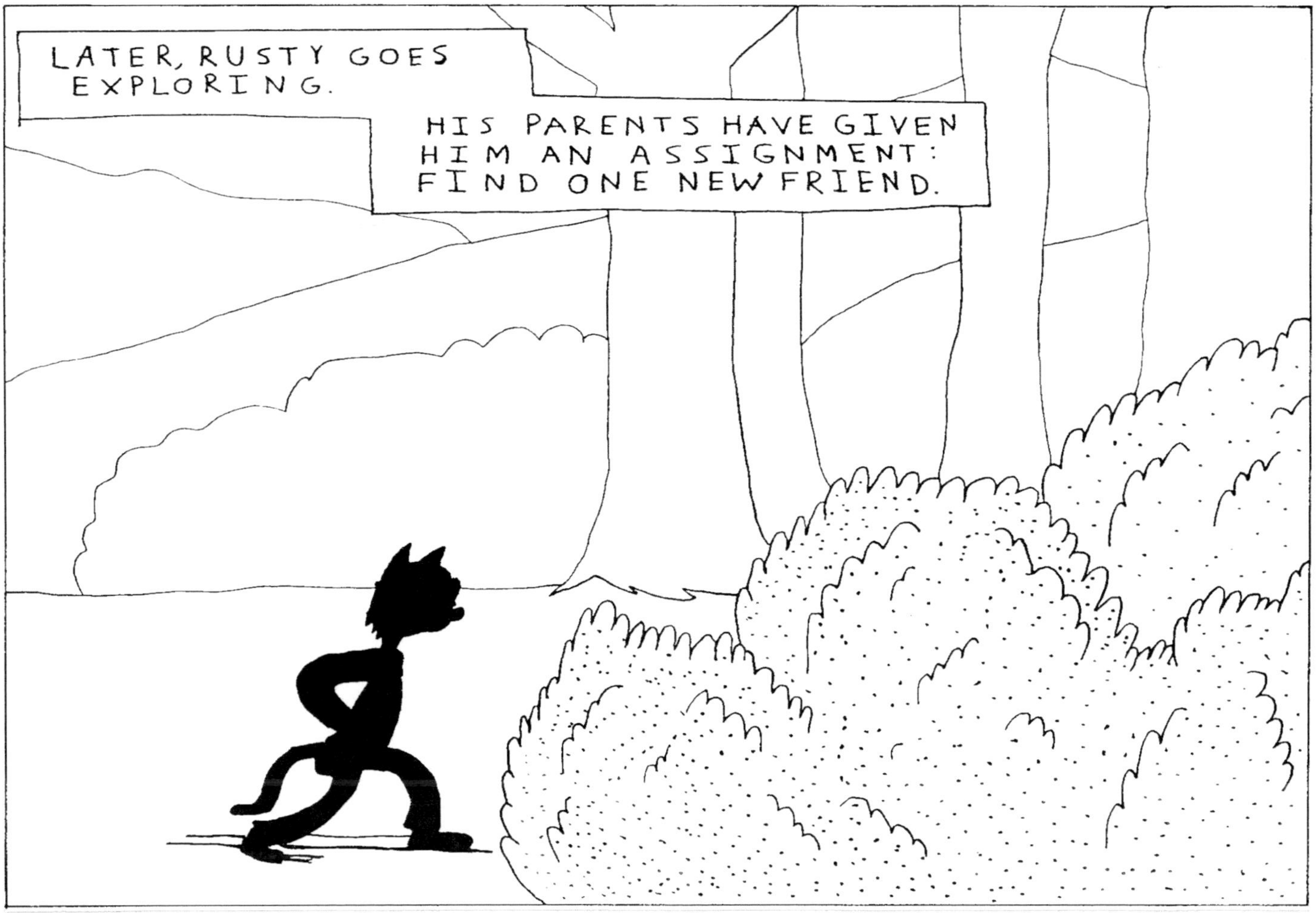
LATER, RUSTY GOES EXPLORING.
HIS PARENTS HAVE GIVEN HIM AN ASSIGNMENT: FIND ONE NEW FRIEND.

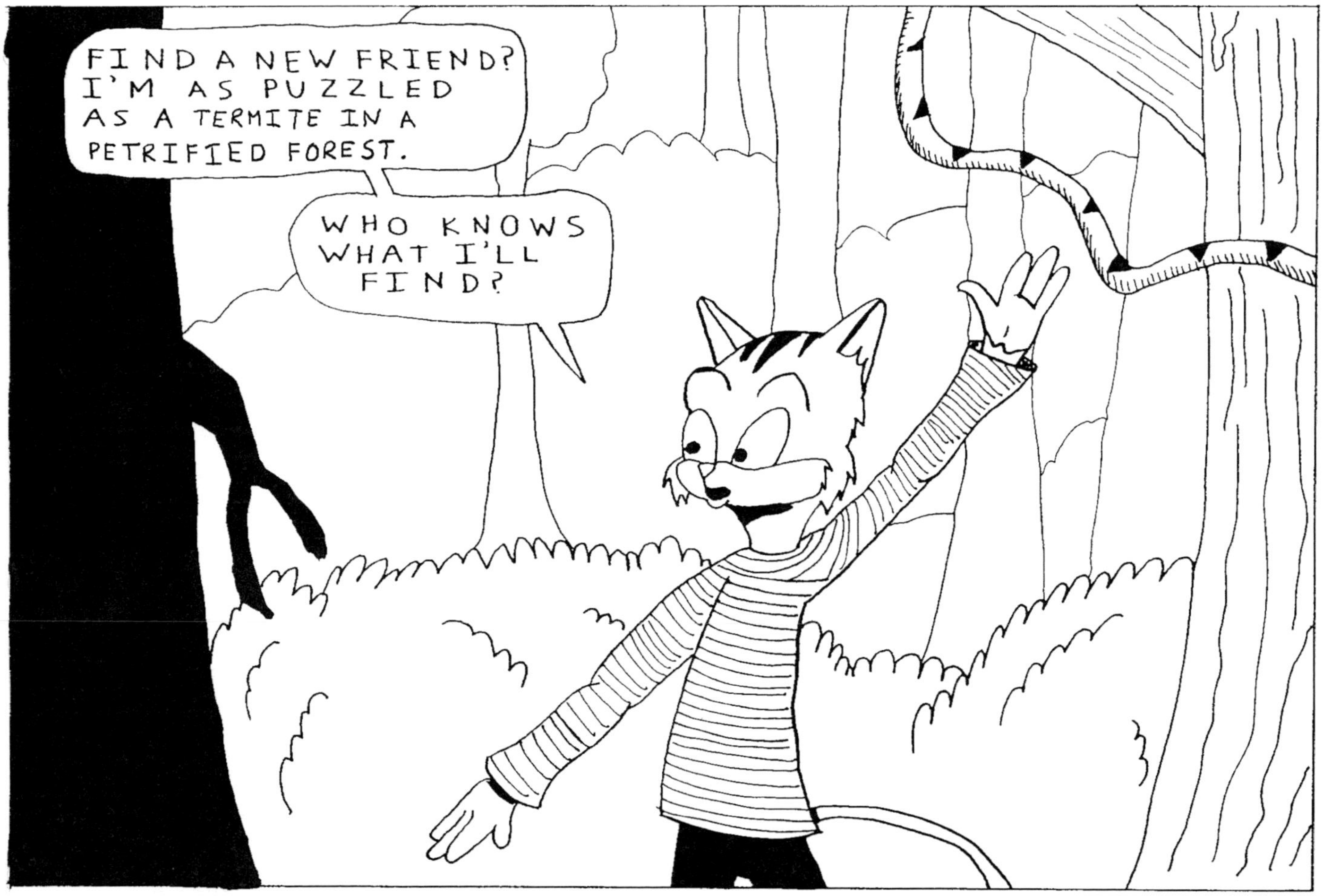
FIND A NEW FRIEND? I'M AS PUZZLED AS A TERMITE IN A PETRIFIED FOREST.
WHO KNOWS WHAT I'LL FIND?

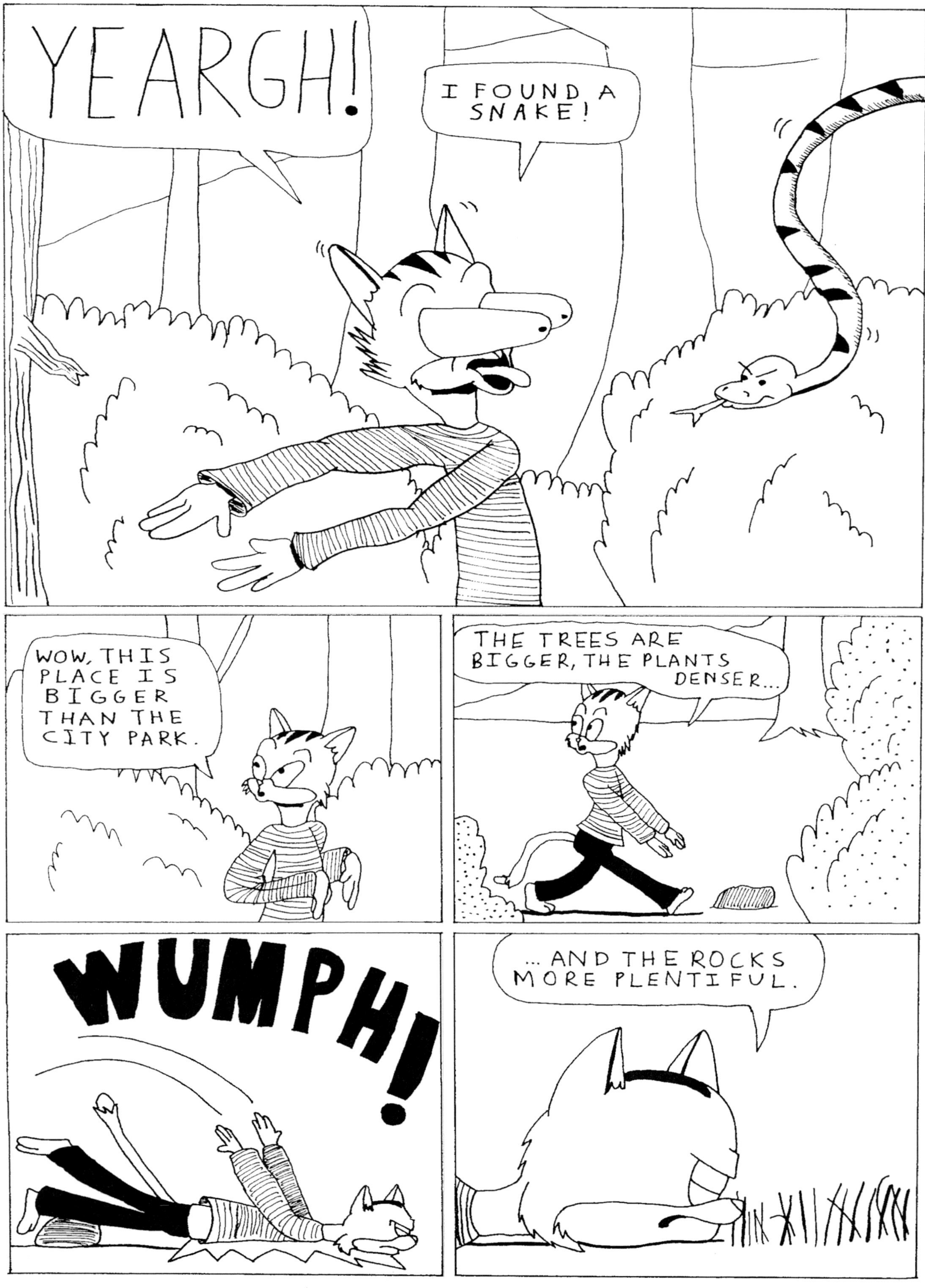
YEARGH!
I FOUND A SNAKE!
WOW, THIS PLACE IS BIGGER THAN THE CITY PARK.
THE TREES ARE BIGGER, THE PLANTS DENSER...
WUMPH!
...AND THE ROCKS MORE PLENTIFUL.

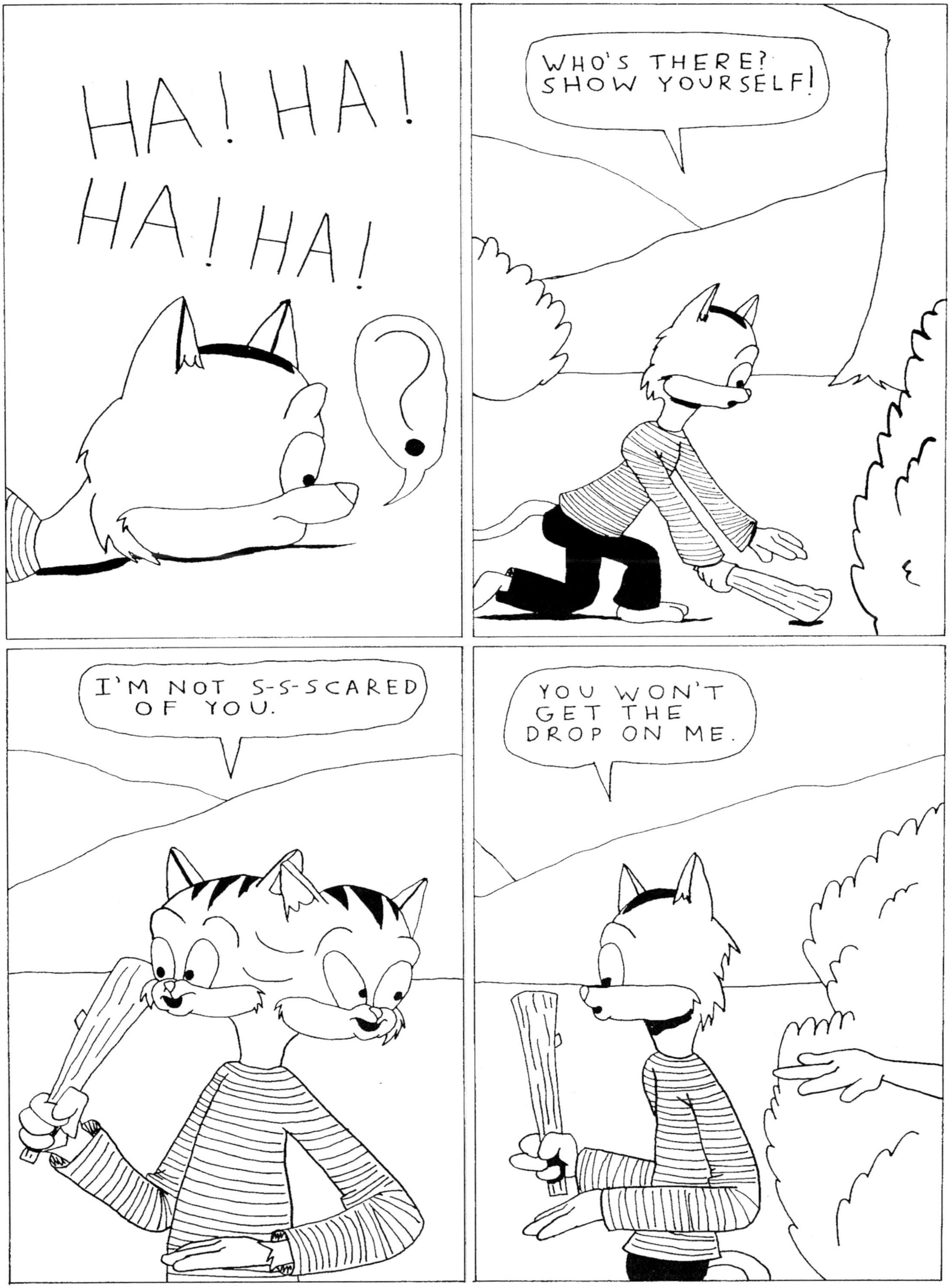
HA! HA! HA! HA!
WHO'S THERE? SHOW YOURSELF!
I'M NOT S-S-SCARED OF YOU.
YOU WON'T GET THE DROP ON ME.

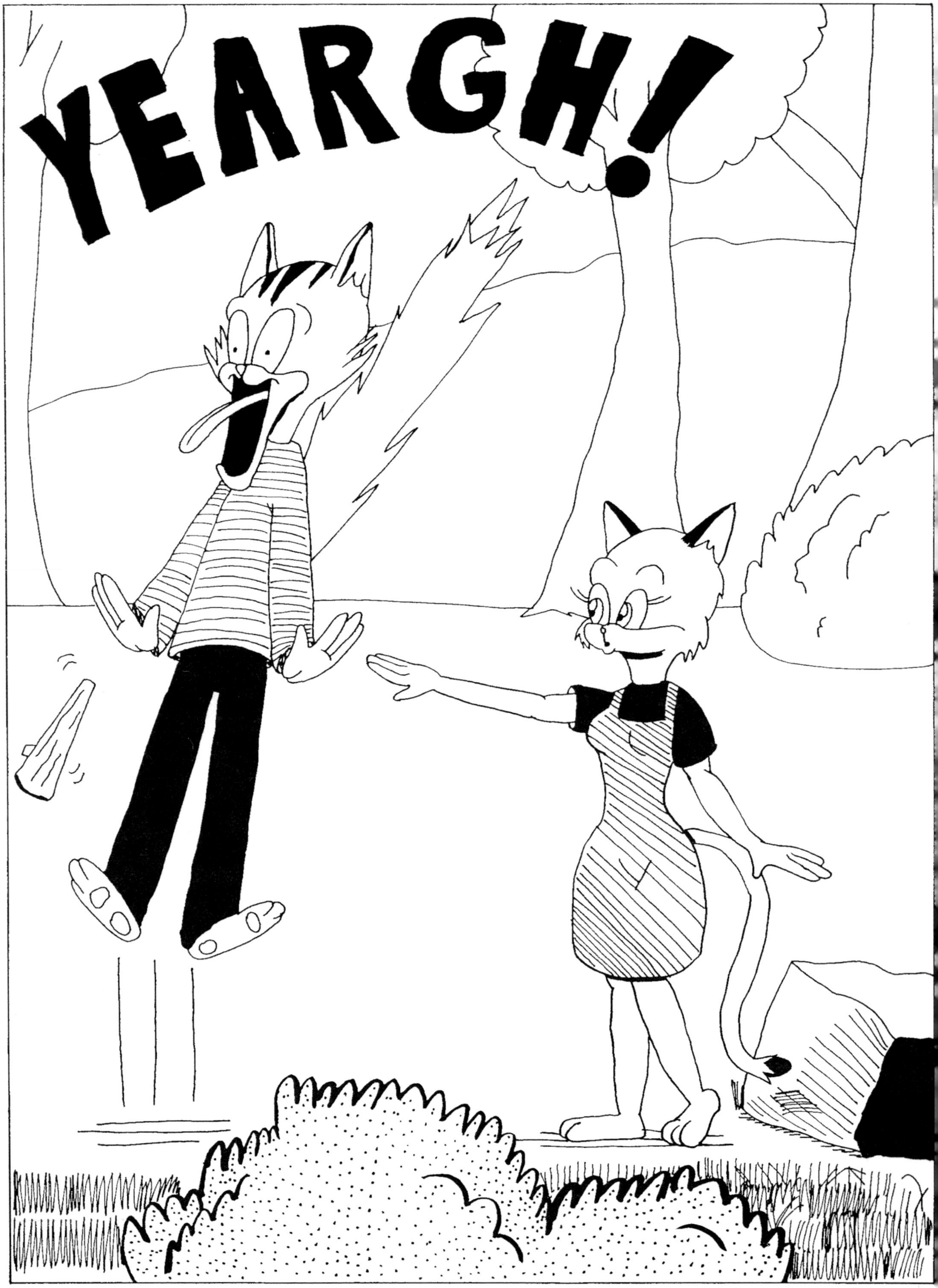
YEARGH!

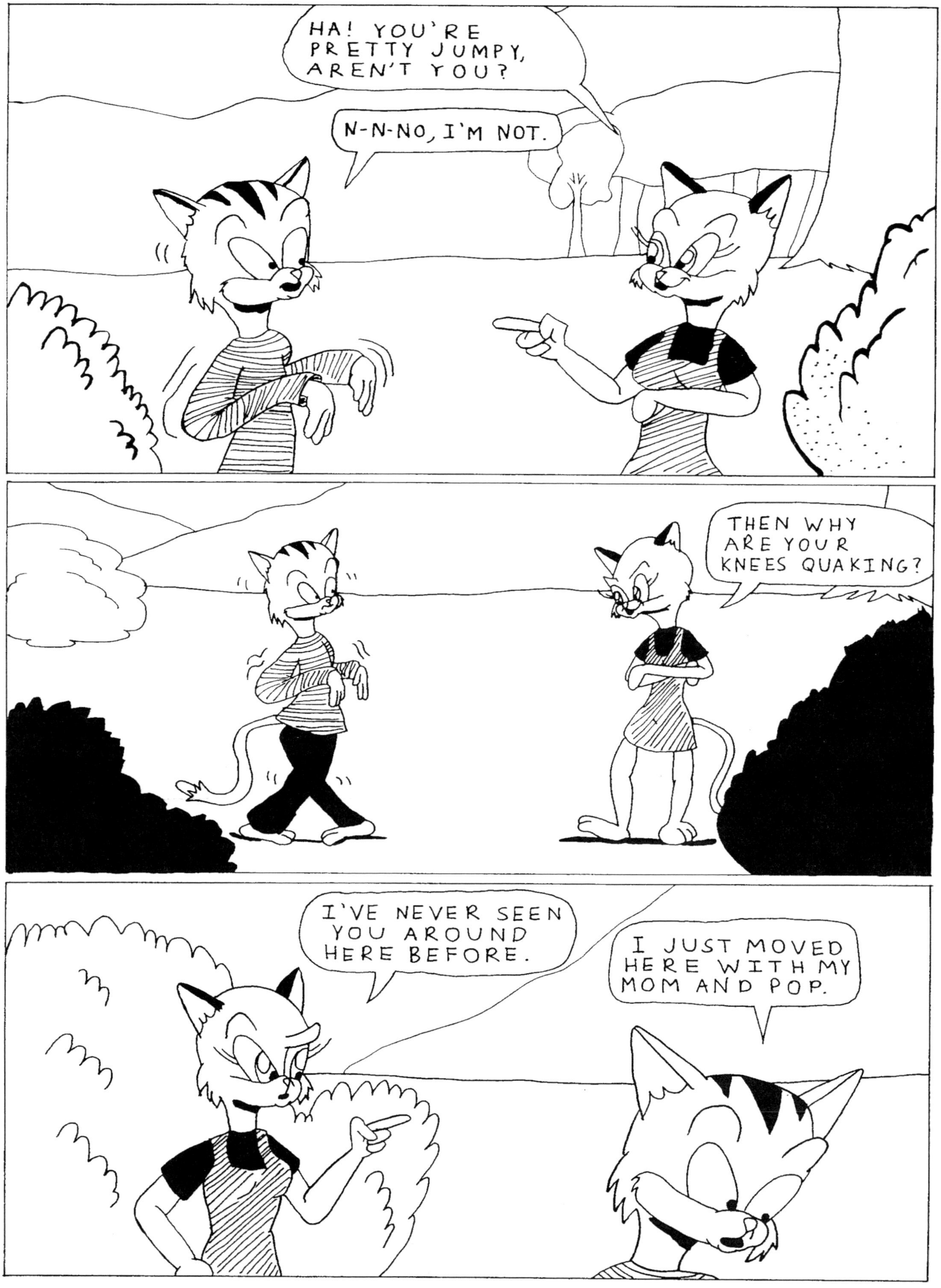
HA! YOU'RE PRETTY JUMPY, AREN'T YOU?
N-N-NO, I'M NOT.
THEN WHY ARE YOUR KNEES QUAKING?
I'VE NEVER SEEN YOU AROUND HERE BEFORE.
I JUST MOVED HERE WITH MY MOM AND POP.

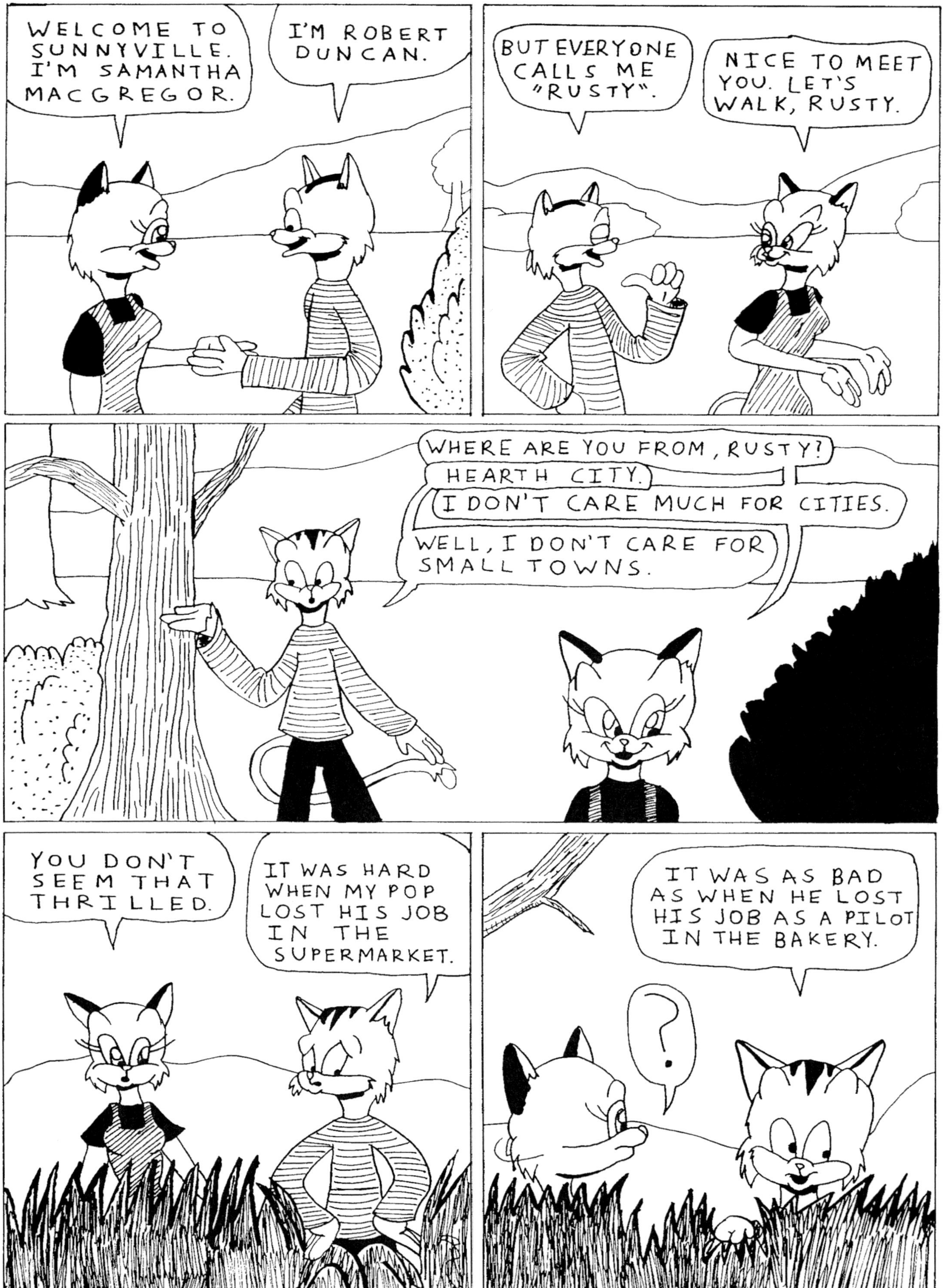
WELCOME TO SUNNYVILLE. I'M SAMANTHA MACGREGOR.
I'M ROBERT DUNCAN.
BUT EVERYONE CALLS ME "RUSTY".
NICE TO MEET YOU. LET'S WALK, RUSTY.
WHERE ARE YOU FROM, RUSTY?
HEARTH CITY.
I DON'T CARE MUCH FOR CITIES.
WELL, I DON'T CARE FOR SMALL TOWNS.
YOU DON'T SEEM THAT THRILLED.
IT WAS HARD WHEN MY POP LOST HIS JOB IN THE SUPERMARKET.
IT WAS AS BAD AS WHEN HE LOST HIS JOB AS A PILOT IN THE BAKERY.
?

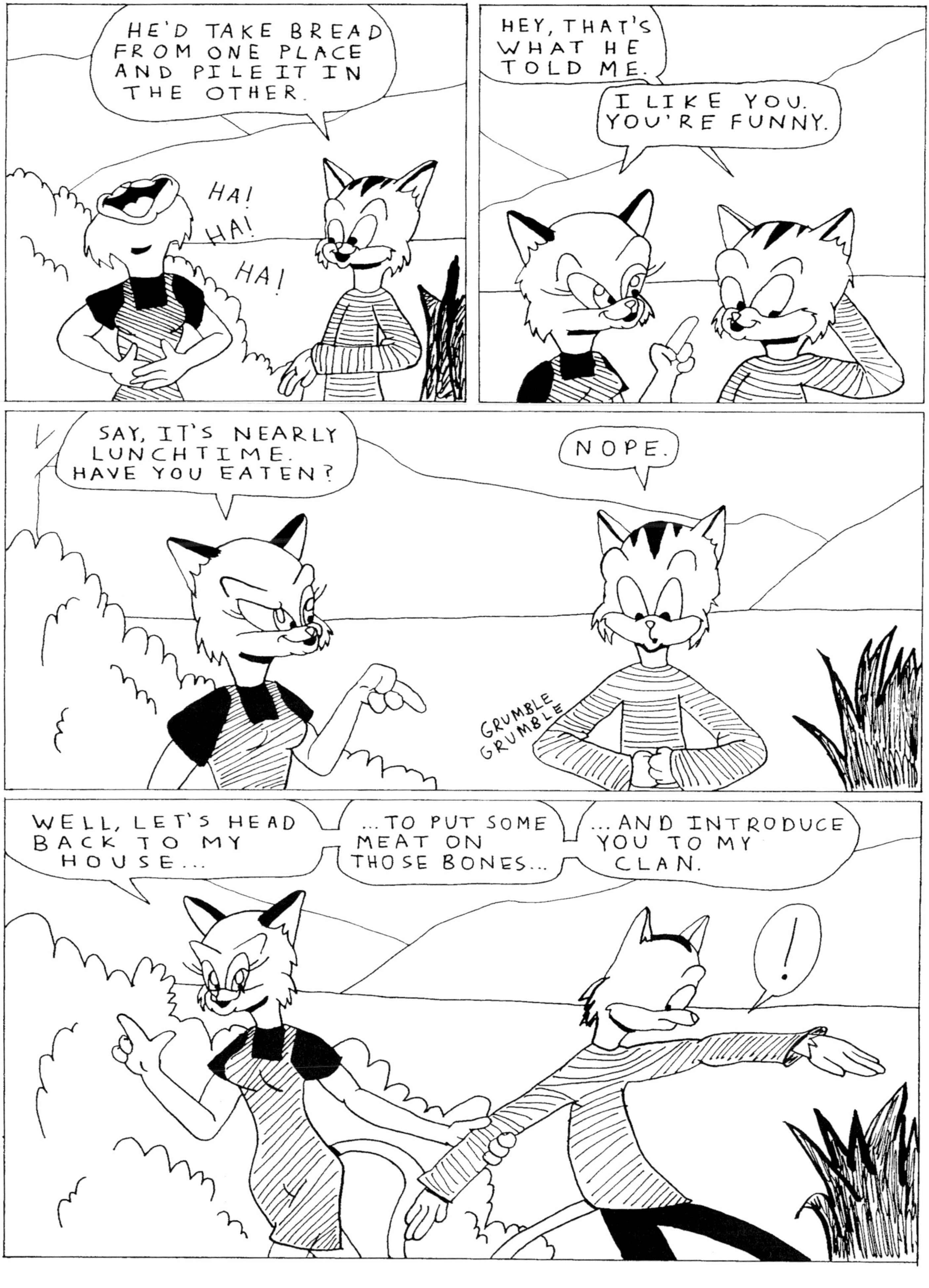
HE'D TAKE BREAD FROM ONE PLACE AND PILE IT IN THE OTHER.
HA! HA! HA!
HEY, THAT'S WHAT HE TOLD ME.
I LIKE YOU. YOU'RE FUNNY.
SAY, IT'S NEARLY LUNCHTIME. HAVE YOU EATEN?
NOPE.
GRUMBLE GRUMBLE
WELL, LET'S HEAD BACK TO MY HOUSE...
...TO PUT SOME MEAT ON THOSE BONES...
...AND INTRODUCE YOU TO MY CLAN.
!

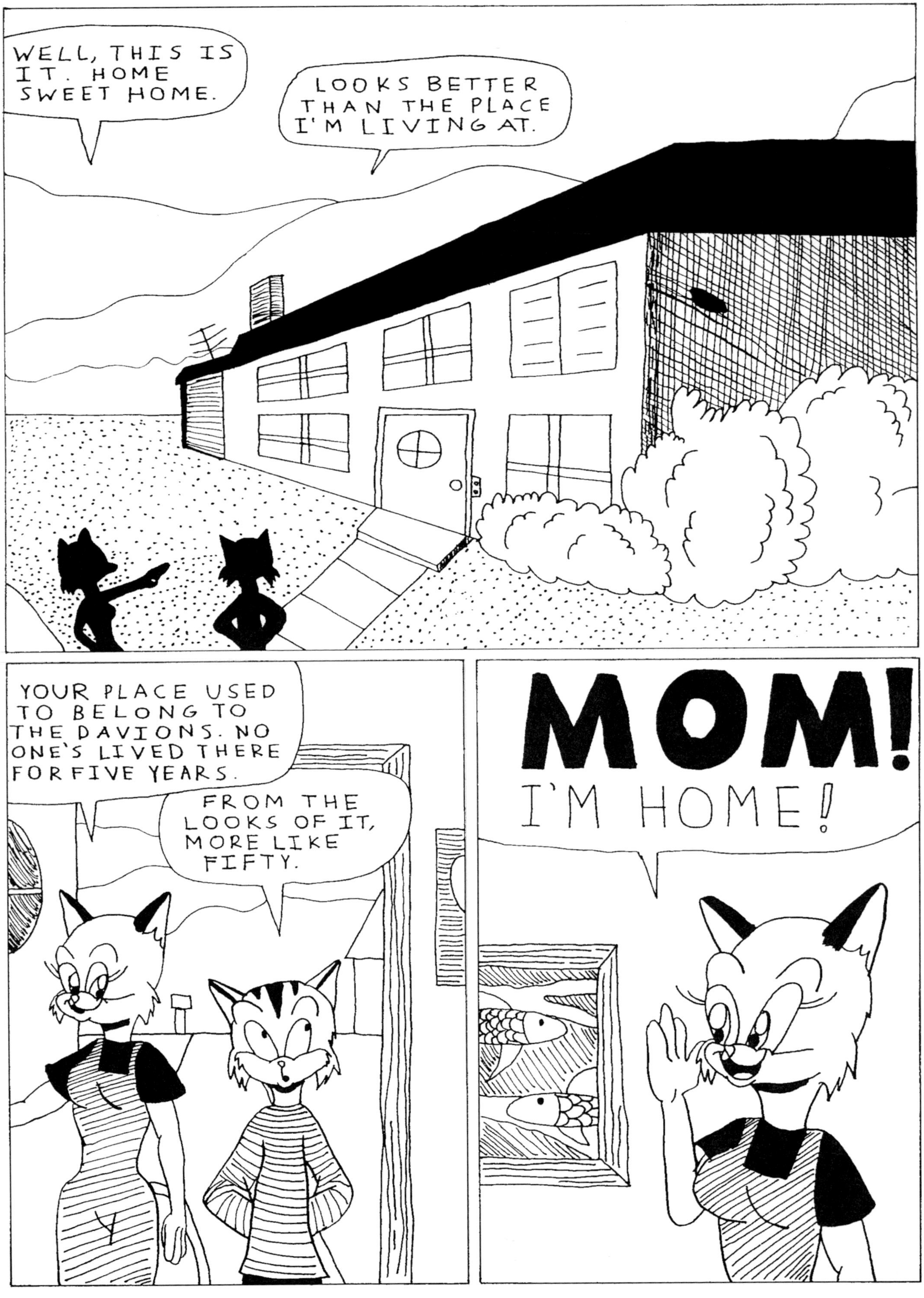
WELL, THIS IS IT. HOME SWEET HOME.
LOOKS BETTER THAN THE PLACE I'M LIVING AT.
YOUR PLACE USED TO BELONG TO THE DAVIONS. NO ONE'S LIVED THERE FOR FIVE YEARS.
FROM THE LOOKS OF IT, MORE LIKE FIFTY.
MOM! I'M HOME!

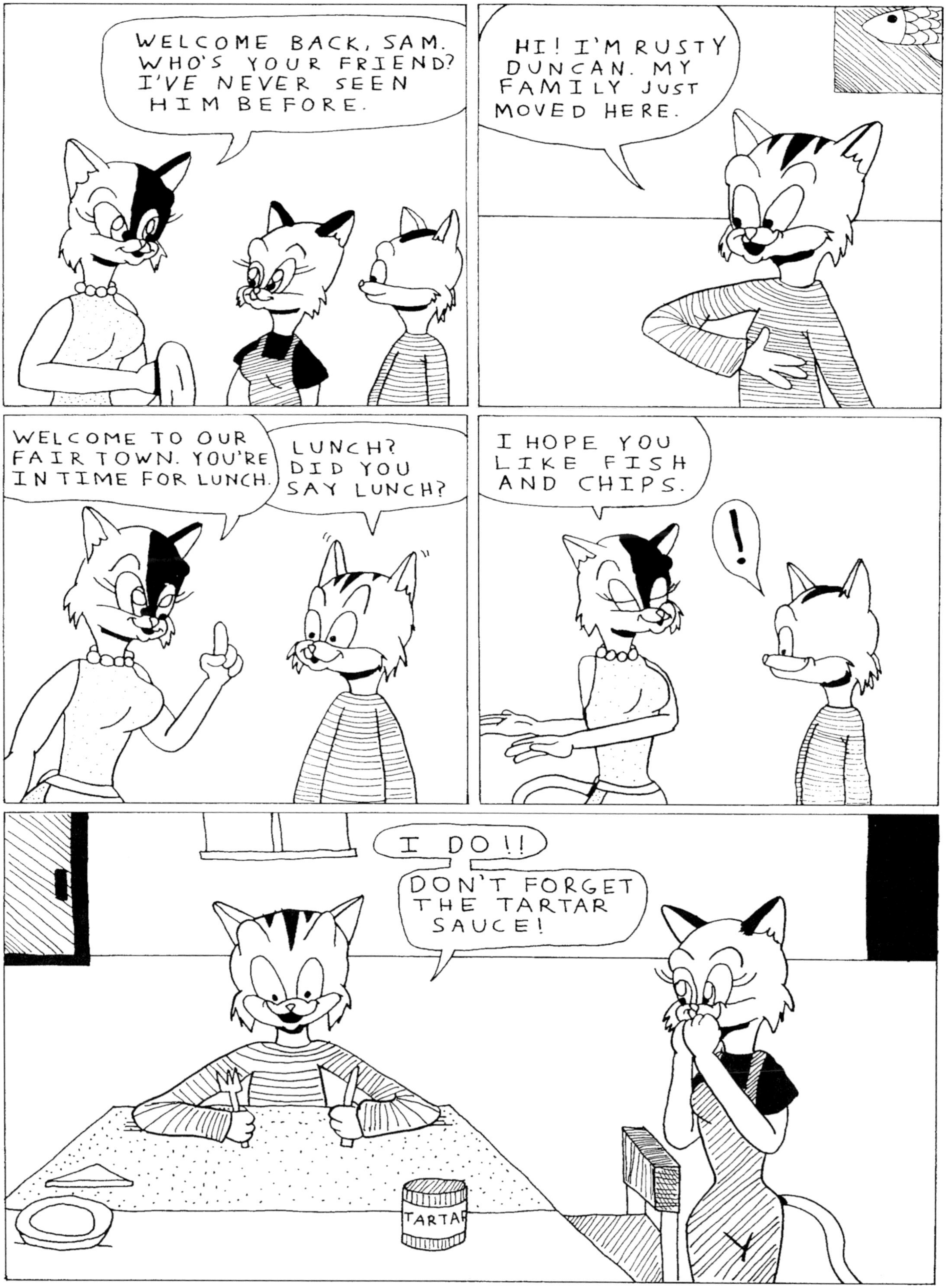
WELCOME BACK, SAM. WHO'S YOUR FRIEND? I'VE NEVER SEEN HIM BEFORE.
HI! I'M RUSTY DUNCAN. MY FAMILY JUST MOVED HERE.
WELCOME TO OUR FAIR TOWN. YOU'RE IN TIME FOR LUNCH.
LUNCH? DID YOU SAY LUNCH?
I HOPE YOU LIKE FISH AND CHIPS.
!
I DO!!
DON'T FORGET THE TARTAR SAUCE!
TARTAR

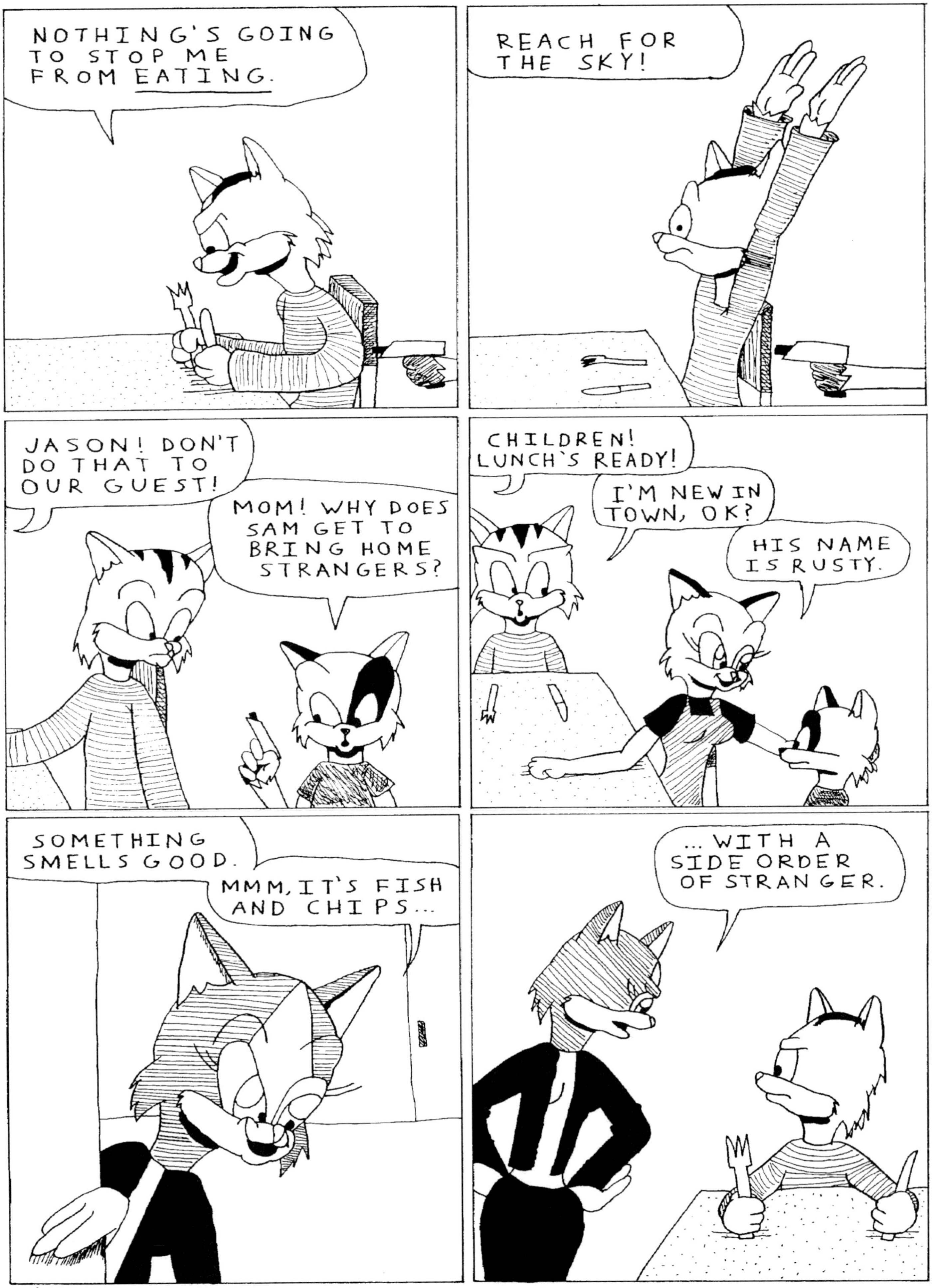

NOTHING'S GOING TO STOP ME FROM EATING.
REACH FOR THE SKY!
JASON! DON'T DO THAT TO OUR GUEST!
MOM! WHY DOES SAM GET TO BRING HOME STRANGERS?
CHILDREN! LUNCH'S READY!
I'M NEW IN TOWN, OK?
HIS NAME IS RUSTY.
SOMETHING SMELLS GOOD.
MMM, IT'S FISH AND CHIPS...
... WITH A SIDE ORDER OF STRANGER.

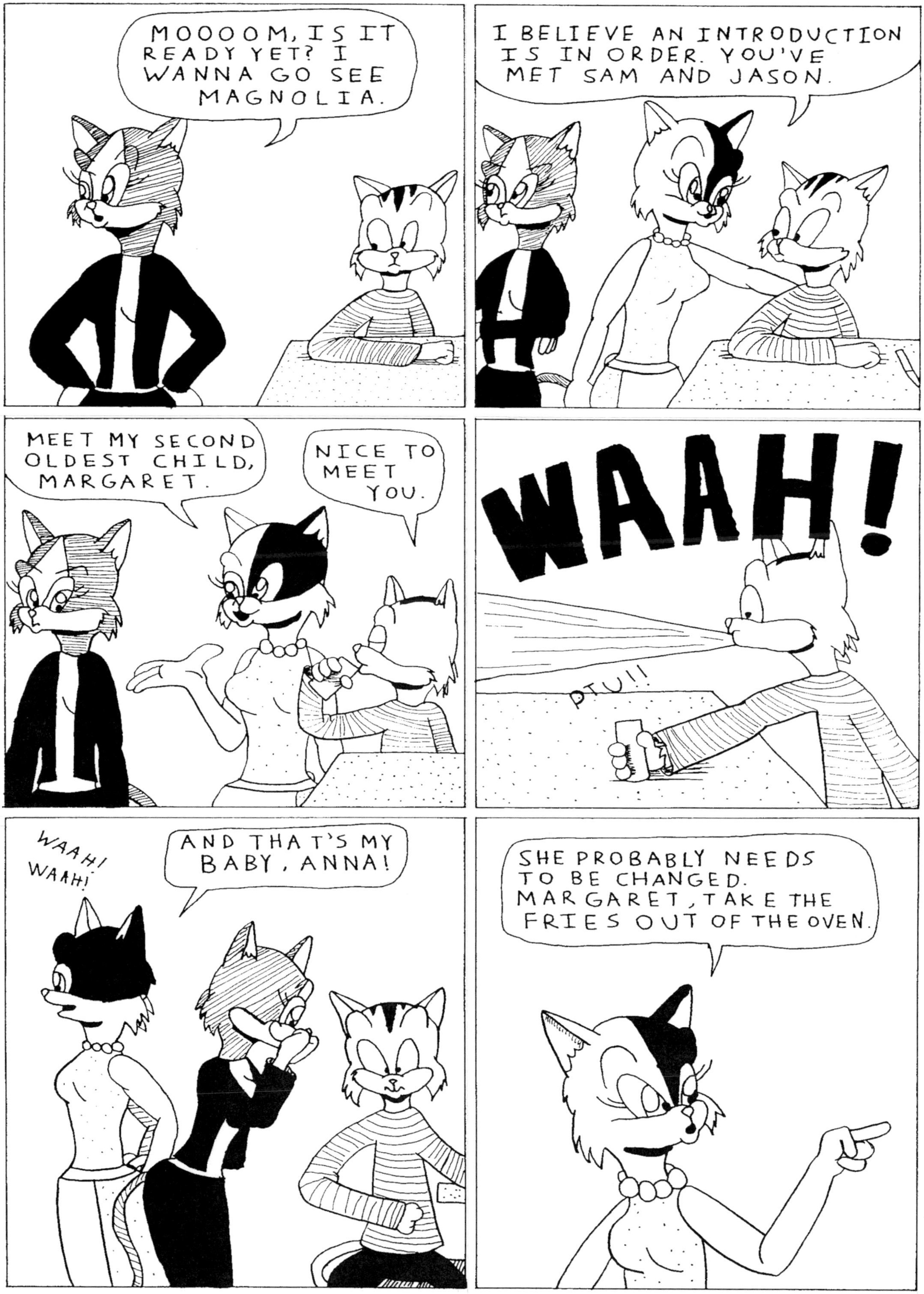
MOOOOM, IS IT READY YET? I WANNA GO SEE MAGNOLIA.
I BELIEVE AN INTRODUCTION IS IN ORDER. YOU'VE MET SAM AND JASON.
MEET MY SECOND OLDEST CHILD, MARGARET.
NICE TO MEET YOU.
WAAH!
PTUI!
WAAH! WAAH!
AND THAT'S MY BABY, ANNA!
SHE PROBABLY NEEDS TO BE CHANGED. MARGARET, TAKE THE FRIES OUT OF THE OVEN.

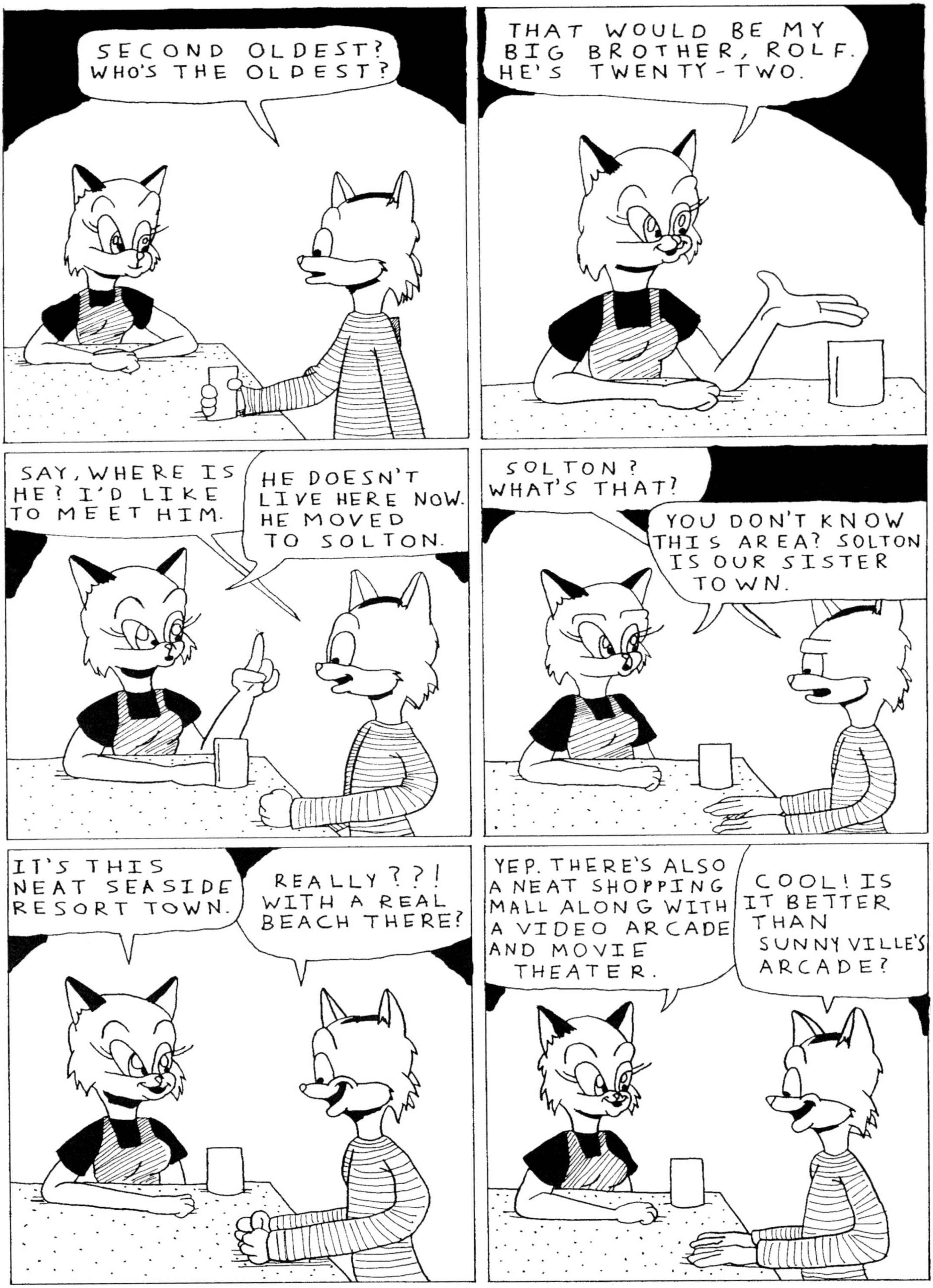
SECOND OLDEST? WHO'S THE OLDEST?
THAT WOULD BE MY BIG BROTHER, ROLF. HE'S TWENTY-TWO.
SAY, WHERE IS HE? I'D LIKE TO MEET HIM.
HE DOESN'T LIVE HERE NOW. HE MOVED TO SOLTON.
SOLTON? WHAT'S THAT?
YOU DON'T KNOW THIS AREA? SOLTON IS OUR SISTER TOWN.
IT'S THIS NEAT SEASIDE RESORT TOWN.
REALLY??! WITH A REAL BEACH THERE?
YEP. THERE'S ALSO A NEAT SHOPPING MALL ALONG WITH A VIDEO ARCADE AND MOVIE THEATER.
COOL! IS IT BETTER THAN SUNNYVILLE'S ARCADE?

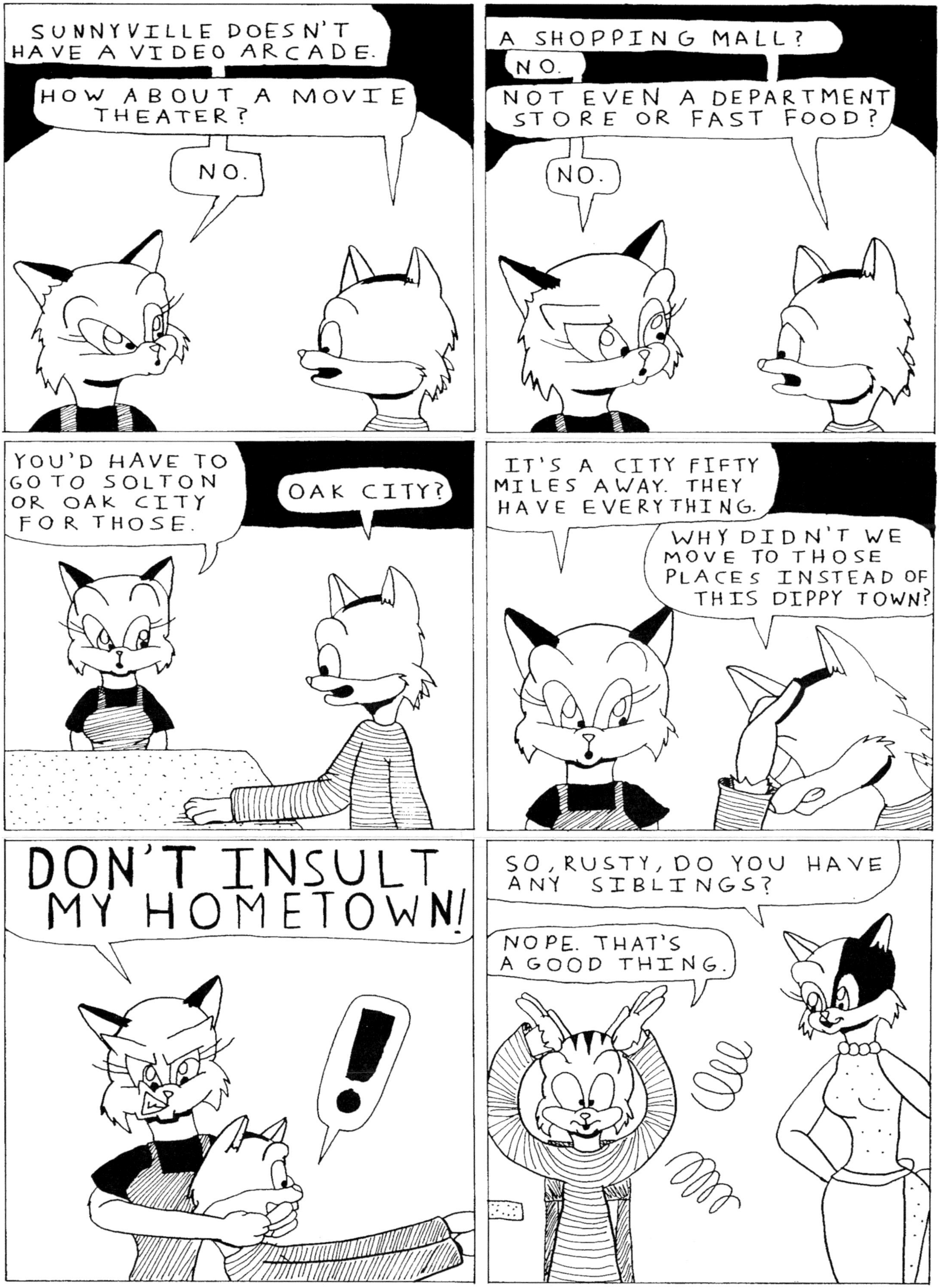
SUNNYVILLE DOESN'T HAVE A VIDEO ARCADE.
HOW ABOUT A MOVIE THEATER?
NO.
A SHOPPING MALL?
NO.
NOT EVEN A DEPARTMENT STORE OR FAST FOOD?
NO.
YOU'D HAVE TO GO TO SOLTON OR OAK CITY FOR THOSE.
OAK CITY?
IT'S A CITY FIFTY MILES AWAY. THEY HAVE EVERYTHING.
WHY DIDN'T WE MOVE TO THOSE PLACES INSTEAD OF THIS DIPPY TOWN?
DON'T INSULT MY HOMETOWN!
!
SO, RUSTY, DO YOU HAVE ANY SIBLINGS?
NOPE. THAT'S A GOOD THING.

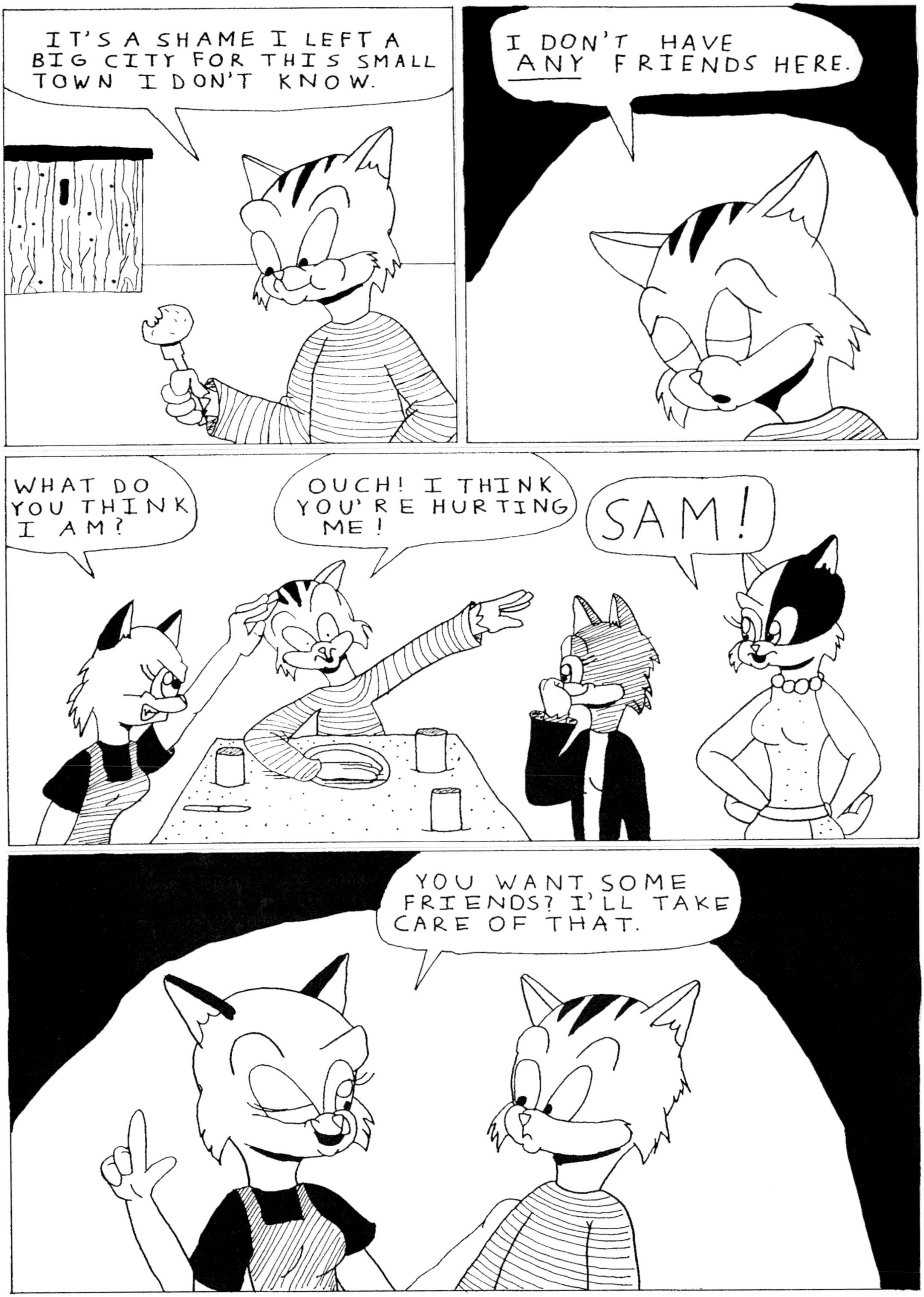
IT'S A SHAME I LEFT A BIG CITY FOR THIS SMALL TOWN I DON'T KNOW.
I DON'T HAVE ANY FRIENDS HERE.
WHAT DO YOU THINK I AM?
OUCH! I THINK YOU'RE HURTING ME!
SAM!
YOU WANT SOME FRIENDS? I'LL TAKE CARE OF THAT.

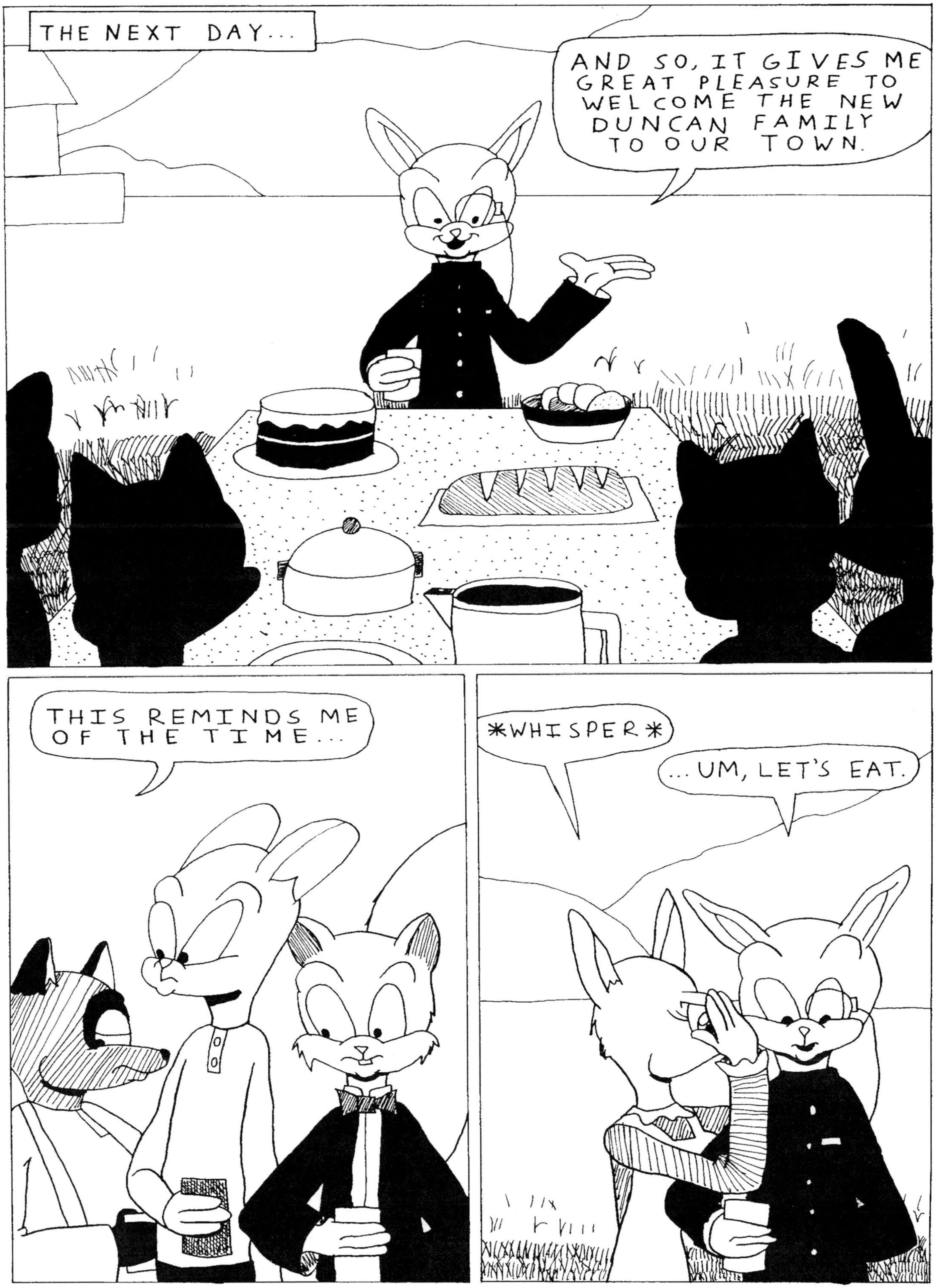
THE NEXT DAY...
AND SO, IT GIVES ME GREAT PLEASURE TO WELCOME THE NEW DUNCAN FAMILY TO OUR TOWN.
THIS REMINDS ME OF THE TIME...
WHISPER
...UM, LET'S EAT.

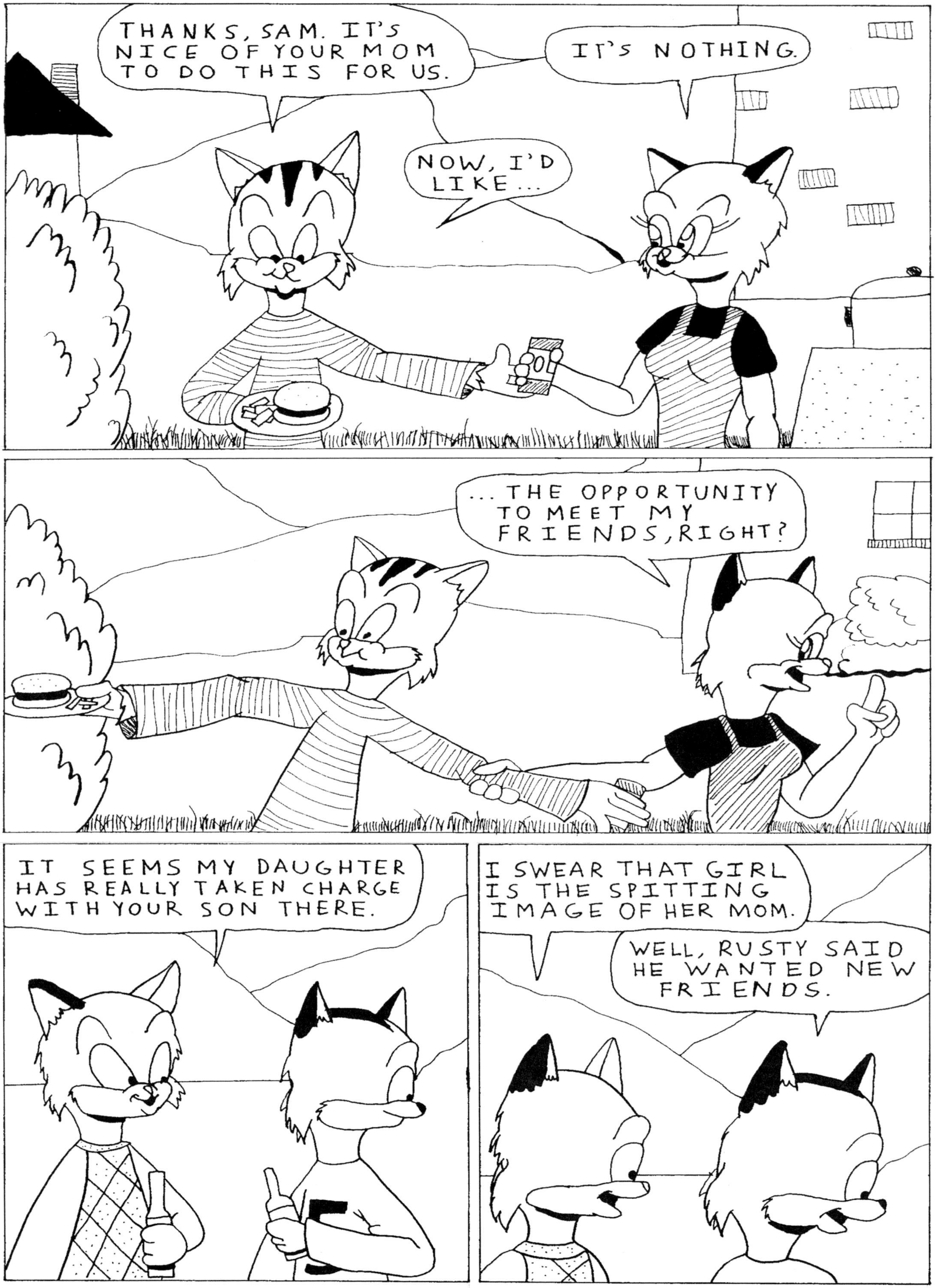
THANKS, SAM. IT'S NICE OF YOUR MOM TO DO THIS FOR US.
IT'S NOTHING.
NOW, I'D LIKE...
...THE OPPORTUNITY TO MEET MY FRIENDS, RIGHT?
IT SEEMS MY DAUGHTER HAS REALLY TAKEN CHARGE WITH YOUR SON THERE.
I SWEAR THAT GIRL IS THE SPITTING IMAGE OF HER MOM.
WELL, RUSTY SAID HE WANTED NEW FRIENDS.

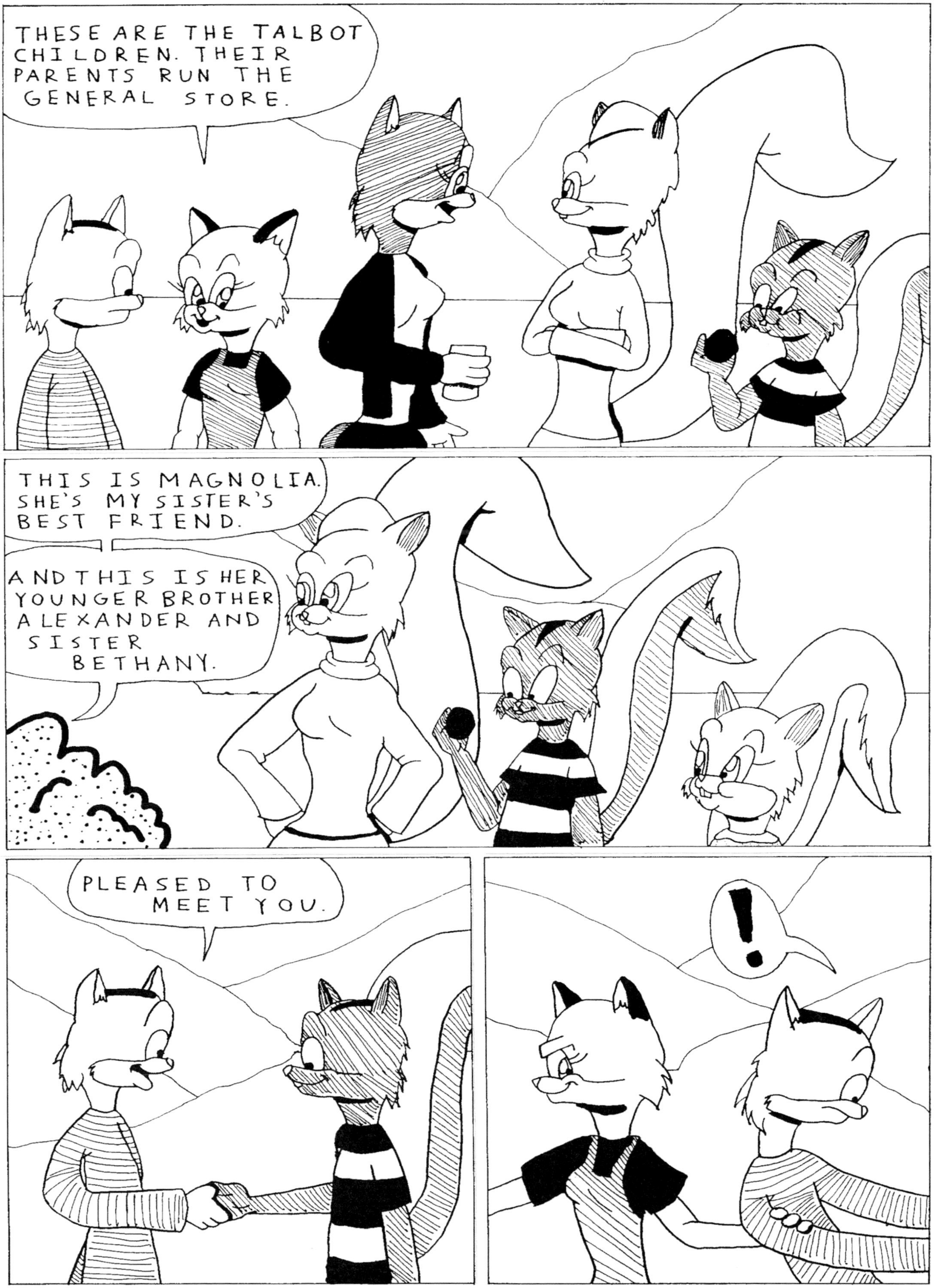
THESE ARE THE TALBOT CHILDREN. THEIR PARENTS RUN THE GENERAL STORE.
THIS IS MAGNOLIA. SHE'S MY SISTER'S BEST FRIEND.
AND THIS IS HER YOUNGER BROTHER ALEXANDER AND SISTER BETHANY.
PLEASED TO MEET YOU.
!

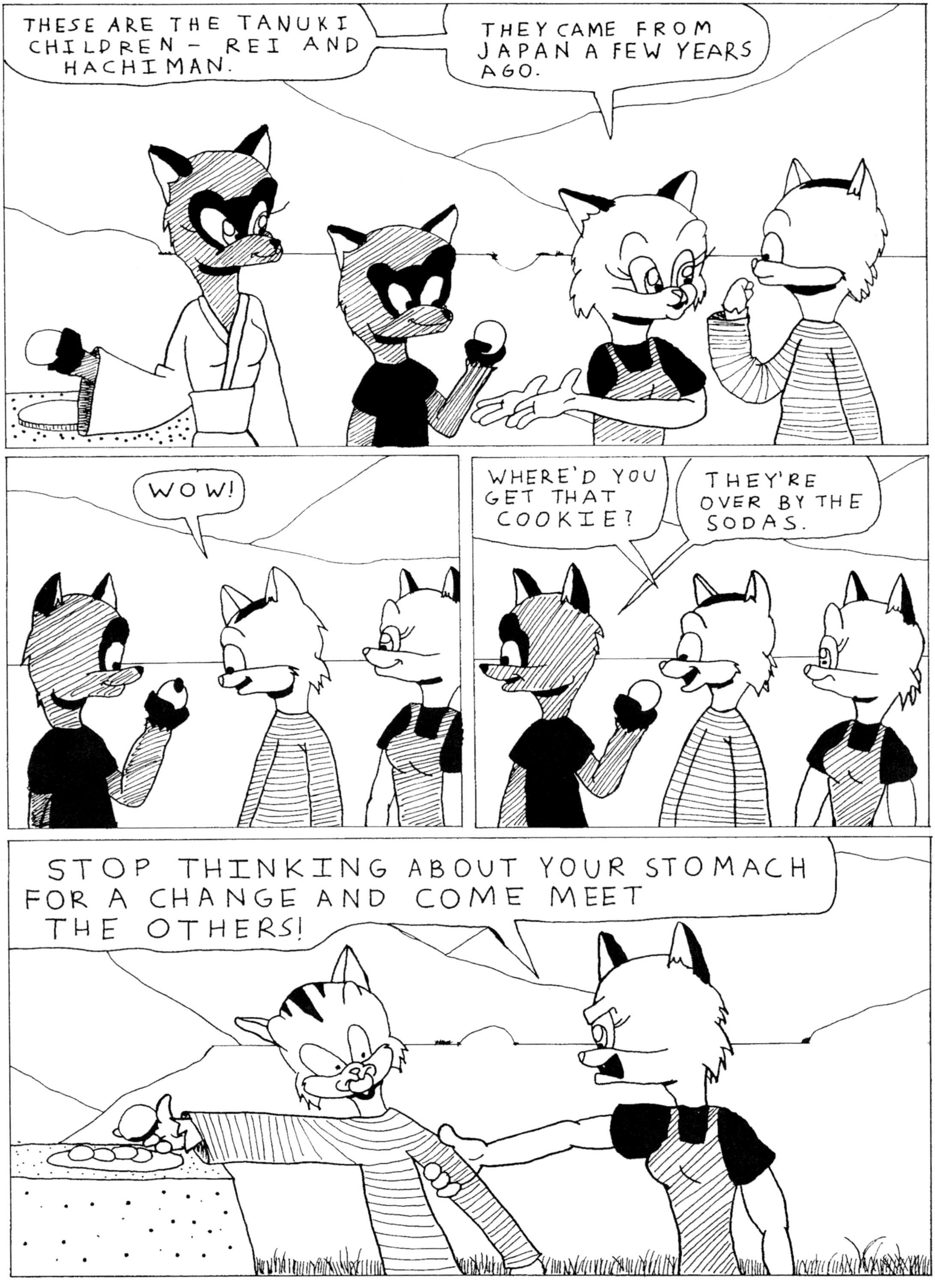
THESE ARE THE TANUKI CHILDREN - REI AND HACHIMAN.
THEY CAME FROM JAPAN A FEW YEARS AGO.
WOW!
WHERE'D YOU GET THAT COOKIE?
THEY'RE OVER BY THE SODAS.
STOP THINKING ABOUT YOUR STOMACH FOR A CHANGE AND COME MEET THE OTHERS!

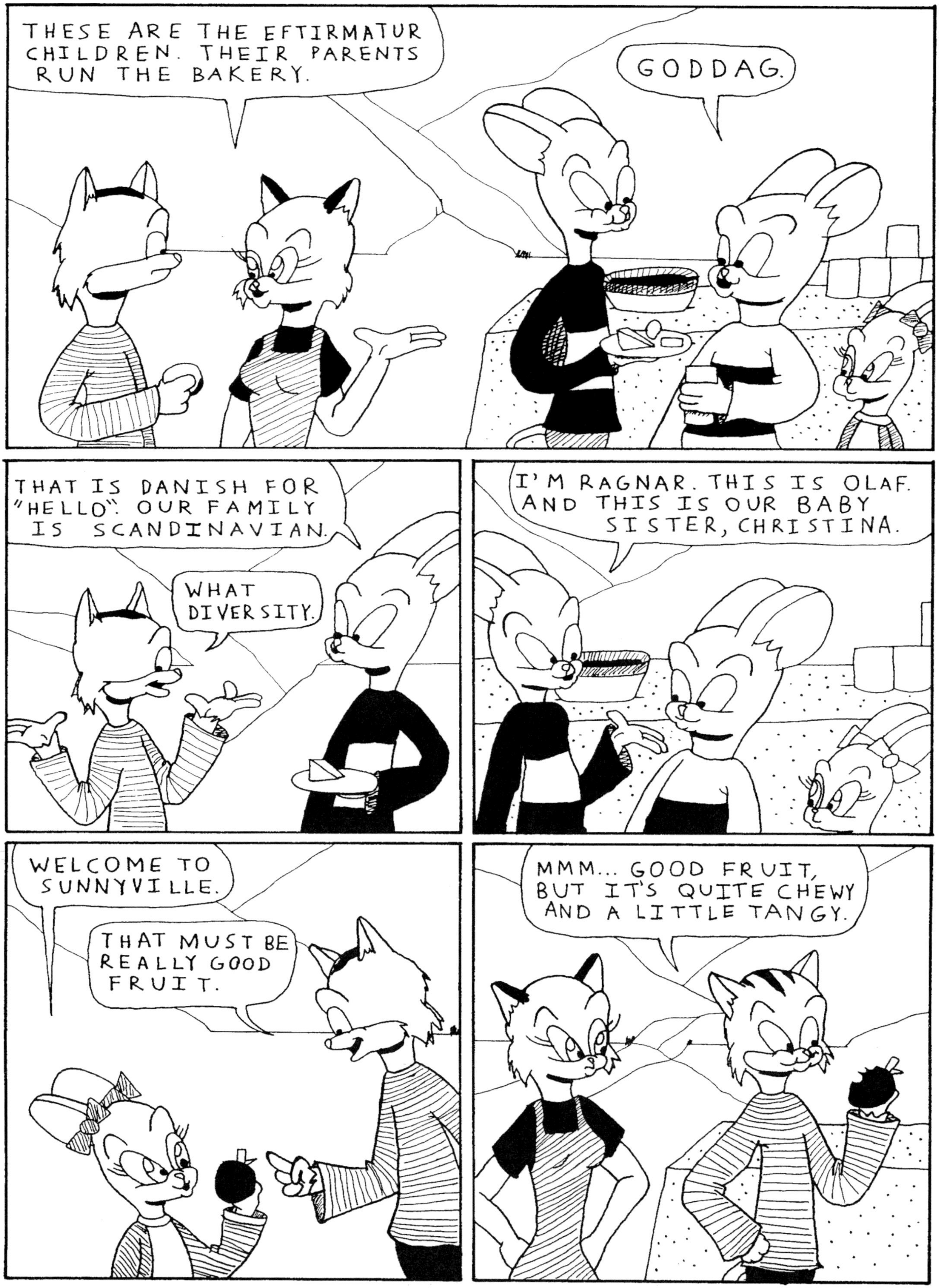
THESE ARE THE EFTIRMATUR CHILDREN. THEIR PARENTS RUN THE BAKERY.
GODDAG.
THAT IS DANISH FOR "HELLO". OUR FAMILY IS SCANDINAVIAN.
WHAT DIVERSITY.
I'M RAGNAR. THIS IS OLAF. AND THIS IS OUR BABY SISTER, CHRISTINA.
WELCOME TO SUNNYVILLE.
THAT MUST BE REALLY GOOD FRUIT.
MMM... GOOD FRUIT, BUT IT'S QUITE CHEWY AND A LITTLE TANGY.

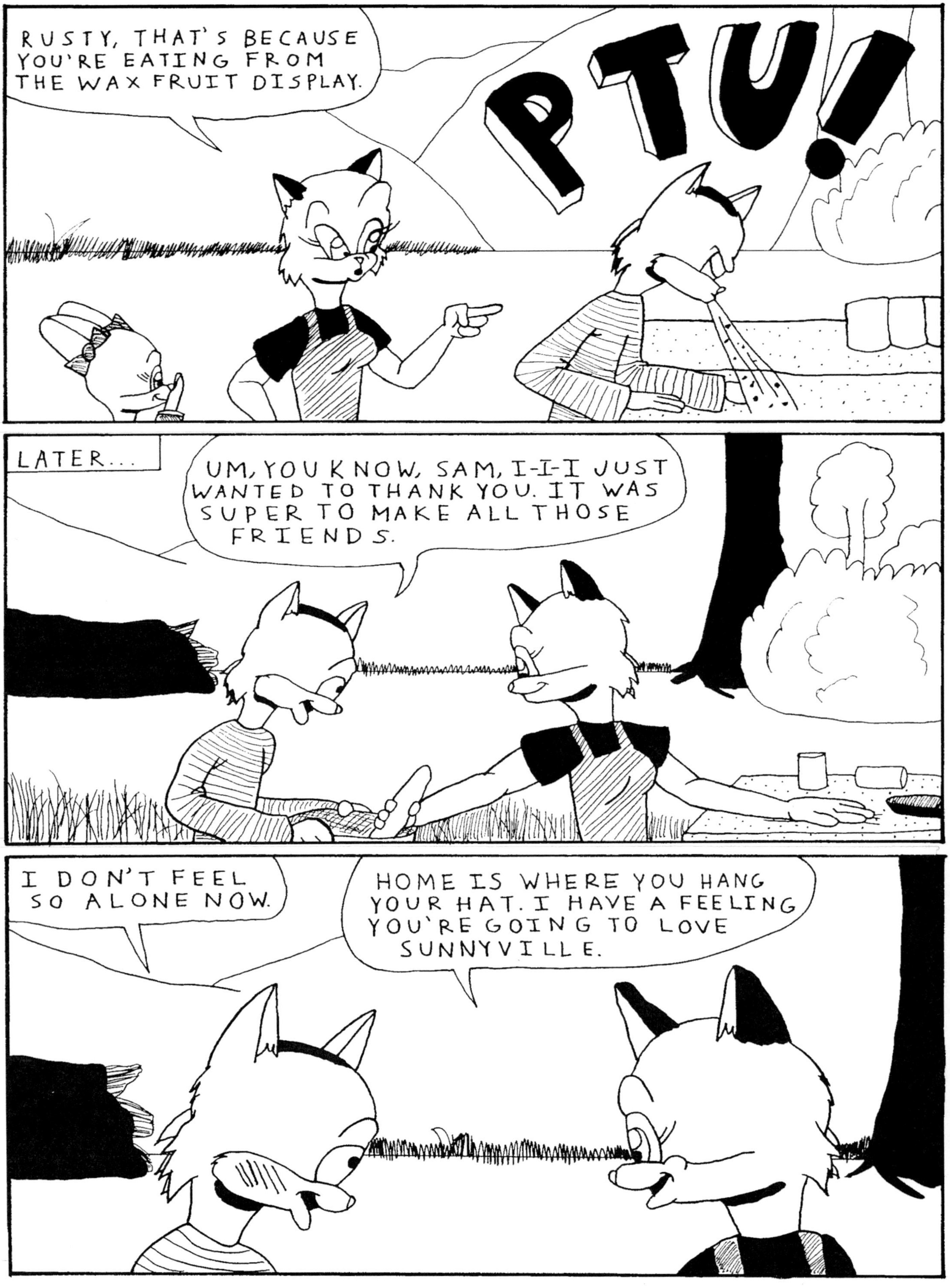
RUSTY, THAT'S BECAUSE YOU'RE EATING FROM THE WAX FRUIT DISPLAY.
PTU!
LATER...
UM, YOU KNOW, SAM, I-I-I JUST WANTED TO THANK YOU. IT WAS SUPER TO MAKE ALL THOSE FRIENDS.
I DON'T FEEL SO ALONE NOW.
HOME IS WHERE YOU HANG YOUR HAT. I HAVE A FEELING YOU'RE GOING TO LOVE SUNNYVILLE.

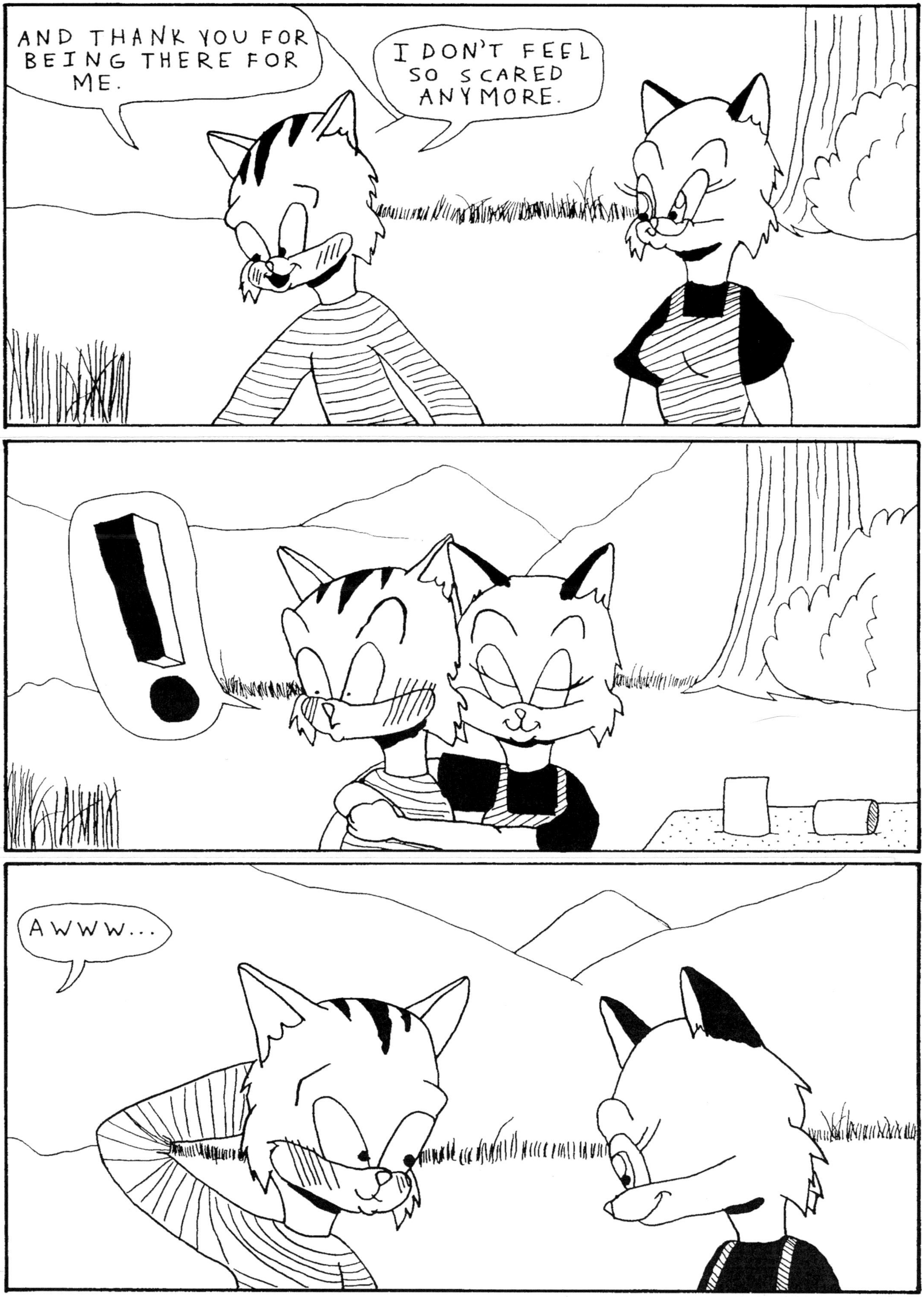
AND THANK YOU FOR BEING THERE FOR ME.
I DON'T FEEL SO SCARED ANYMORE.
!
AWWW...

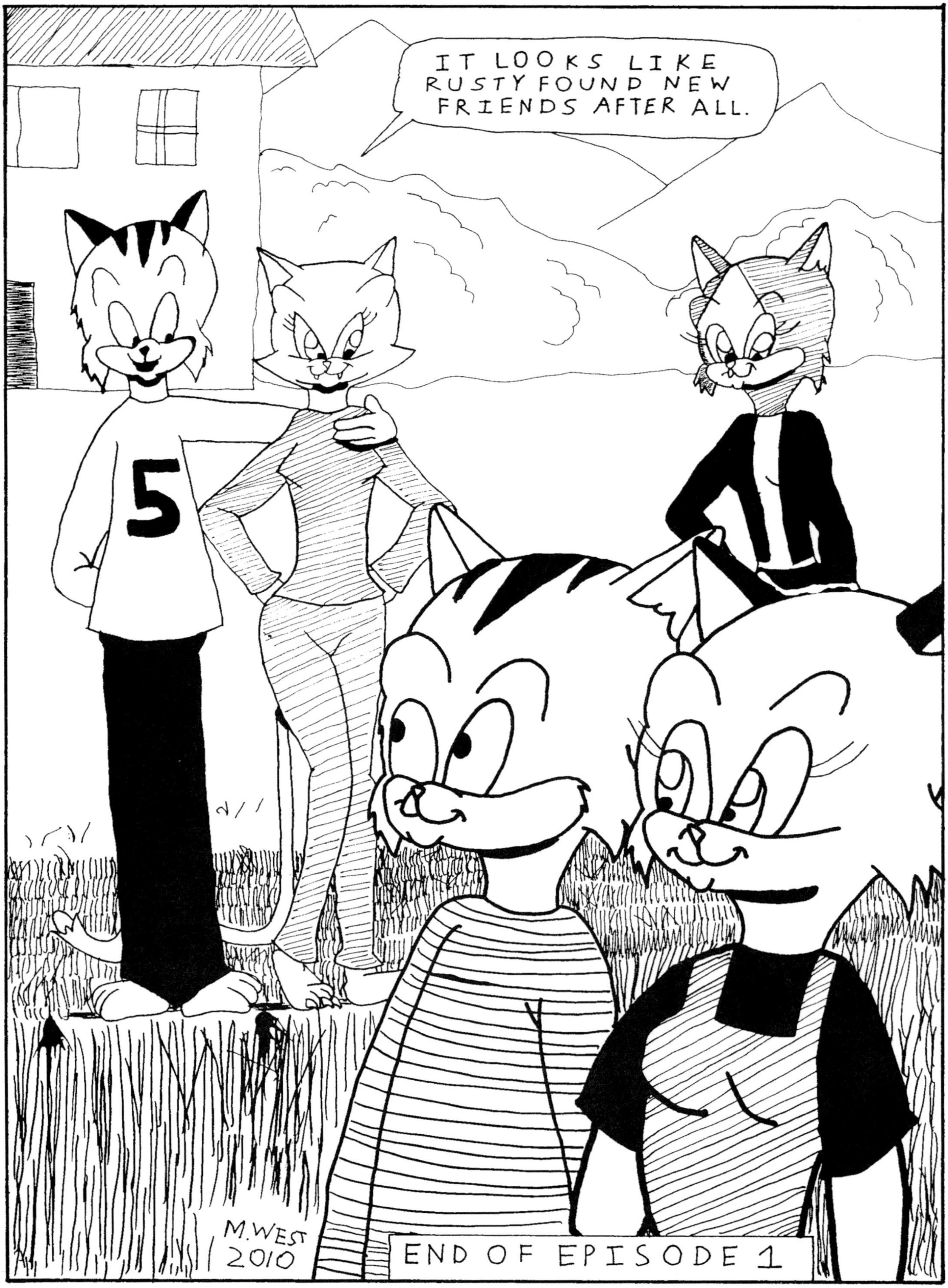
IT LOOKS LIKE RUSTY FOUND NEW FRIENDS AFTER ALL.
5
M.WEST 2010
END OF EPISODE 1

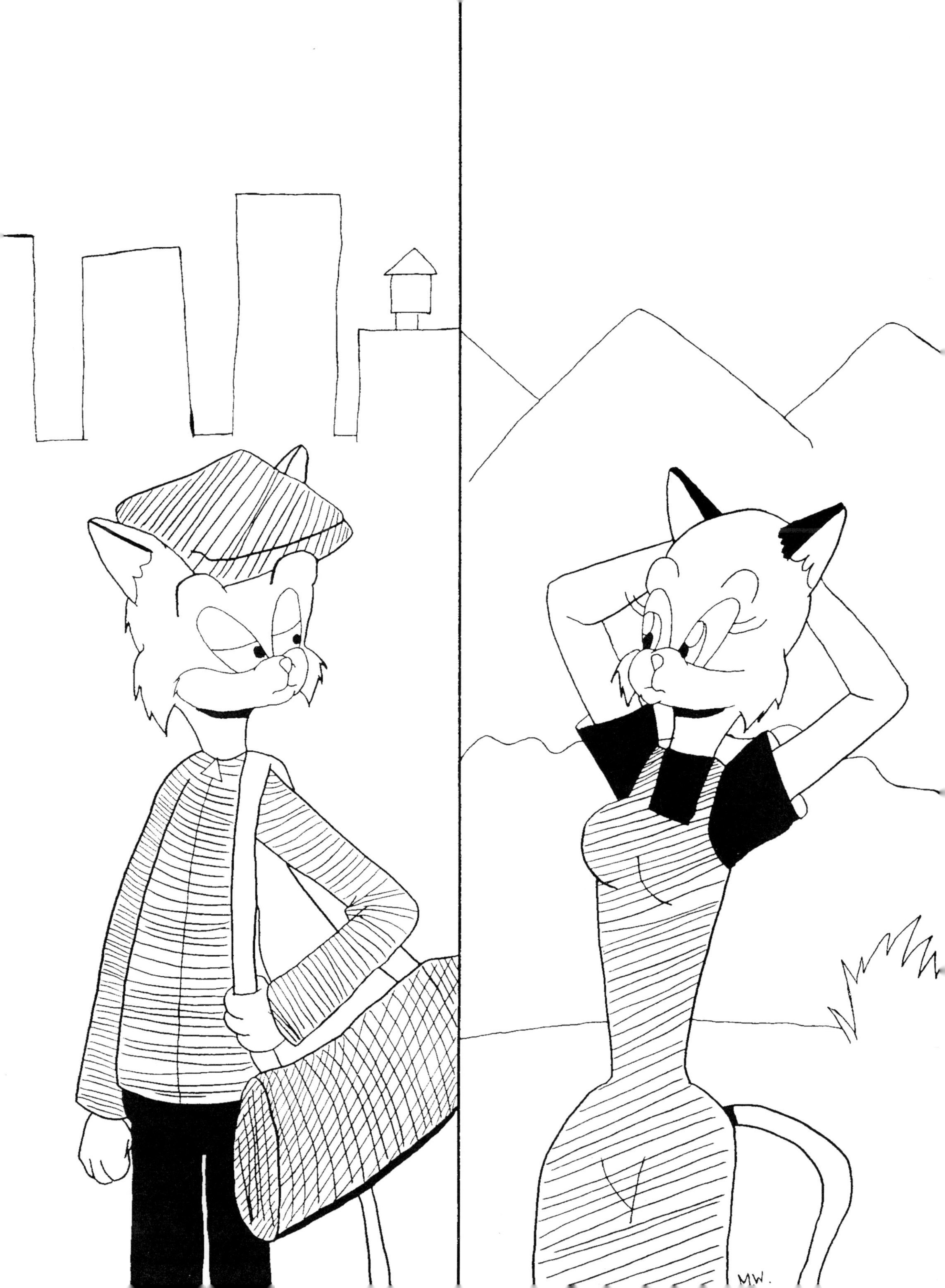
M.W.

Episode 2 - Multiball Madness

Written and Illustrated by
Max West

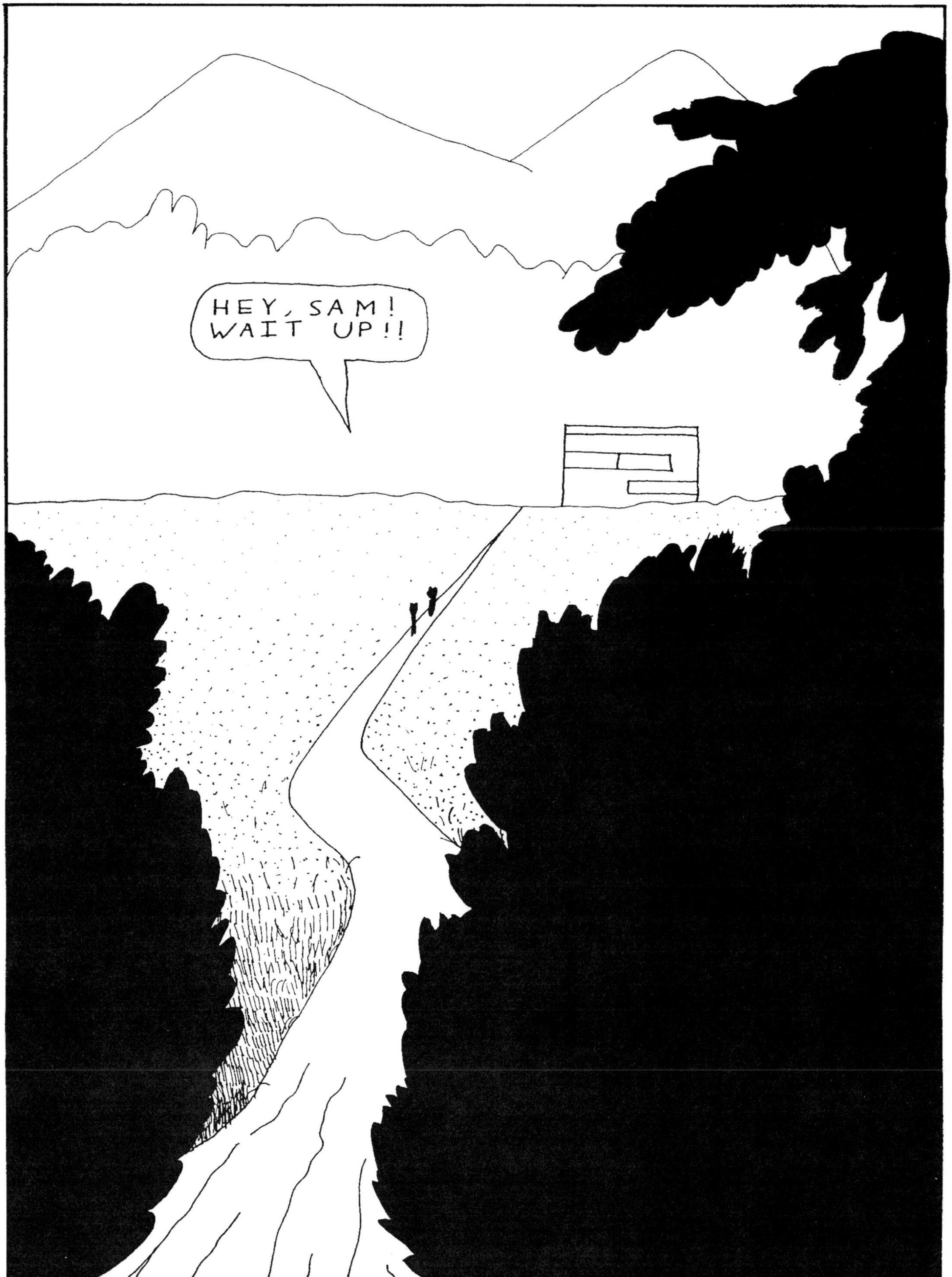
HEY, SAM! WAIT UP!!

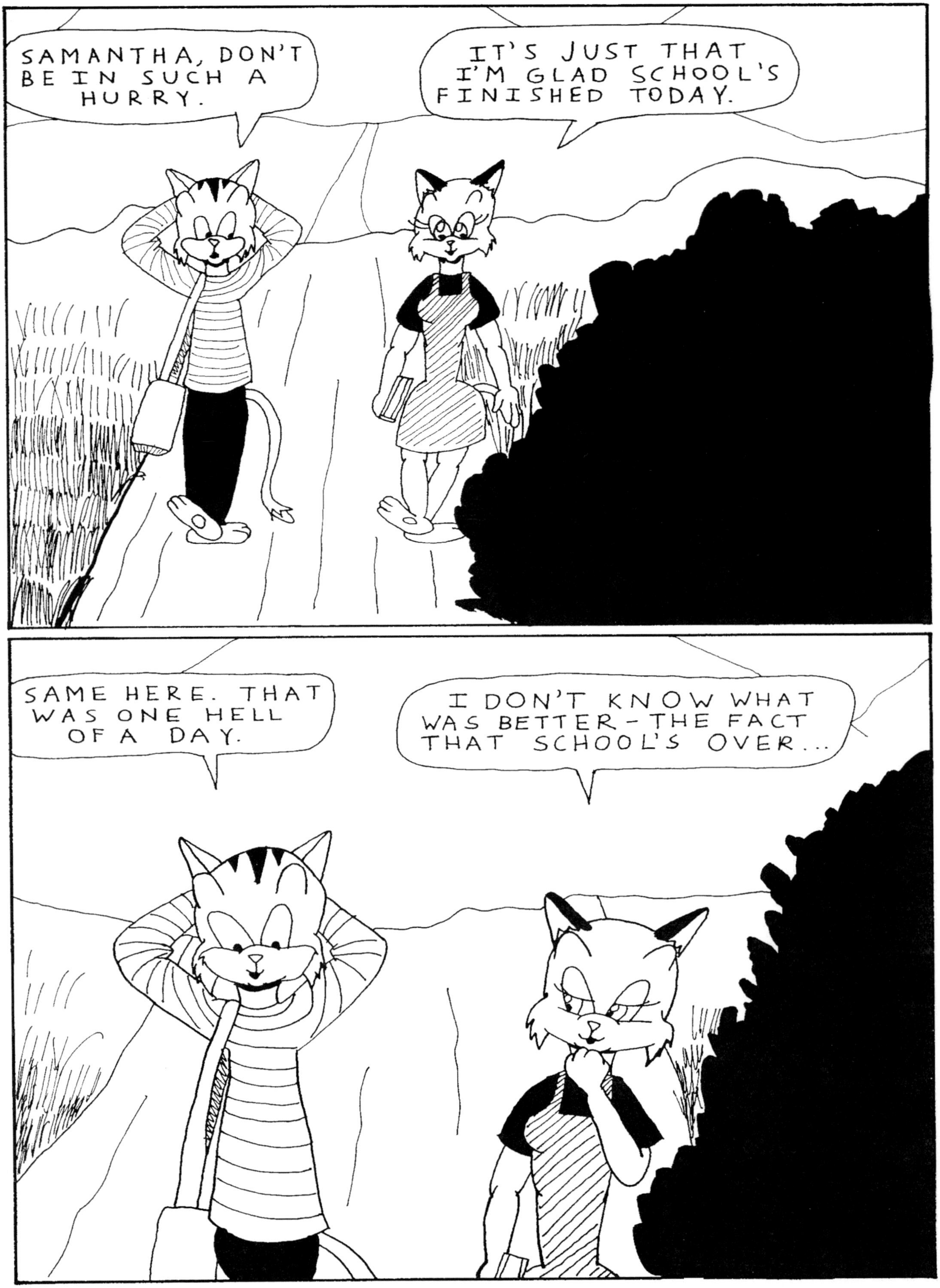
SAMANTHA, DON'T BE IN SUCH A HURRY.
IT'S JUST THAT I'M GLAD SCHOOL'S FINISHED TODAY.
SAME HERE. THAT WAS ONE HELL OF A DAY.
I DON'T KNOW WHAT WAS BETTER - THE FACT THAT SCHOOL'S OVER...

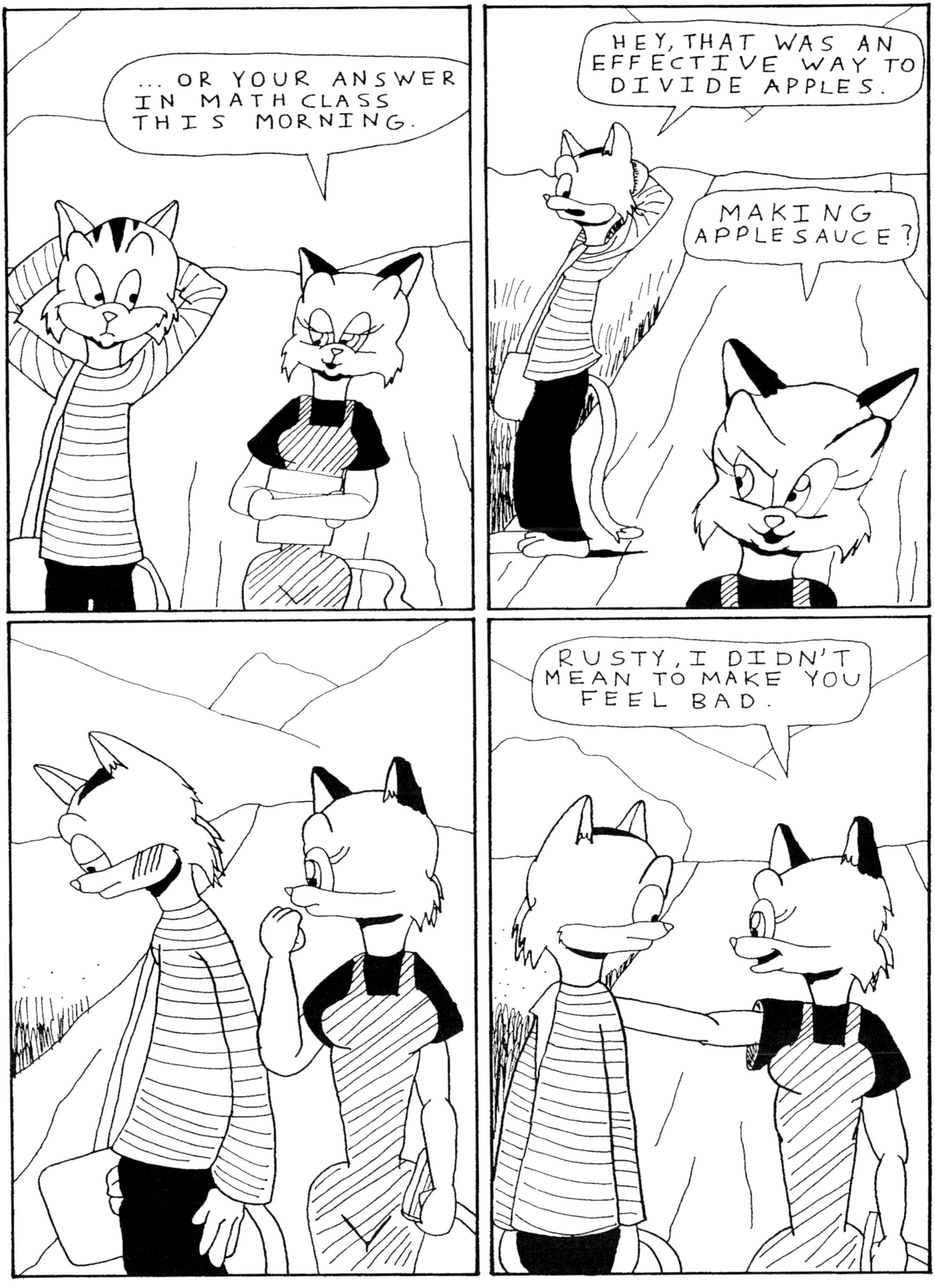

... OR YOUR ANSWER IN MATH CLASS THIS MORNING.
HEY, THAT WAS AN EFFECTIVE WAY TO DIVIDE APPLES.
MAKING APPLESAUCE?
RUSTY, I DIDN'T MEAN TO MAKE YOU FEEL BAD.

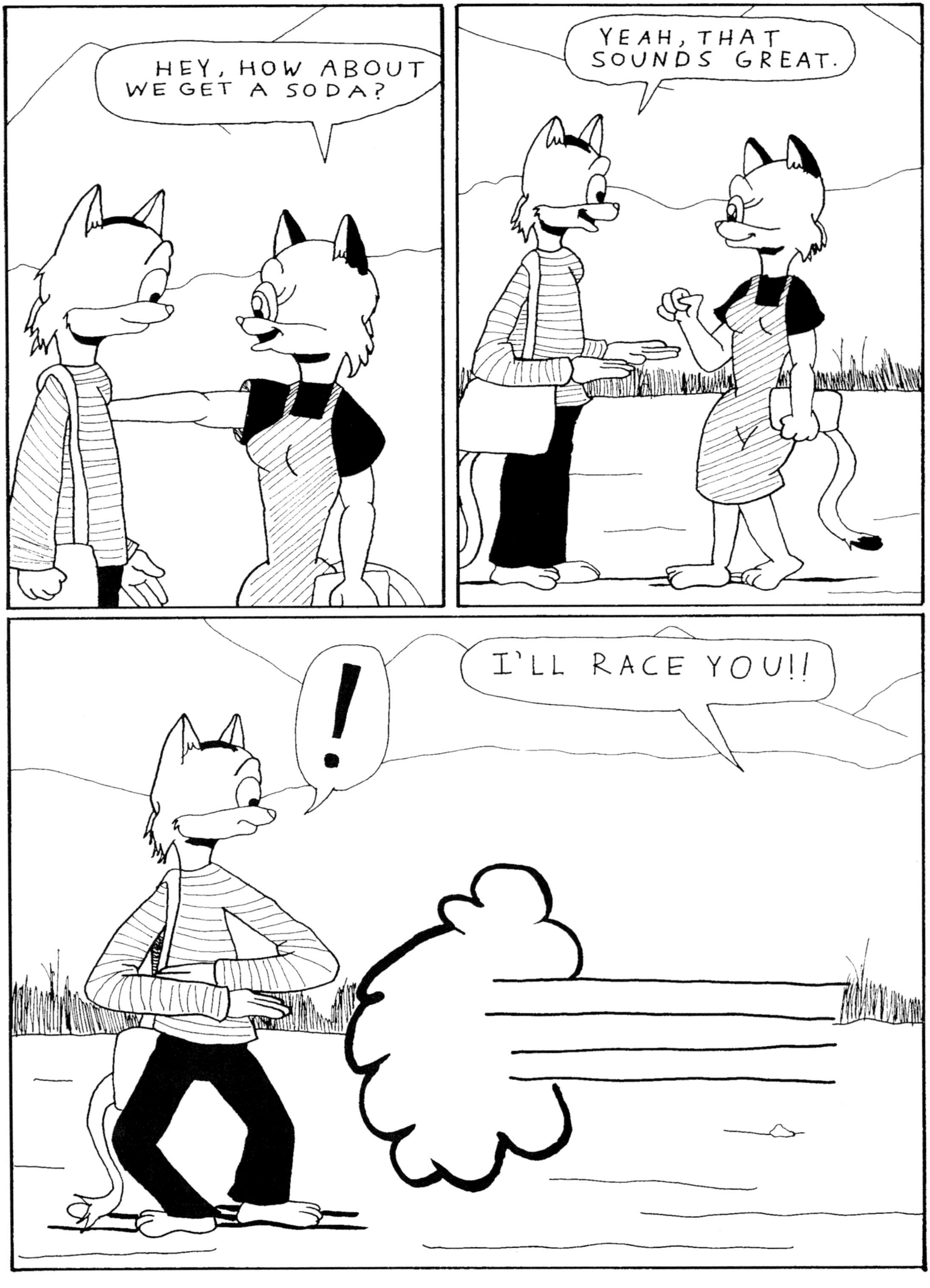
HEY, HOW ABOUT WE GET A SODA?
YEAH, THAT SOUNDS GREAT.
!
I'LL RACE YOU!!

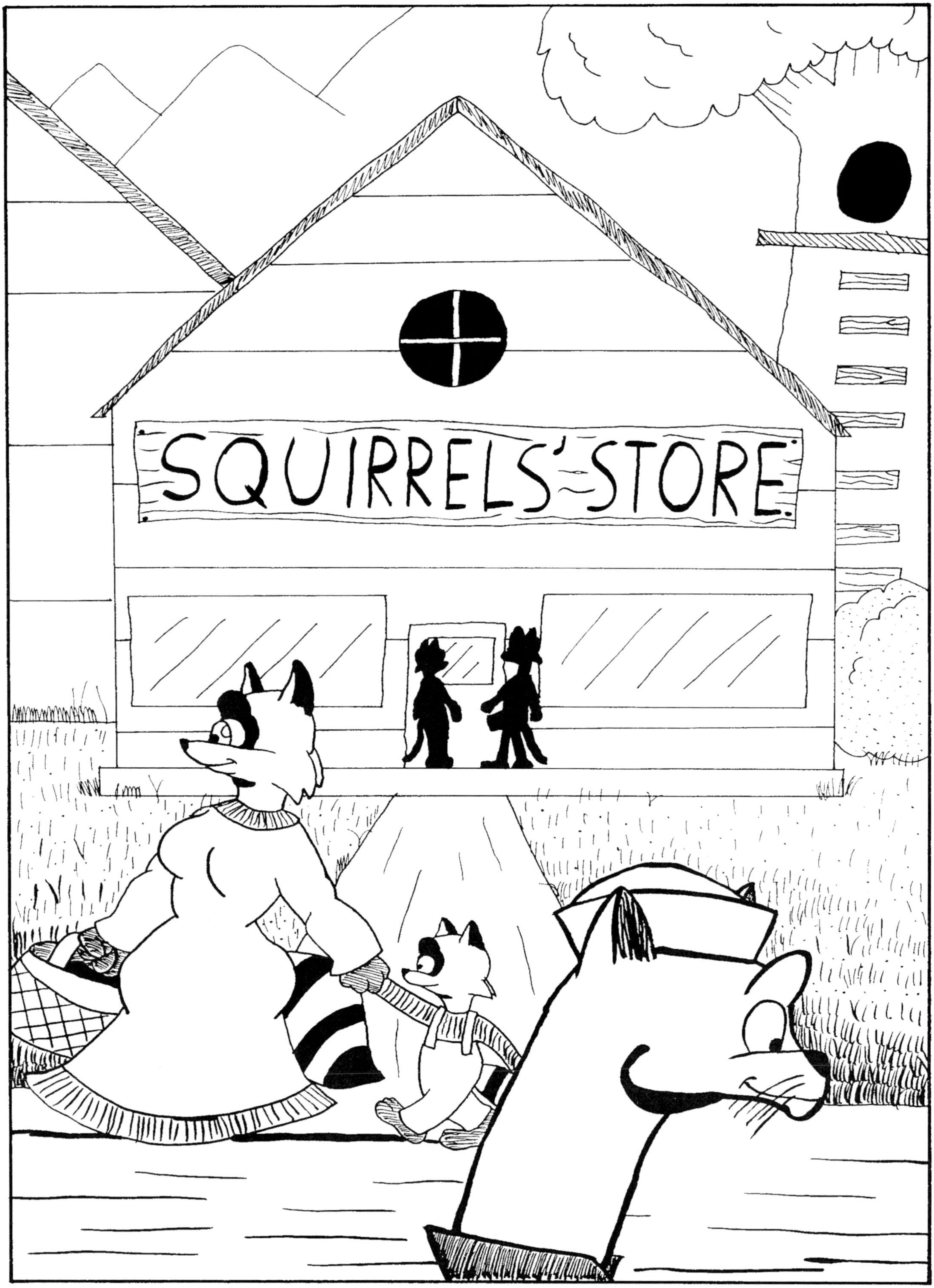
SQUIRRELS' STORE

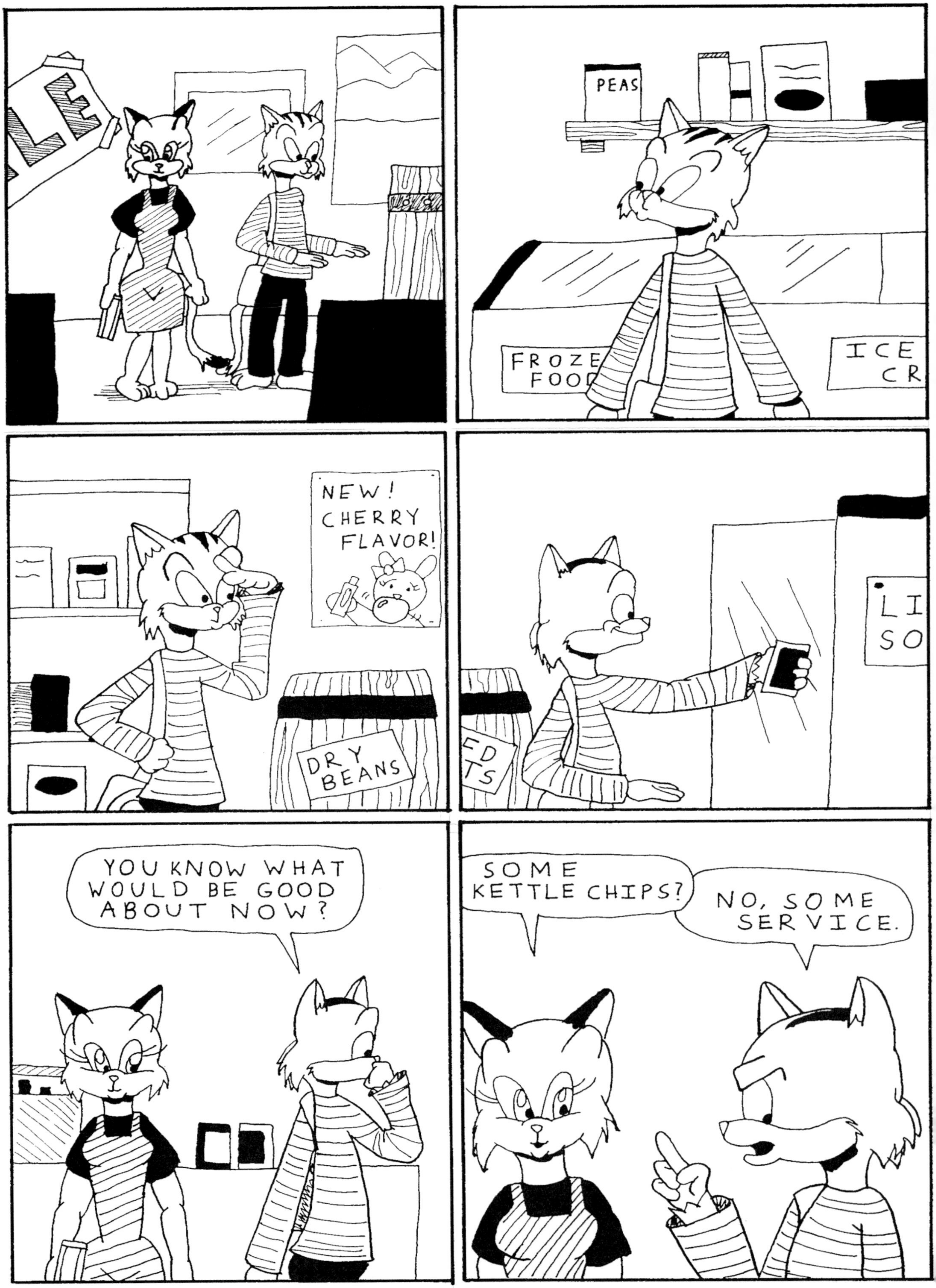

PEAS
FROZE FOOD
ICE CR
NEW! CHERRY FLAVOR!
DRY BEANS
LI SO
YOU KNOW WHAT WOULD BE GOOD ABOUT NOW?
SOME KETTLE CHIPS?
NO, SOME SERVICE.

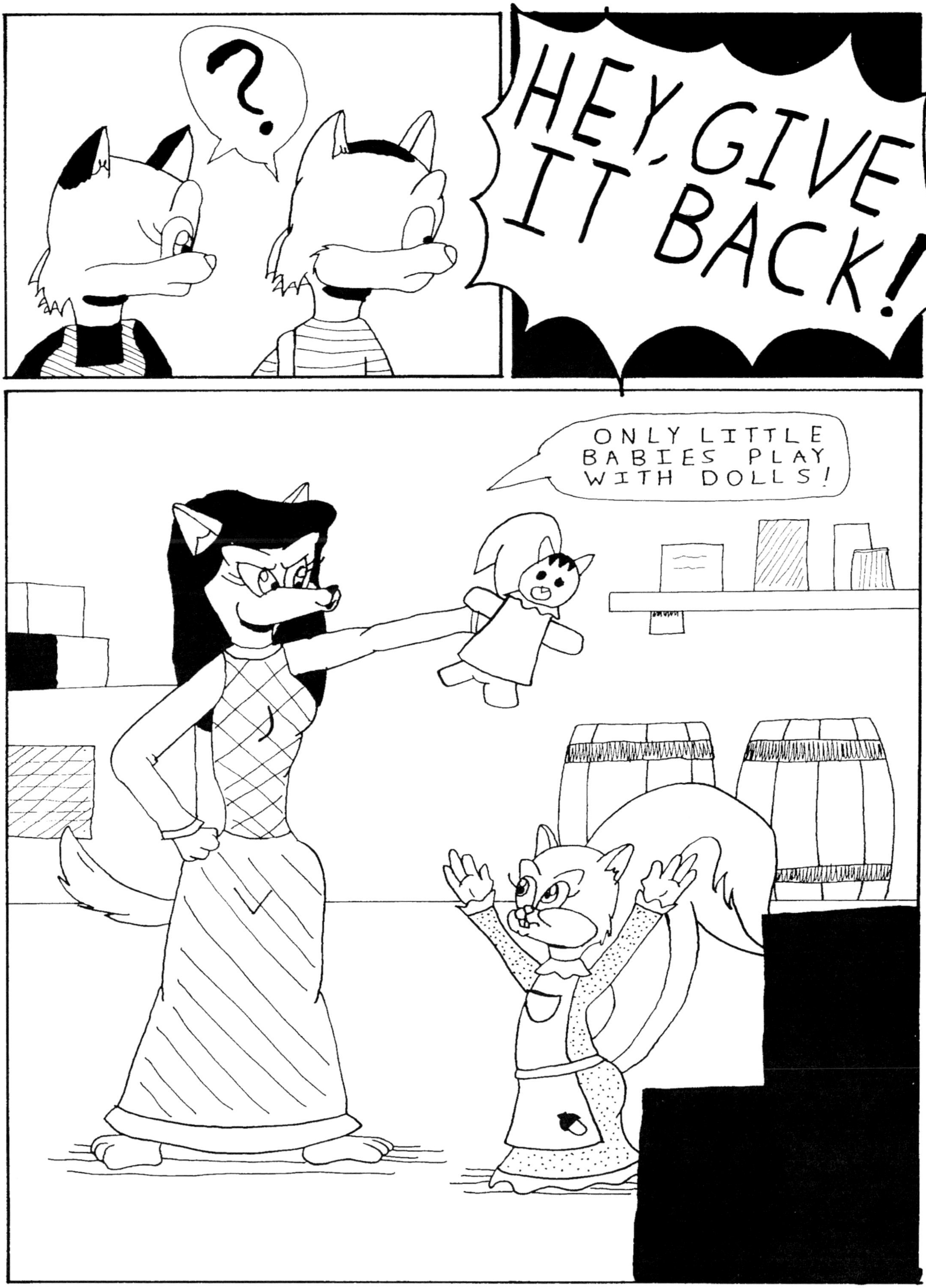
?
HEY, GIVE IT BACK!
ONLY LITTLE BABIES PLAY WITH DOLLS!

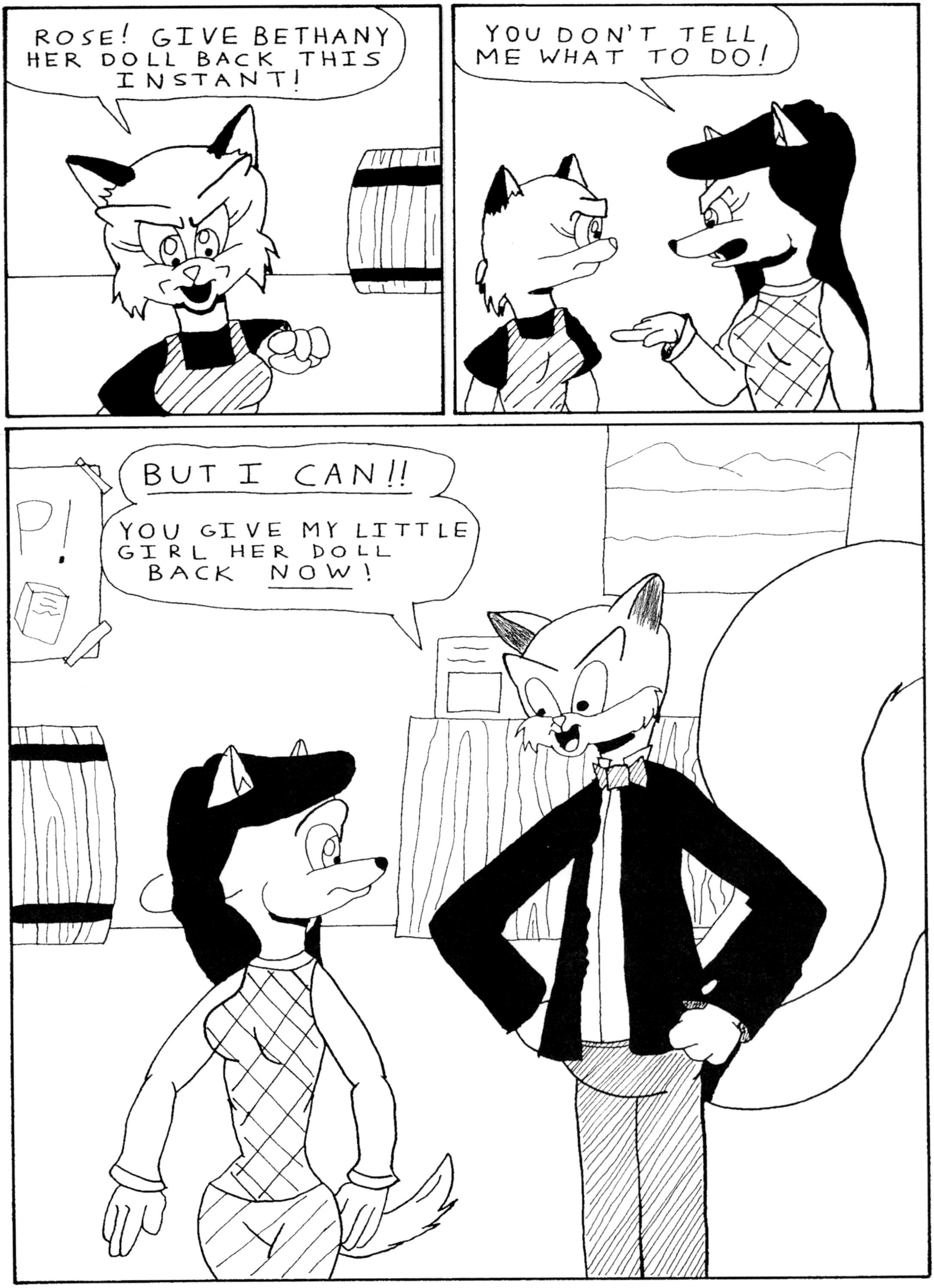
ROSE! GIVE BETHANY HER DOLL BACK THIS INSTANT!
YOU DON'T TELL ME WHAT TO DO!
BUT I CAN!!
YOU GIVE MY LITTLE GIRL HER DOLL BACK NOW!

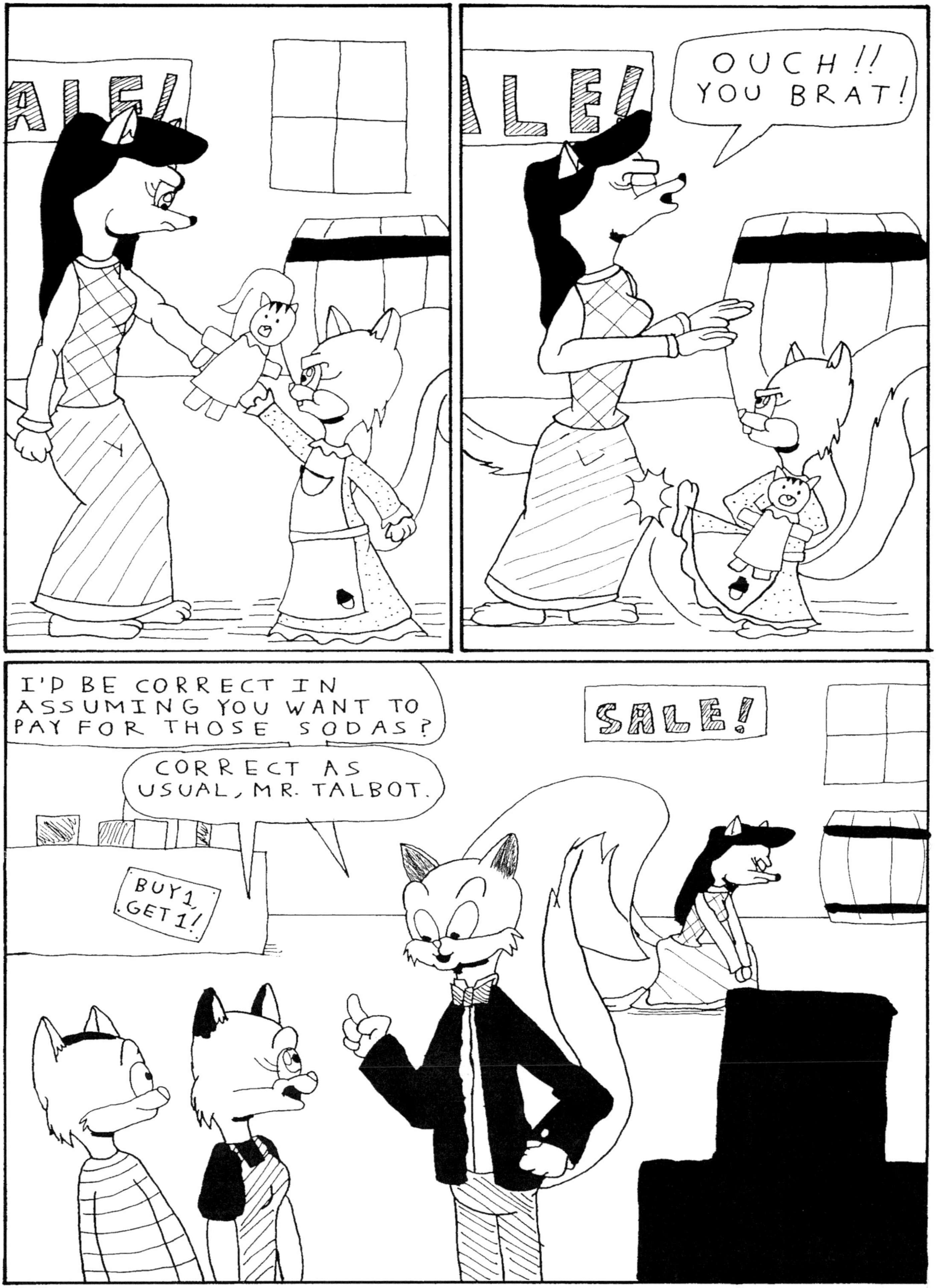
ALE!
ALE!
OUCH!! YOU BRAT!
I'D BE CORRECT IN ASSUMING YOU WANT TO PAY FOR THOSE SODAS?
CORRECT AS USUAL, MR. TALBOT.
SALE!
BUY 1, GET 1!

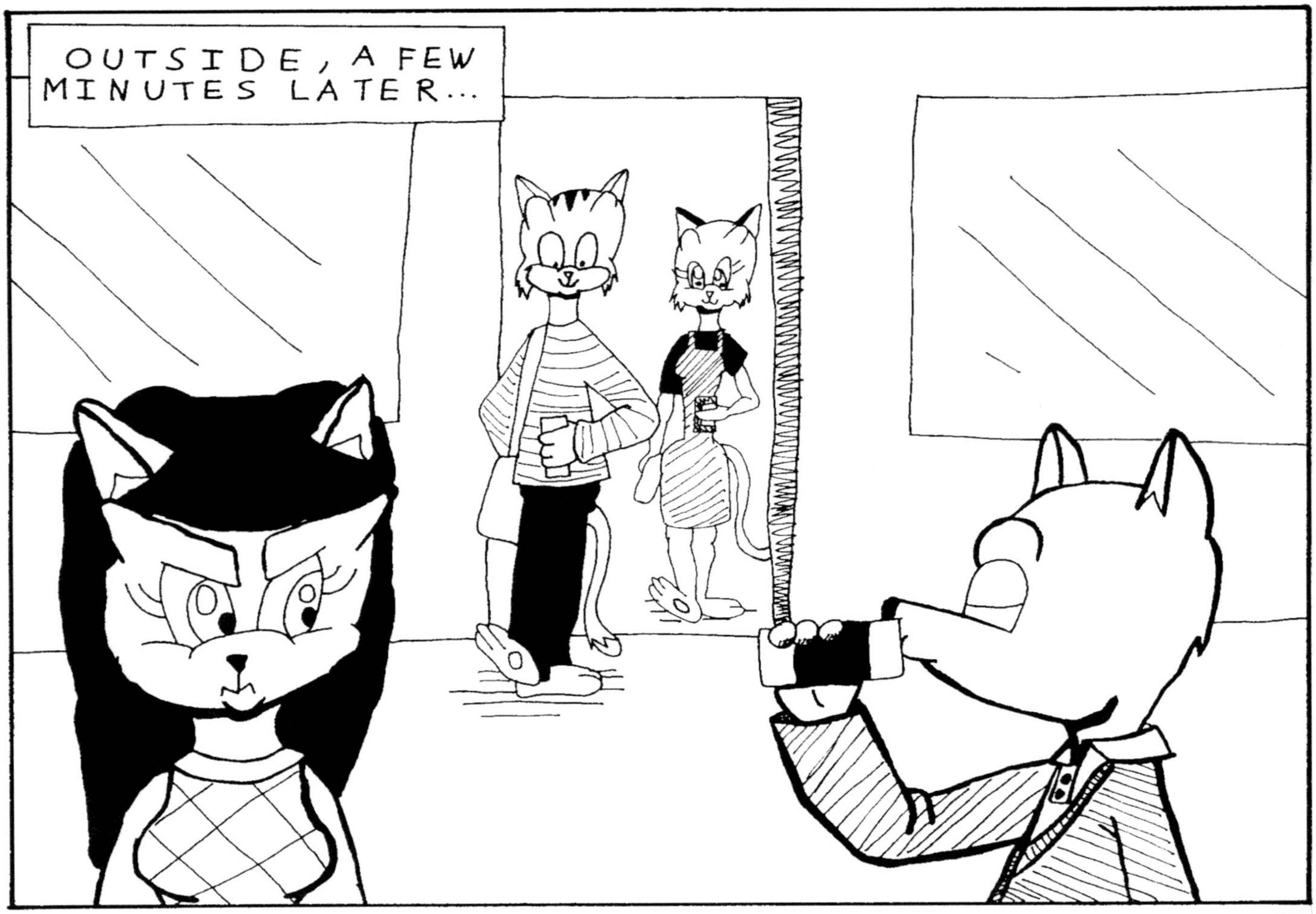
OUTSIDE, A FEW MINUTES LATER...

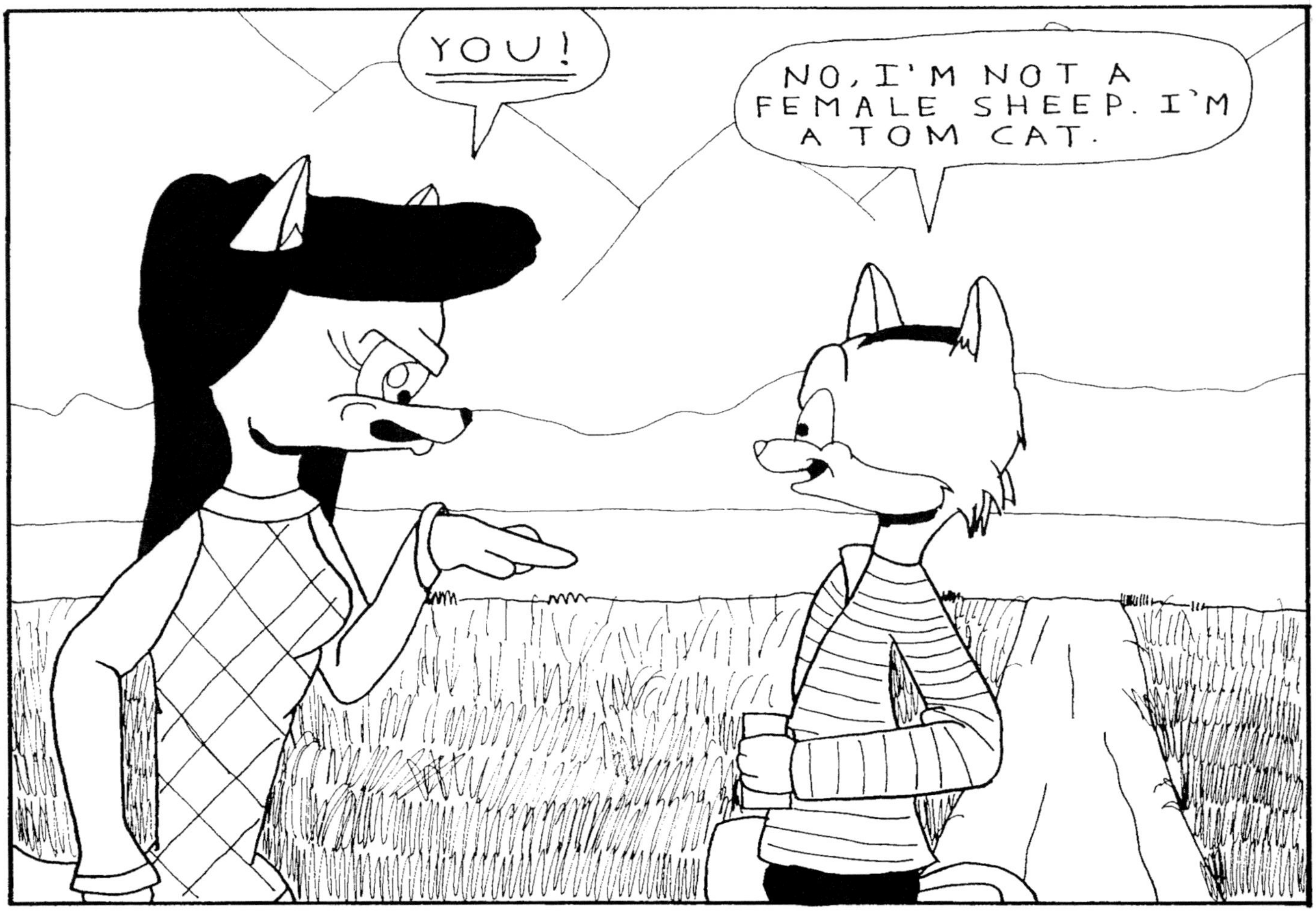
YOU!
NO, I'M NOT A FEMALE SHEEP. I'M A TOM CAT.

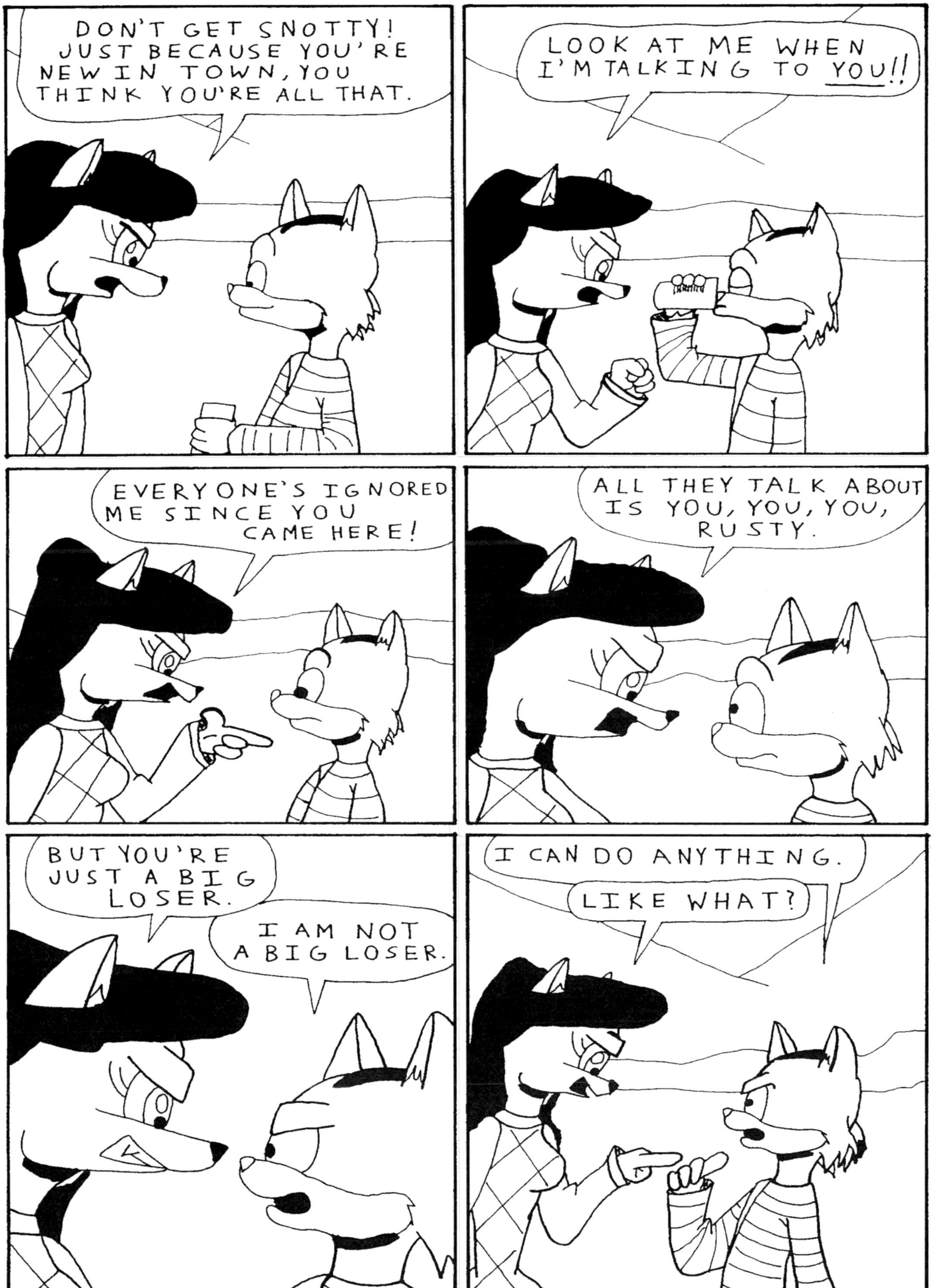
DON'T GET SNOTTY! JUST BECAUSE YOU'RE NEW IN TOWN, YOU THINK YOU'RE ALL THAT.
LOOK AT ME WHEN I'M TALKING TO YOU!!
EVERYONE'S IGNORED ME SINCE YOU CAME HERE!
ALL THEY TALK ABOUT IS YOU, YOU, YOU, RUSTY.
BUT YOU'RE JUST A BIG LOSER.
I AM NOT A BIG LOSER.
I CAN DO ANYTHING.
LIKE WHAT?

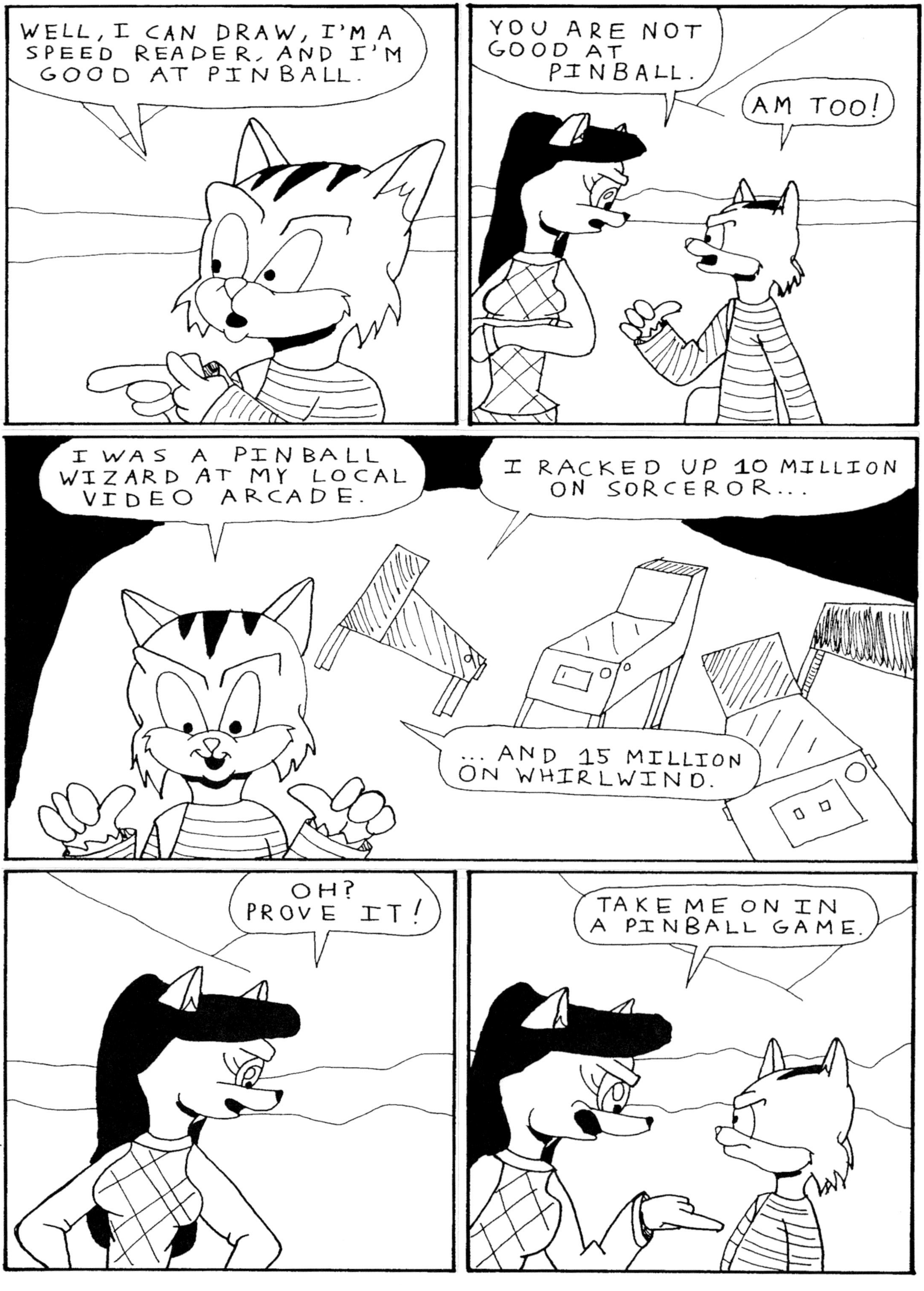
WELL, I CAN DRAW, I'M A SPEED READER, AND I'M GOOD AT PINBALL.
YOU ARE NOT GOOD AT PINBALL.
AM TOO!
I WAS A PINBALL WIZARD AT MY LOCAL VIDEO ARCADE.
I RACKED UP 10 MILLION ON SORCEROR...
... AND 15 MILLION ON WHIRLWIND.
OH? PROVE IT!
TAKE ME ON IN A PINBALL GAME.

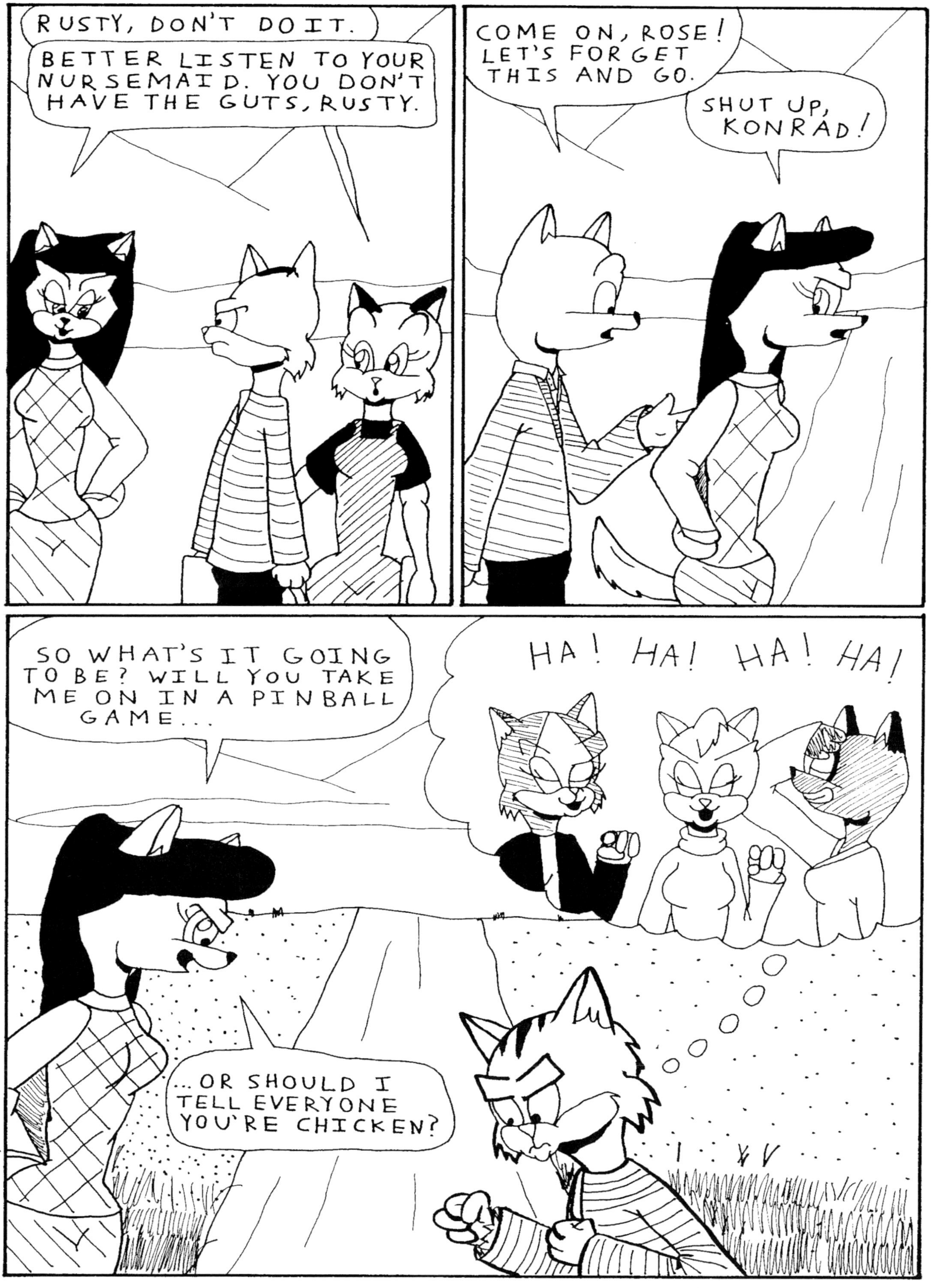
RUSTY, DON'T DO IT.
BETTER LISTEN TO YOUR NURSEMAID. YOU DON'T HAVE THE GUTS, RUSTY.
COME ON, ROSE! LET'S FORGET THIS AND GO.
SHUT UP, KONRAD!
SO WHAT'S IT GOING TO BE? WILL YOU TAKE ME ON IN A PINBALL GAME...
HA! HA! HA! HA!
...OR SHOULD I TELL EVERYONE YOU'RE CHICKEN?

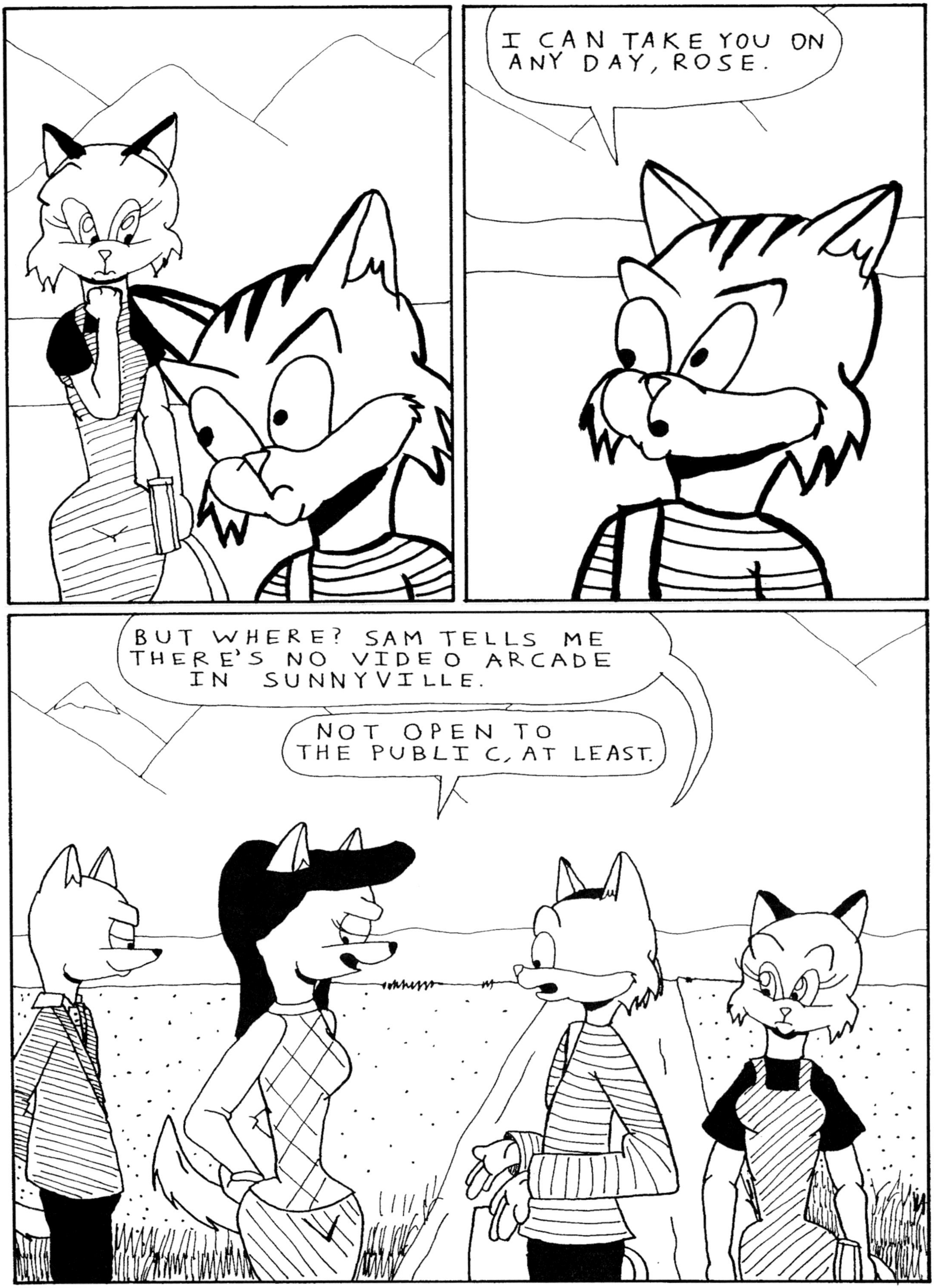
I CAN TAKE YOU ON ANY DAY, ROSE.
BUT WHERE? SAM TELLS ME THERE'S NO VIDEO ARCADE IN SUNNYVILLE.
NOT OPEN TO THE PUBLIC, AT LEAST.

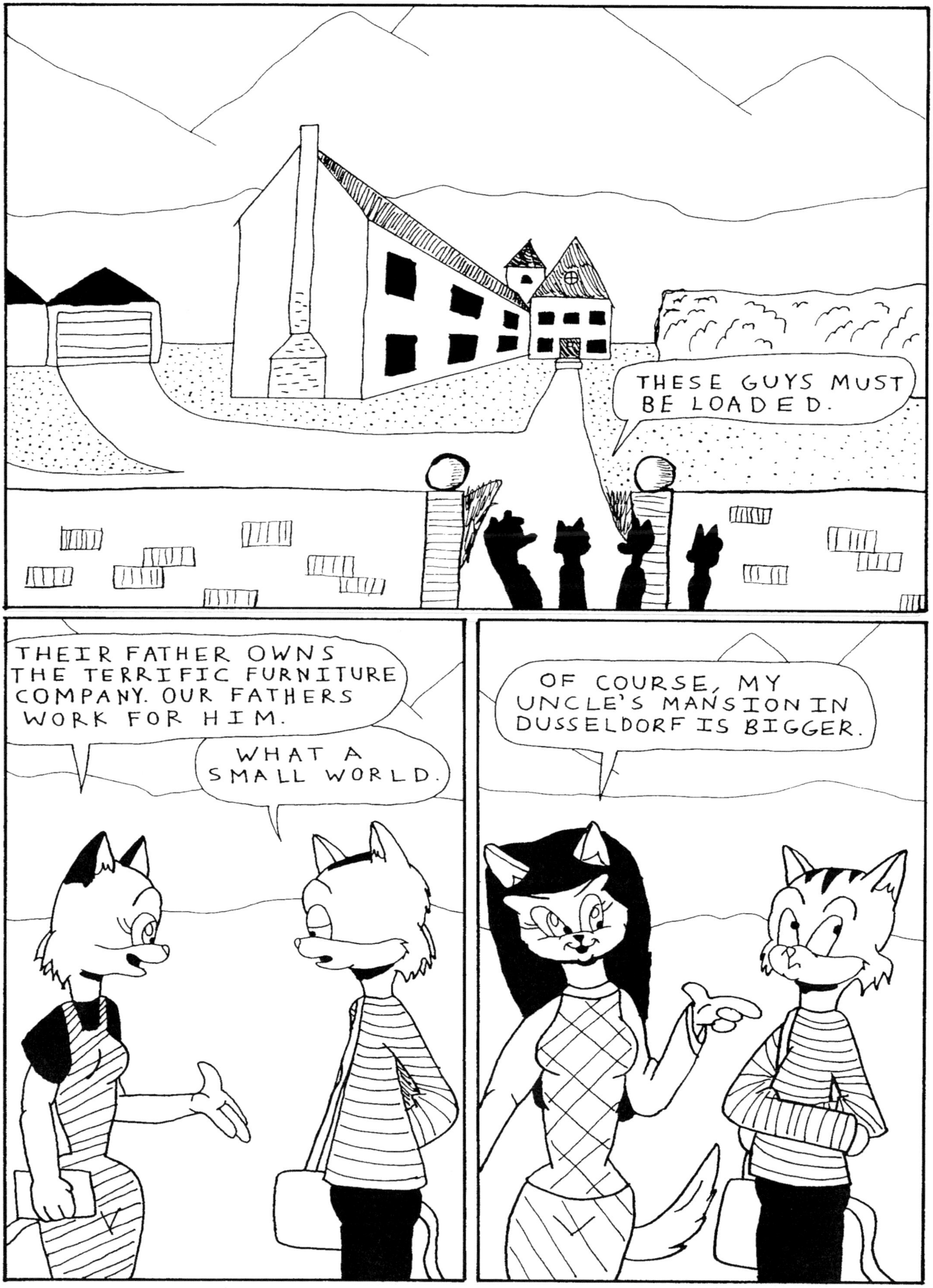
THESE GUYS MUST BE LOADED.
THEIR FATHER OWNS THE TERRIFIC FURNITURE COMPANY. OUR FATHERS WORK FOR HIM.
WHAT A SMALL WORLD.
OF COURSE, MY UNCLE'S MANSION IN DUSSELDORF IS BIGGER.

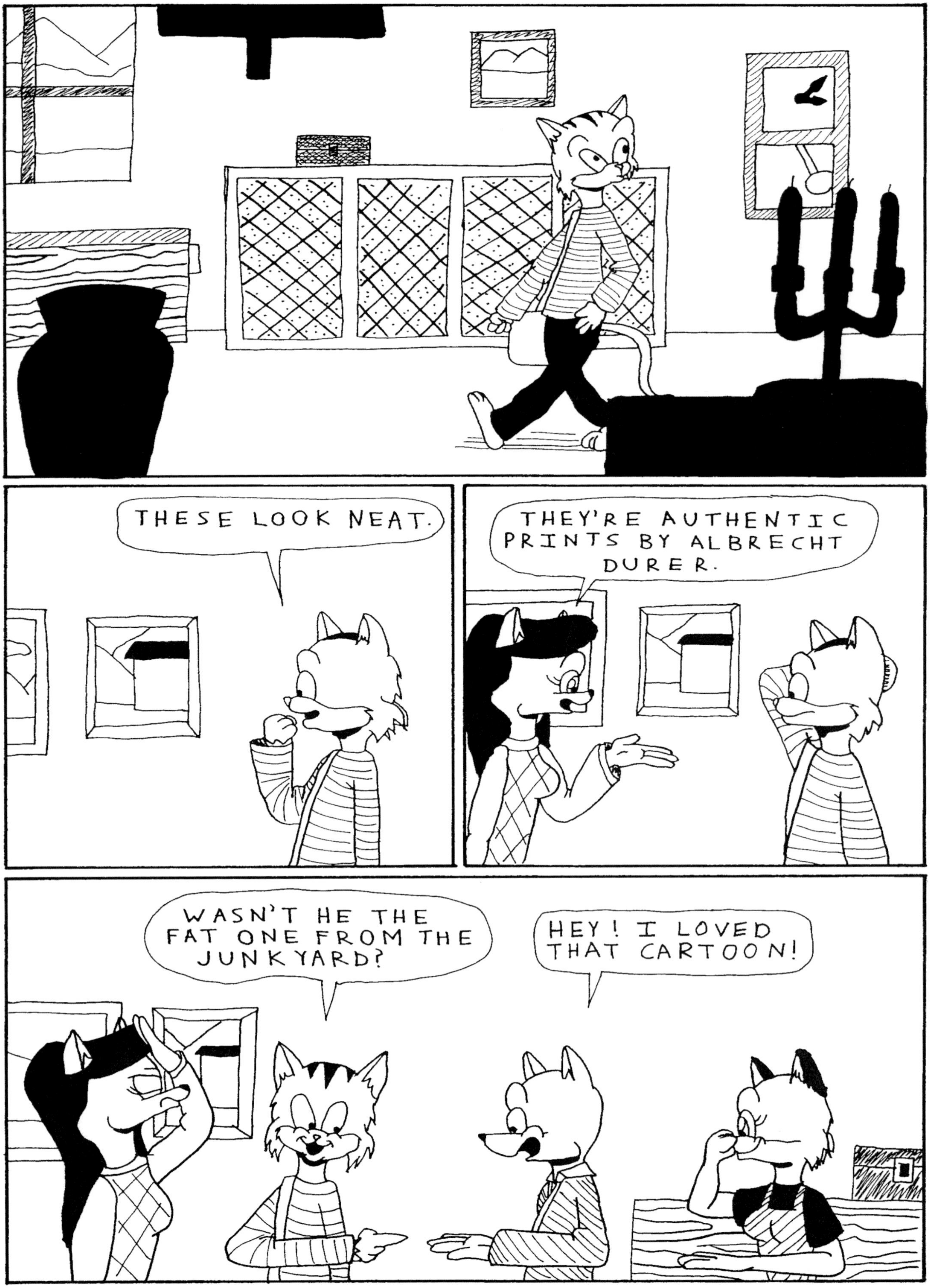
THESE LOOK NEAT.
THEY'RE AUTHENTIC PRINTS BY ALBRECHT DURER.
WASN'T HE THE FAT ONE FROM THE JUNKYARD?
HEY! I LOVED THAT CARTOON!

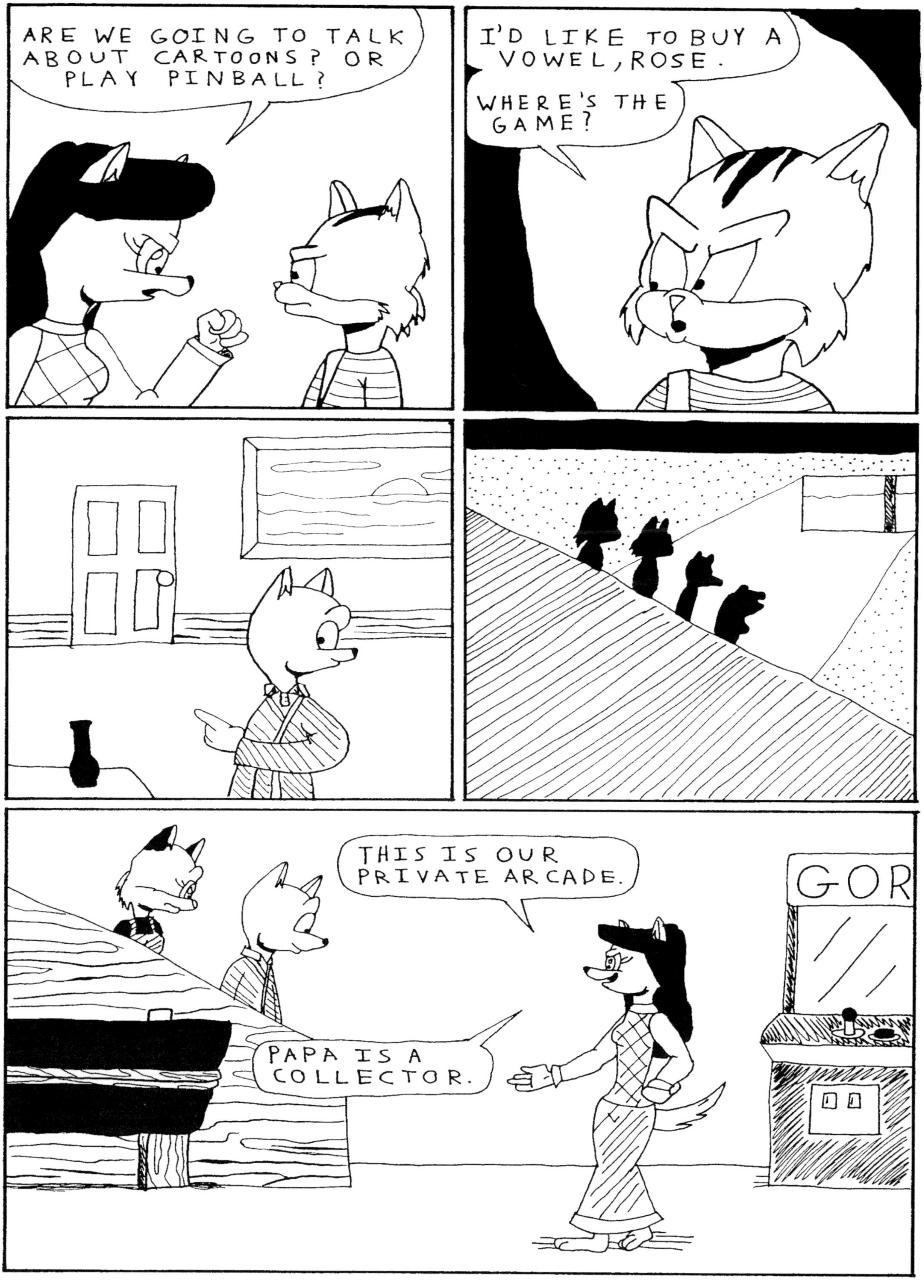
ARE WE GOING TO TALK ABOUT CARTOONS? OR PLAY PINBALL?
I'D LIKE TO BUY A VOWEL, ROSE.
WHERE'S THE GAME?
THIS IS OUR PRIVATE ARCADE.
PAPA IS A COLLECTOR.
GOR

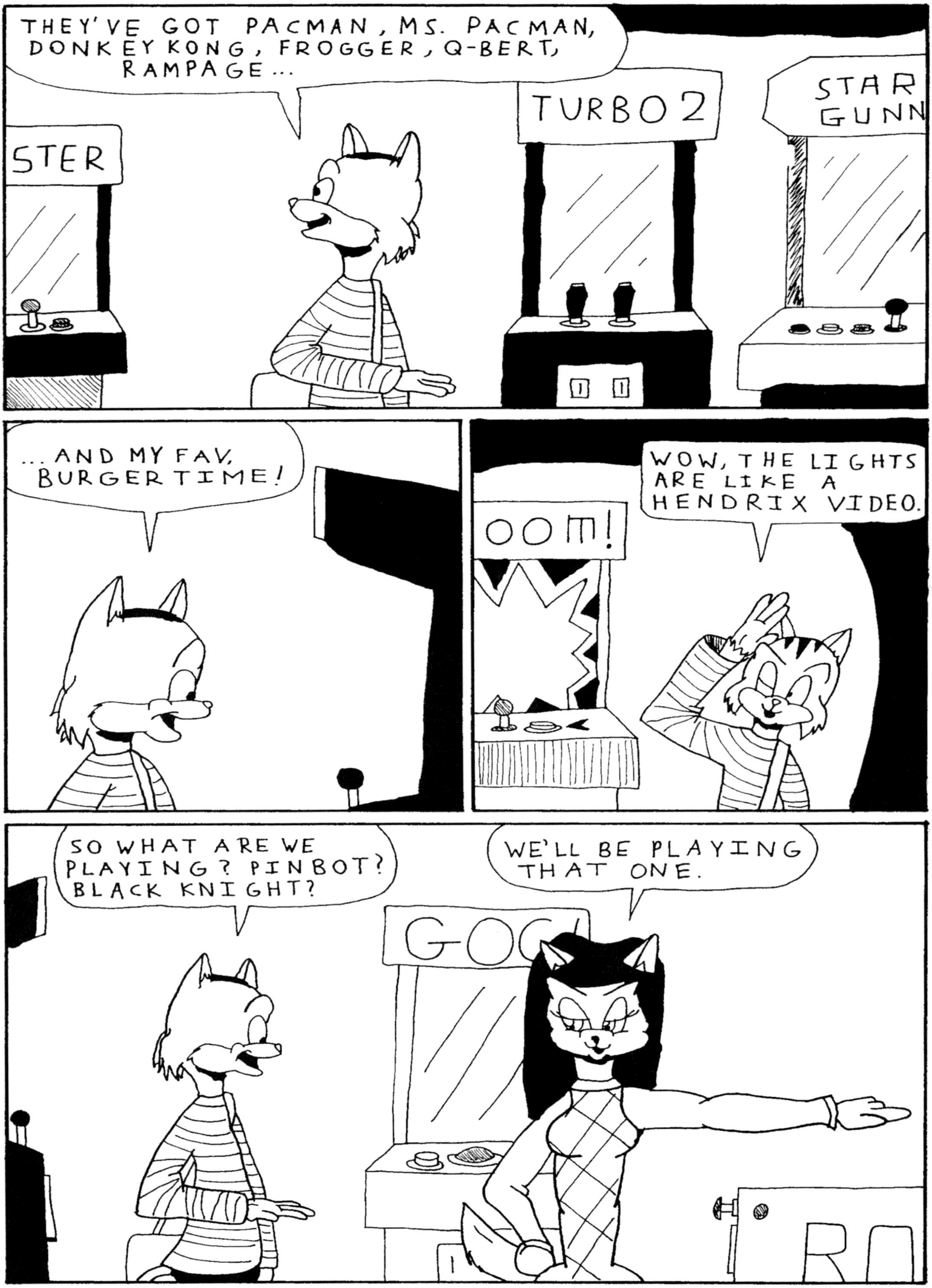
THEY'VE GOT PACMAN, MS. PACMAN, DONKEY KONG, FROGGER, Q-BERT, RAMPAGE...
TURBO 2
STAR GUNN
...AND MY FAV, BURGER TIME!
WOW, THE LIGHTS ARE LIKE A HENDRIX VIDEO.
SO WHAT ARE WE PLAYING? PINBOT? BLACK KNIGHT?
WE'LL BE PLAYING THAT ONE.

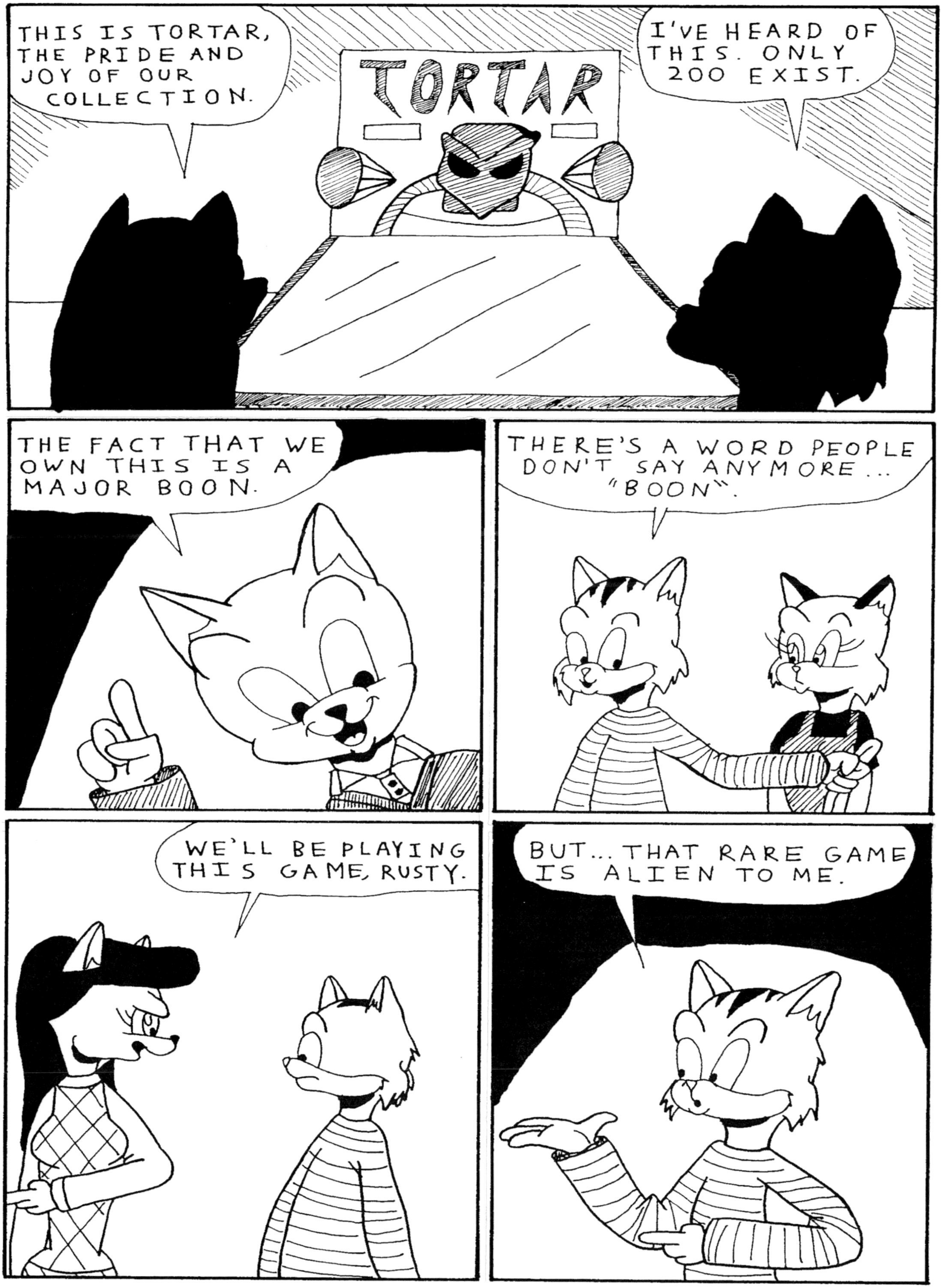
THIS IS TORTAR, THE PRIDE AND JOY OF OUR COLLECTION.
TORTAR
I'VE HEARD OF THIS. ONLY 200 EXIST.
THE FACT THAT WE OWN THIS IS A MAJOR BOON.
THERE'S A WORD PEOPLE DON'T SAY ANYMORE... "BOON".
WE'LL BE PLAYING THIS GAME, RUSTY.
BUT... THAT RARE GAME IS ALIEN TO ME.

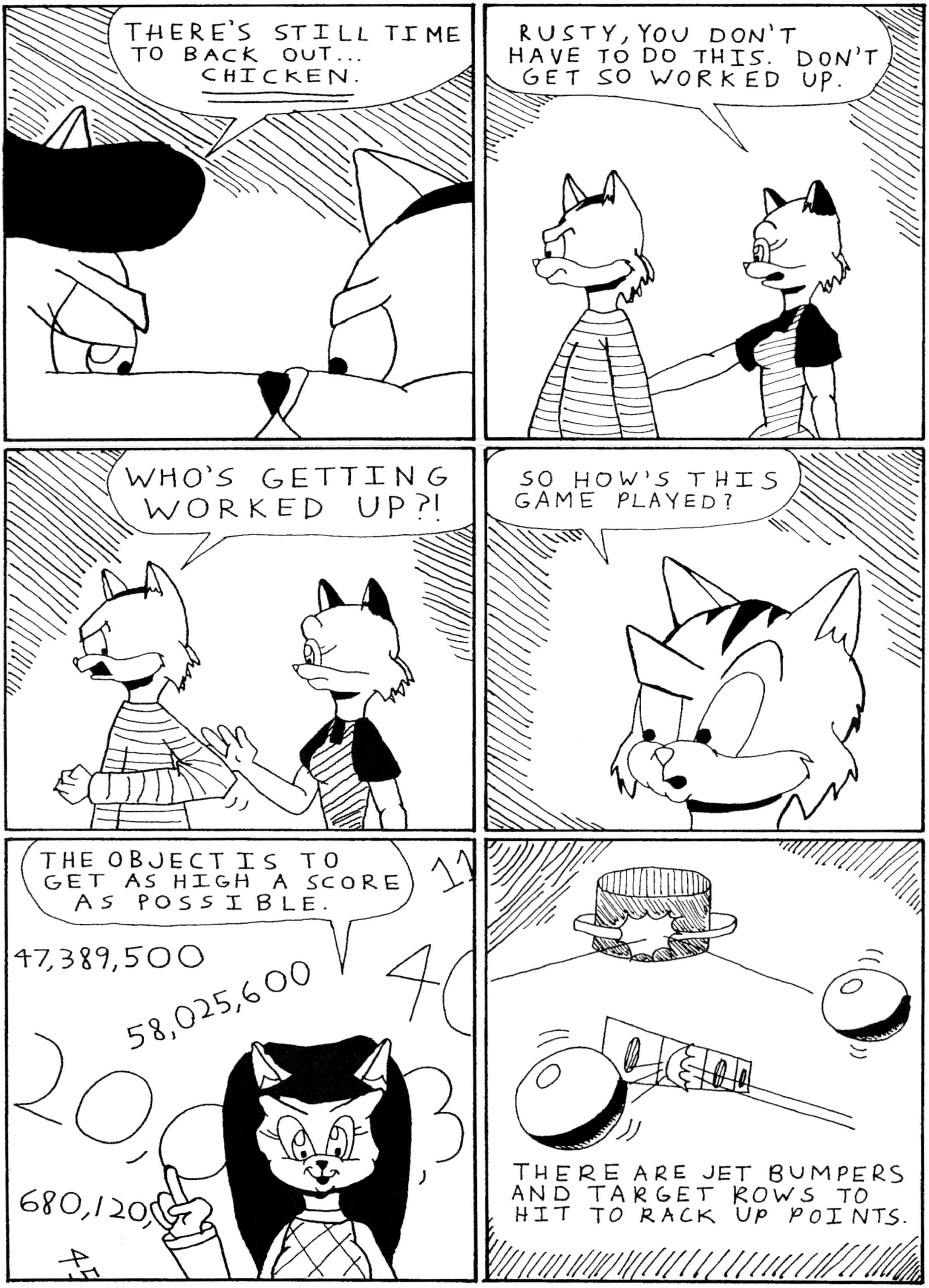
THERE'S STILL TIME TO BACK OUT... CHICKEN.
RUSTY, YOU DON'T HAVE TO DO THIS. DON'T GET SO WORKED UP.
WHO'S GETTING WORKED UP?!
SO HOW'S THIS GAME PLAYED?
THE OBJECT IS TO GET AS HIGH A SCORE AS POSSIBLE.
47,389,500
58,025,600
680,120,
THERE ARE JET BUMPERS AND TARGET ROWS TO HIT TO RACK UP POINTS.

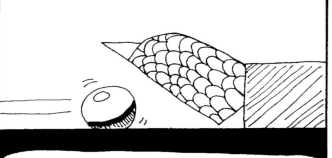

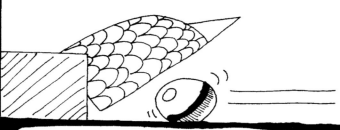

THE BEST WAY TO EARN POINTS IS TO ACTIVATE MULTIBALL.

THIS IS DONE BY LOCKING A BALL IN TORTAR'S CLAW.

LOCK A SECOND BALL IN THE OTHER CLAW TO ACTIVATE MULTIBALL.

DURING MULTIBALL, ALL POINT VALUES ARE DOUBLED.

BUT IF YOU'RE A REAL PINBALL WIZARD, YOU CAN GO FOR...

MULTIBALL MADNESS!

I DON'T KNOW WHAT THAT IS, BUT I THINK I'M ABOUT TO LEARN.

MULTIBALL MADNESS CAN ONLY BE DONE DURING MULTIBALL.

SHOOT A BALL INTO HIS MOUTH TO GET TEN MILLION POINTS.

HIT THE LEFT AND RIGHT GREEN JET BUMPERS TO MAKE TORTAR OPEN HIS MOUTH.

10,000,000

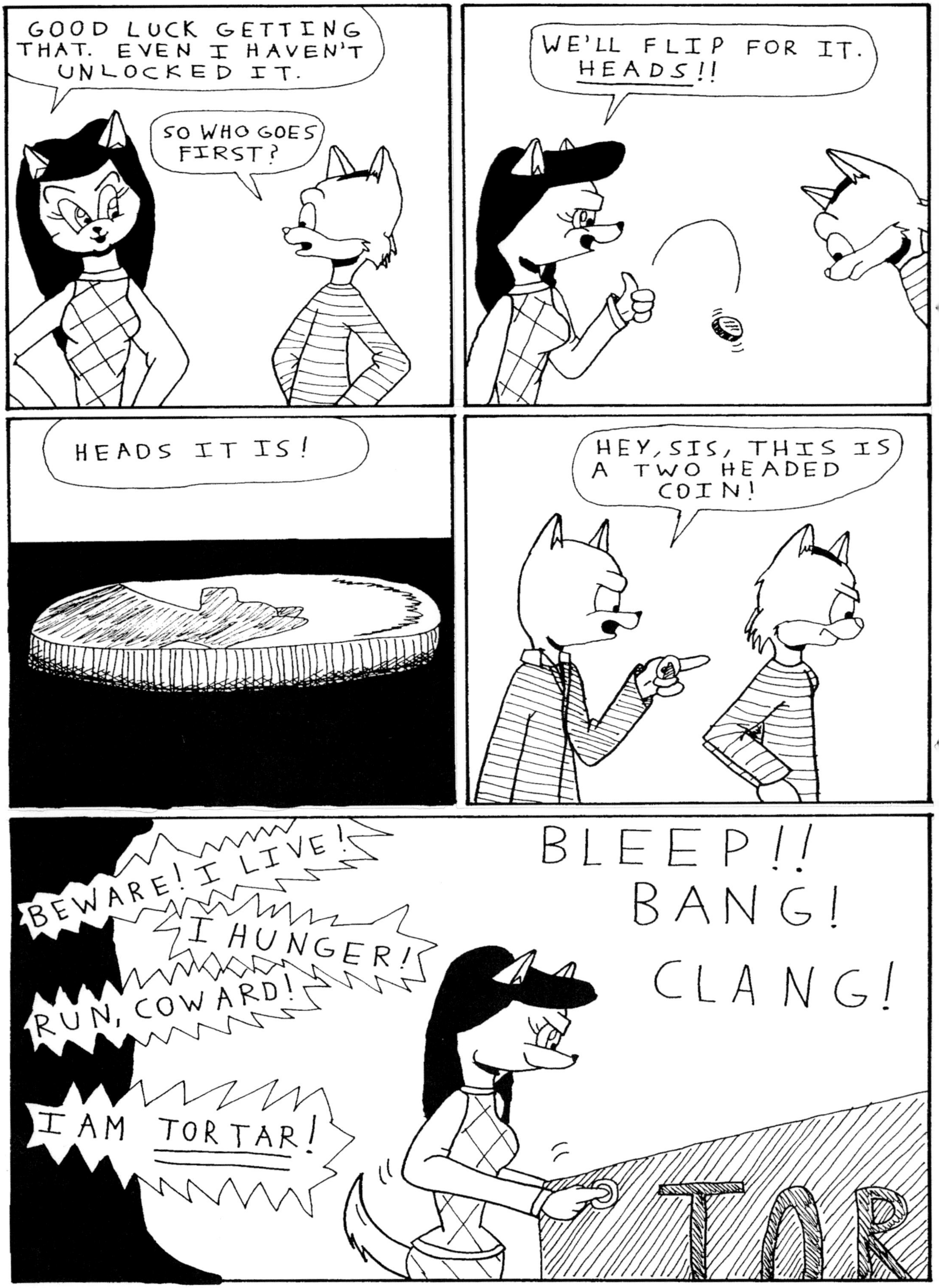
GOOD LUCK GETTING THAT. EVEN I HAVEN'T UNLOCKED IT.
SO WHO GOES FIRST?
WE'LL FLIP FOR IT. HEADS!!
HEADS IT IS!
HEY, SIS, THIS IS A TWO HEADED COIN!
BEWARE! I LIVE!
I HUNGER!
RUN, COWARD!
I AM TORTAR!
BLEEP!!
BANG!
CLANG!
TOR

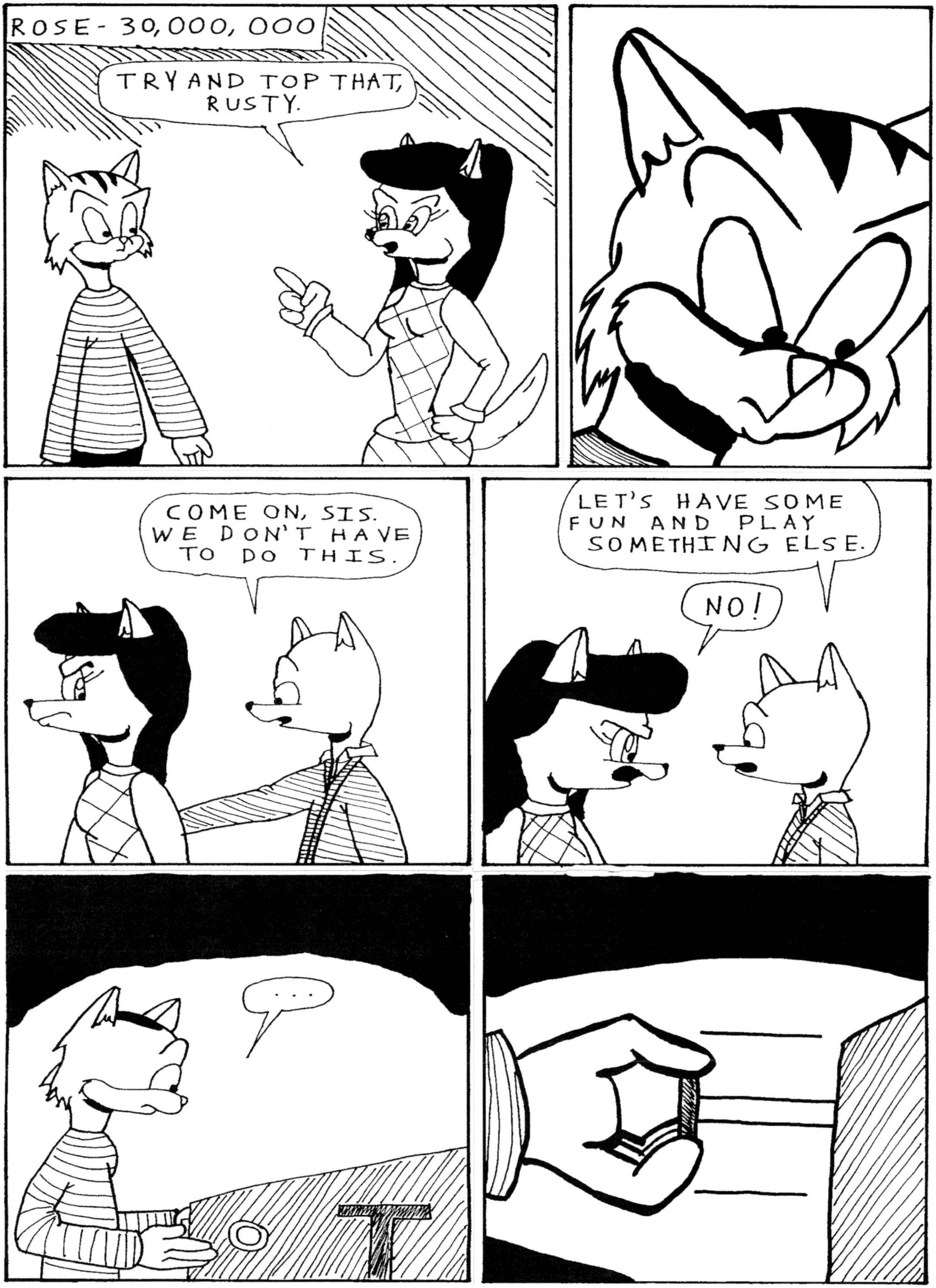
ROSE- 30,000,000
TRY AND TOP THAT, RUSTY.
COME ON, SIS. WE DON'T HAVE TO DO THIS.
LET'S HAVE SOME FUN AND PLAY SOMETHING ELSE.
NO!
. . .

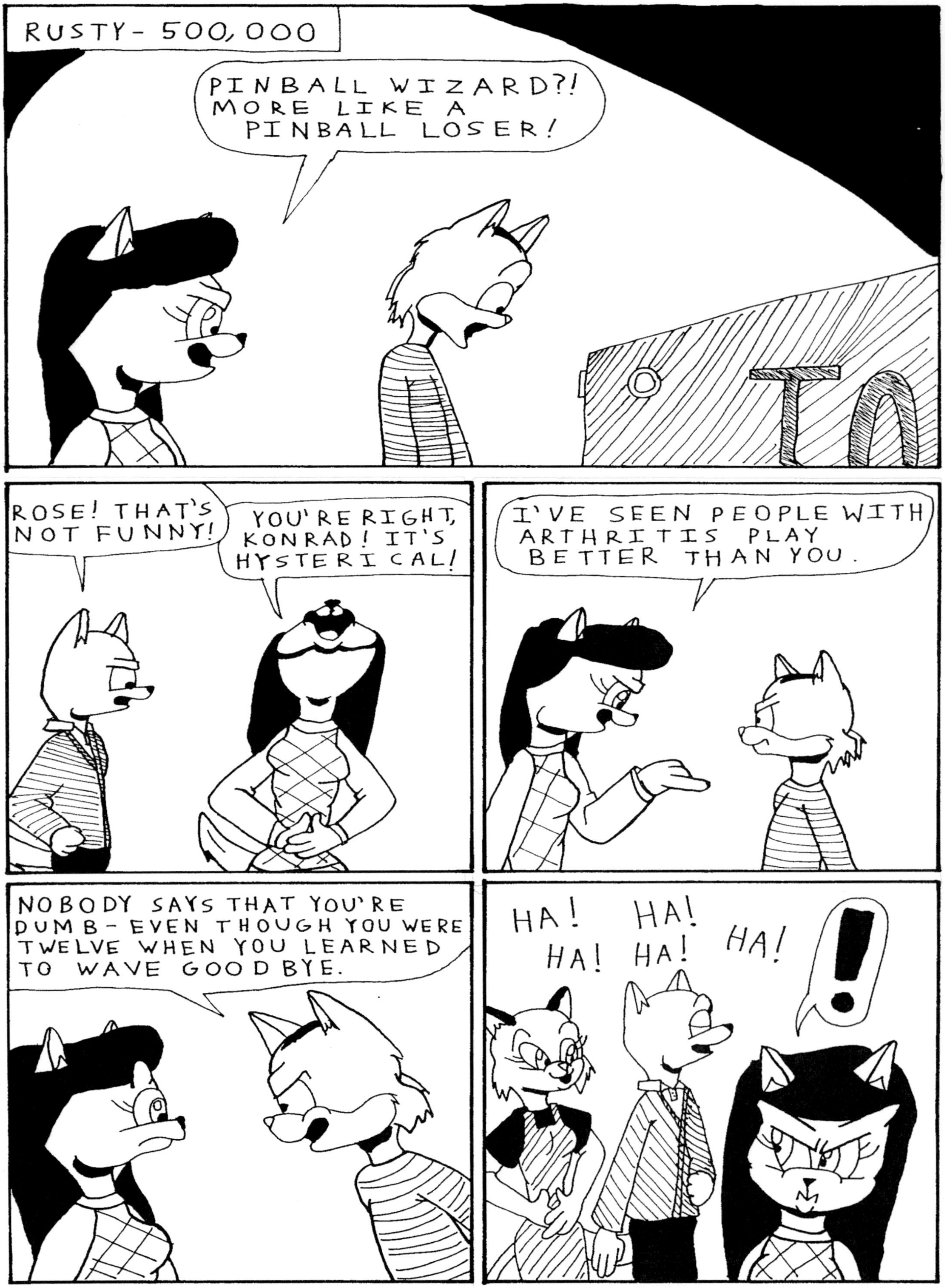
RUSTY- 500,000
PINBALL WIZARD?! MORE LIKE A PINBALL LOSER!
ROSE! THAT'S NOT FUNNY!
YOU'RE RIGHT, KONRAD! IT'S HYSTERICAL!
I'VE SEEN PEOPLE WITH ARTHRITIS PLAY BETTER THAN YOU.
NOBODY SAYS THAT YOU'RE DUMB - EVEN THOUGH YOU WERE TWELVE WHEN YOU LEARNED TO WAVE GOODBYE.
HA! HA! HA! HA! HA!
!

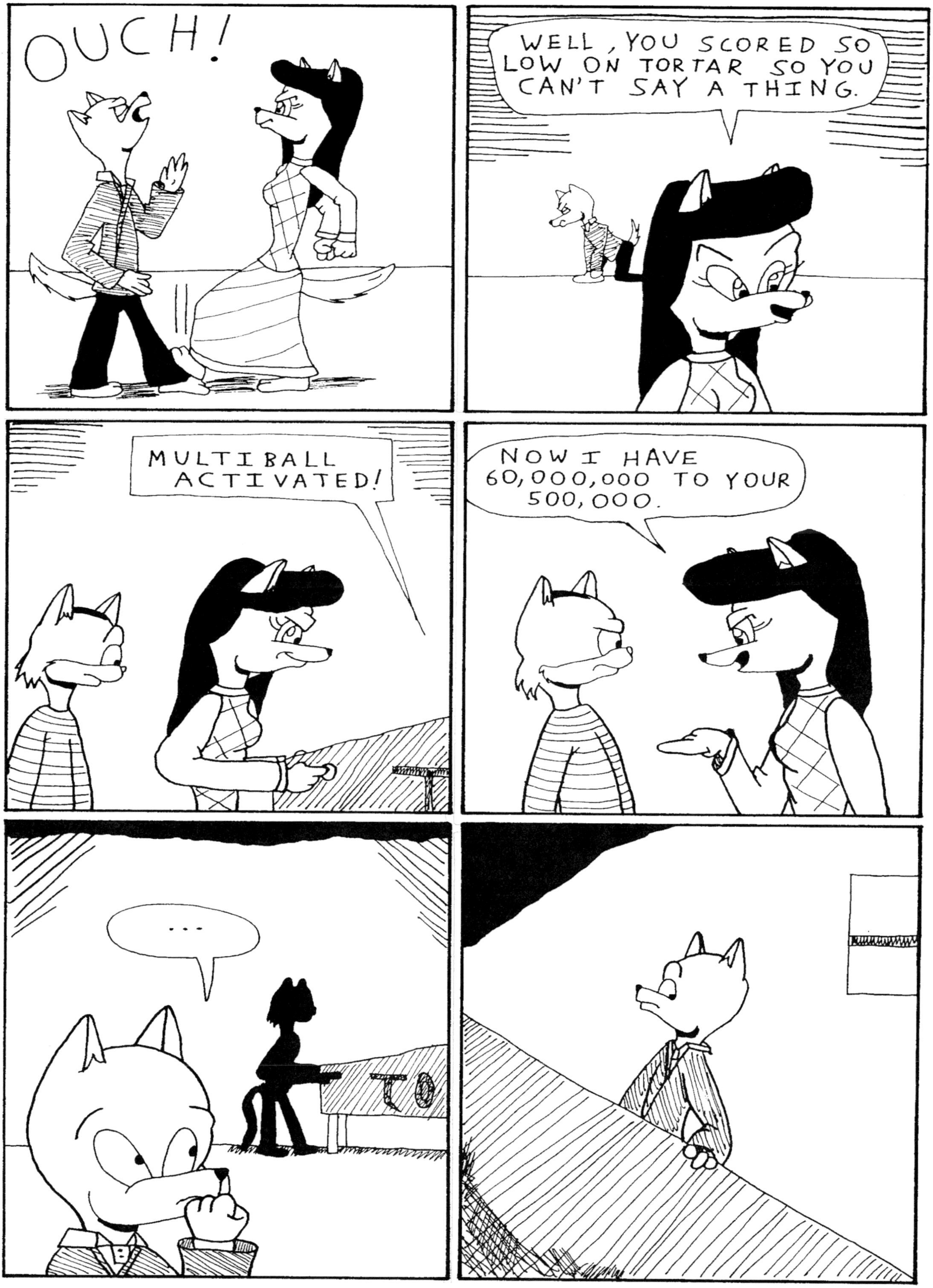
OUCH!
WELL, YOU SCORED SO LOW ON TORTAR SO YOU CAN'T SAY A THING.
MULTIBALL ACTIVATED!
NOW I HAVE 60,000,000 TO YOUR 500,000.
...

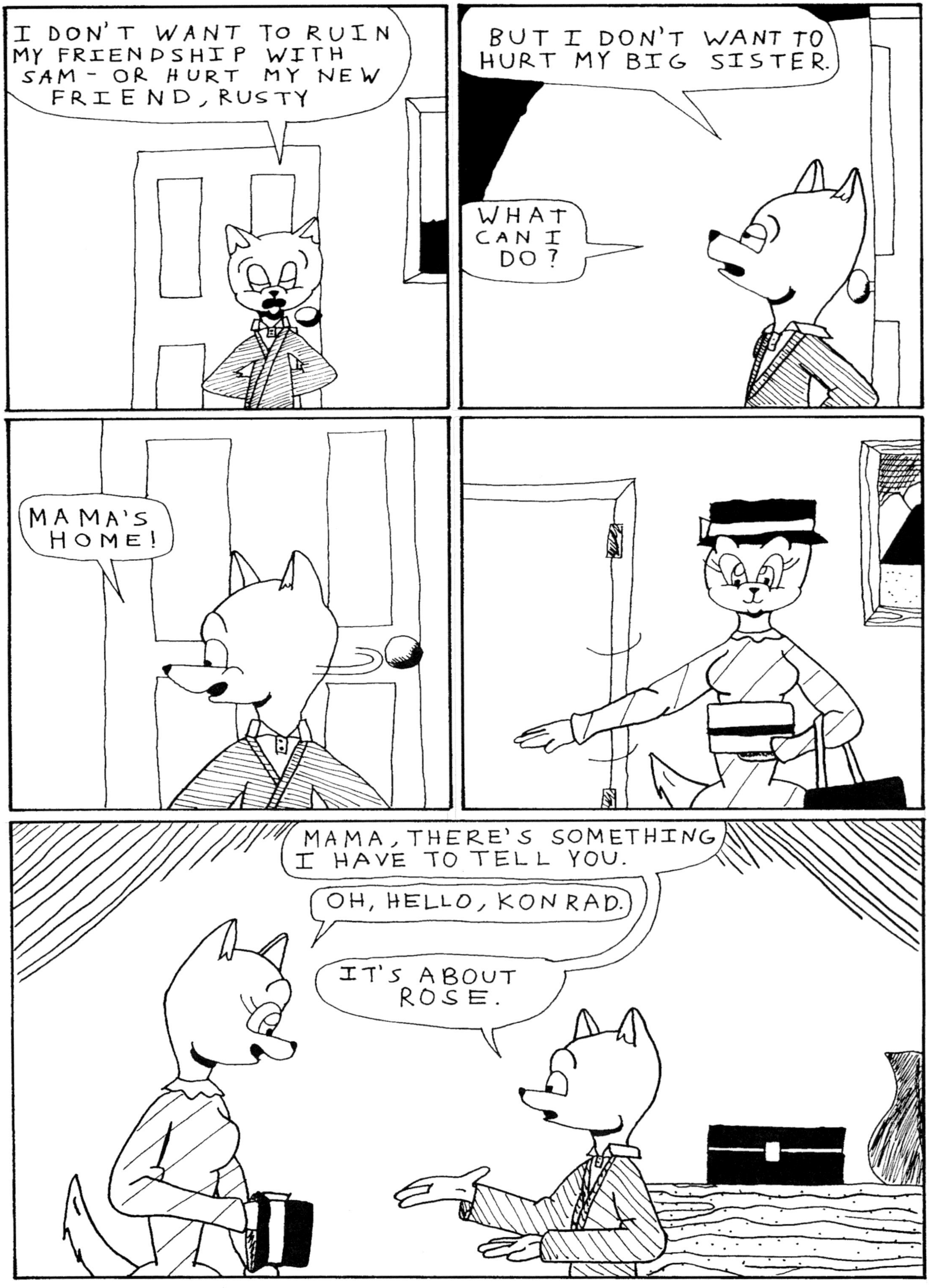
I DON'T WANT TO RUIN MY FRIENDSHIP WITH SAM - OR HURT MY NEW FRIEND, RUSTY
BUT I DON'T WANT TO HURT MY BIG SISTER.
WHAT CAN I DO?
MAMA'S HOME!
MAMA, THERE'S SOMETHING I HAVE TO TELL YOU.
OH, HELLO, KONRAD.
IT'S ABOUT ROSE.

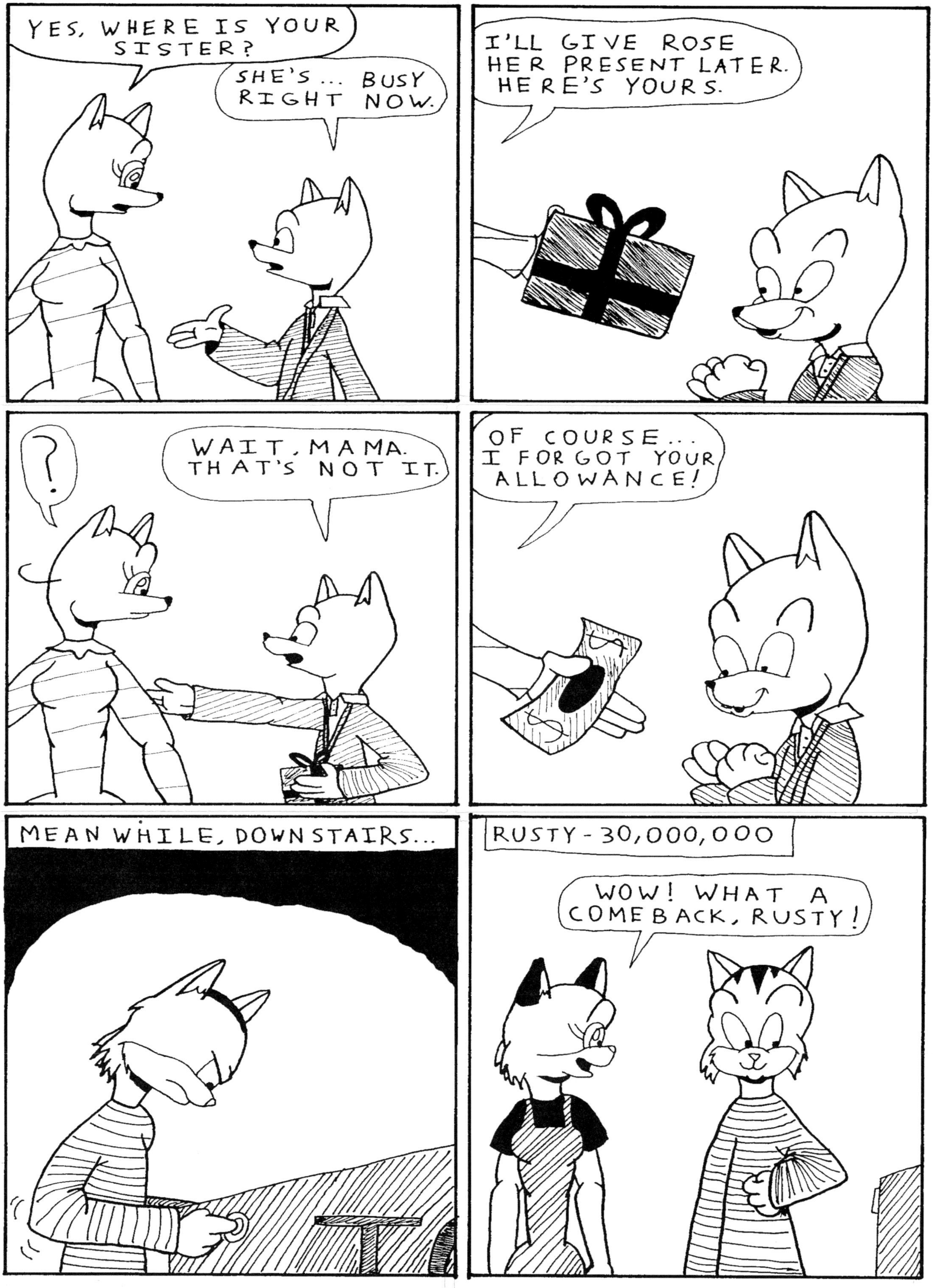
YES, WHERE IS YOUR SISTER?
SHE'S... BUSY RIGHT NOW.
I'LL GIVE ROSE HER PRESENT LATER. HERE'S YOURS.
?
WAIT, MAMA. THAT'S NOT IT.
OF COURSE... I FORGOT YOUR ALLOWANCE!
MEANWHILE, DOWNSTAIRS...
RUSTY - 30,000,000
WOW! WHAT A COMEBACK, RUSTY!

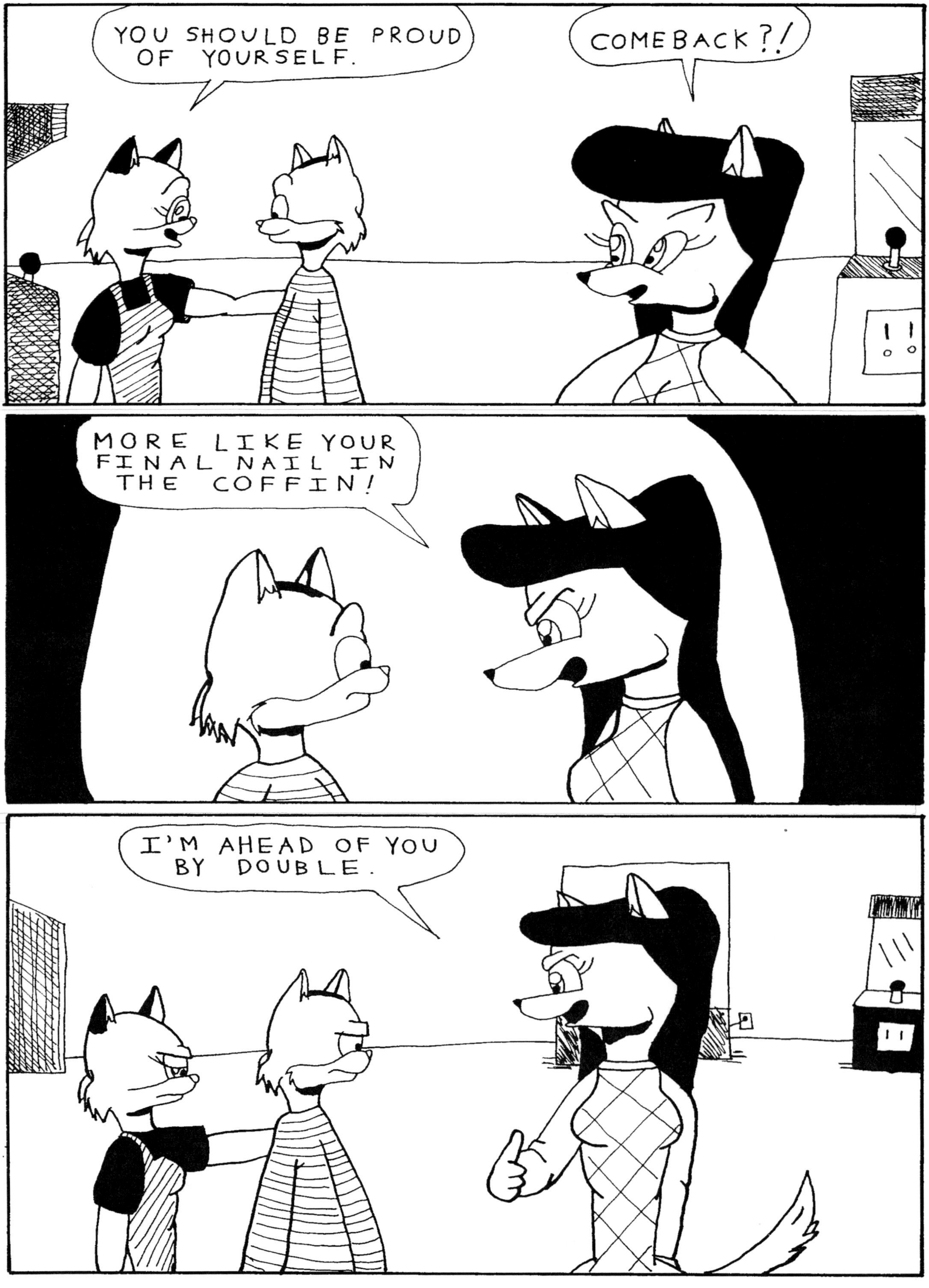
YOU SHOULD BE PROUD OF YOURSELF.
COMEBACK?!
MORE LIKE YOUR FINAL NAIL IN THE COFFIN!
I'M AHEAD OF YOU BY DOUBLE.

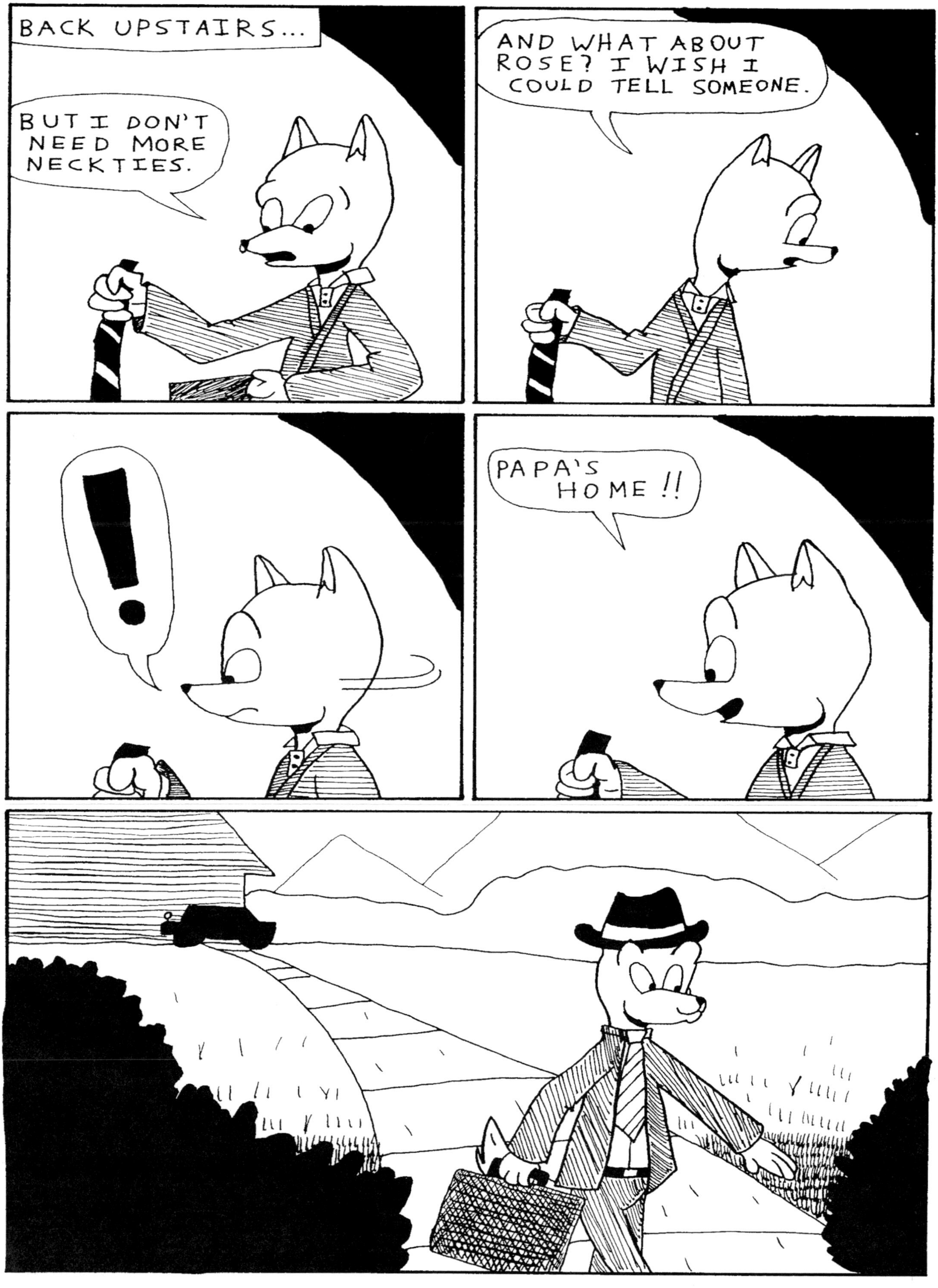
BACK UPSTAIRS...
BUT I DON'T NEED MORE NECKTIES.
AND WHAT ABOUT ROSE? I WISH I COULD TELL SOMEONE.
!
PAPA'S HOME !!

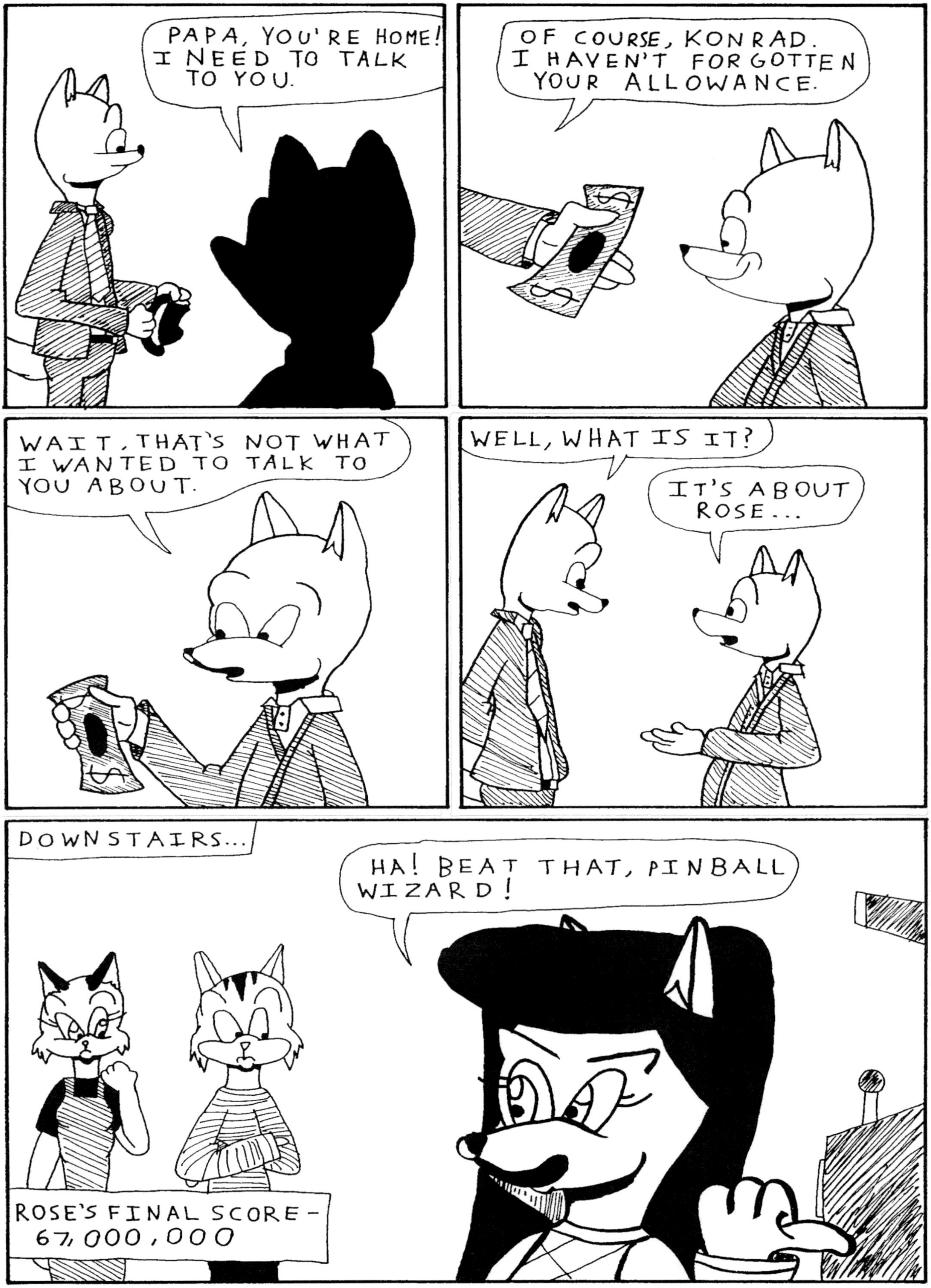
PAPA, YOU'RE HOME! I NEED TO TALK TO YOU.
OF COURSE, KONRAD. I HAVEN'T FORGOTTEN YOUR ALLOWANCE.
WAIT, THAT'S NOT WHAT I WANTED TO TALK TO YOU ABOUT.
WELL, WHAT IS IT?
IT'S ABOUT ROSE...
DOWNSTAIRS...
HA! BEAT THAT, PINBALL WIZARD!
ROSE'S FINAL SCORE - 67,000,000

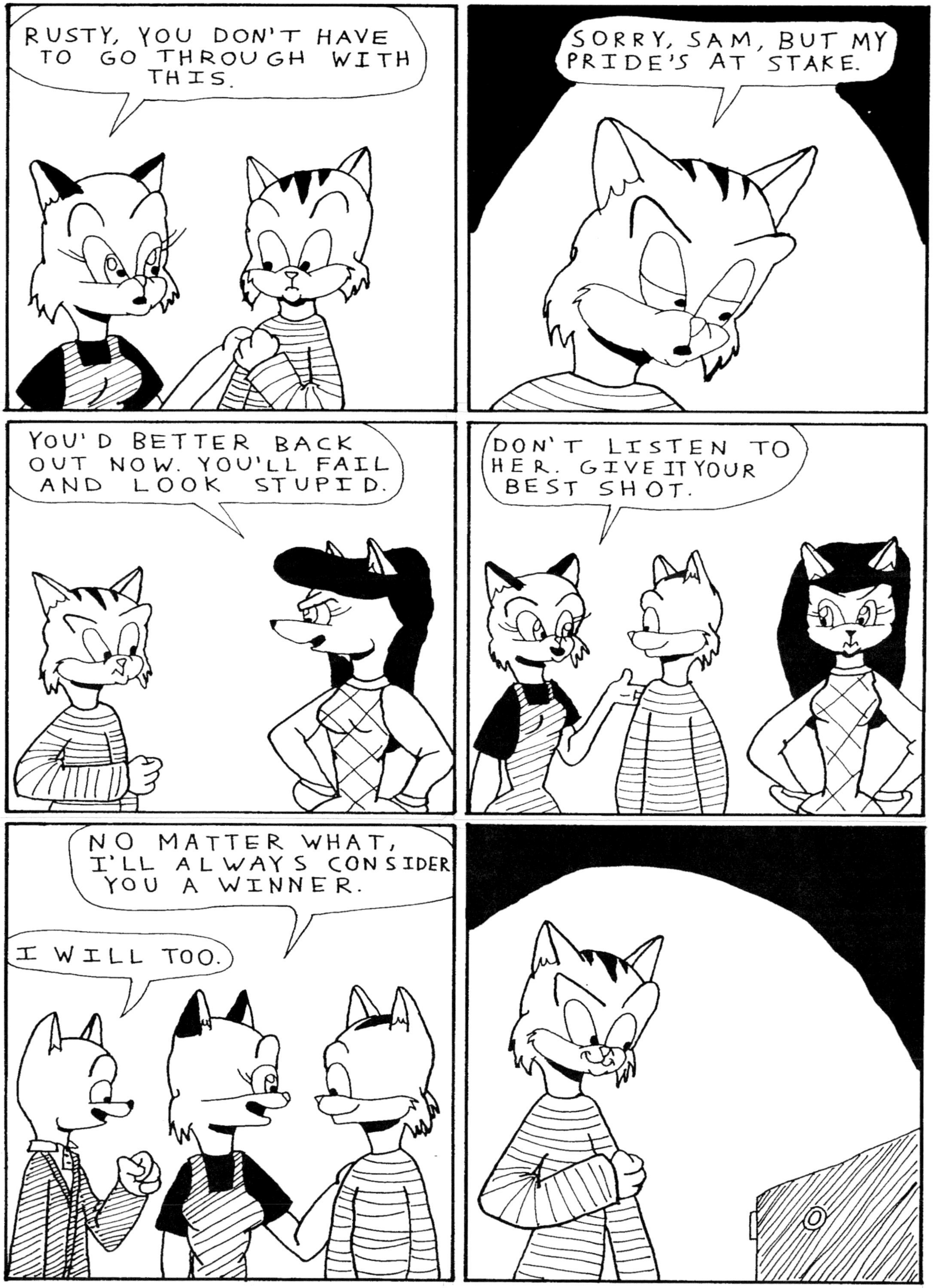
RUSTY, YOU DON'T HAVE TO GO THROUGH WITH THIS.
SORRY, SAM, BUT MY PRIDE'S AT STAKE.
YOU'D BETTER BACK OUT NOW. YOU'LL FAIL AND LOOK STUPID.
DON'T LISTEN TO HER. GIVE IT YOUR BEST SHOT.
NO MATTER WHAT, I'LL ALWAYS CONSIDER YOU A WINNER.
I WILL TOO.

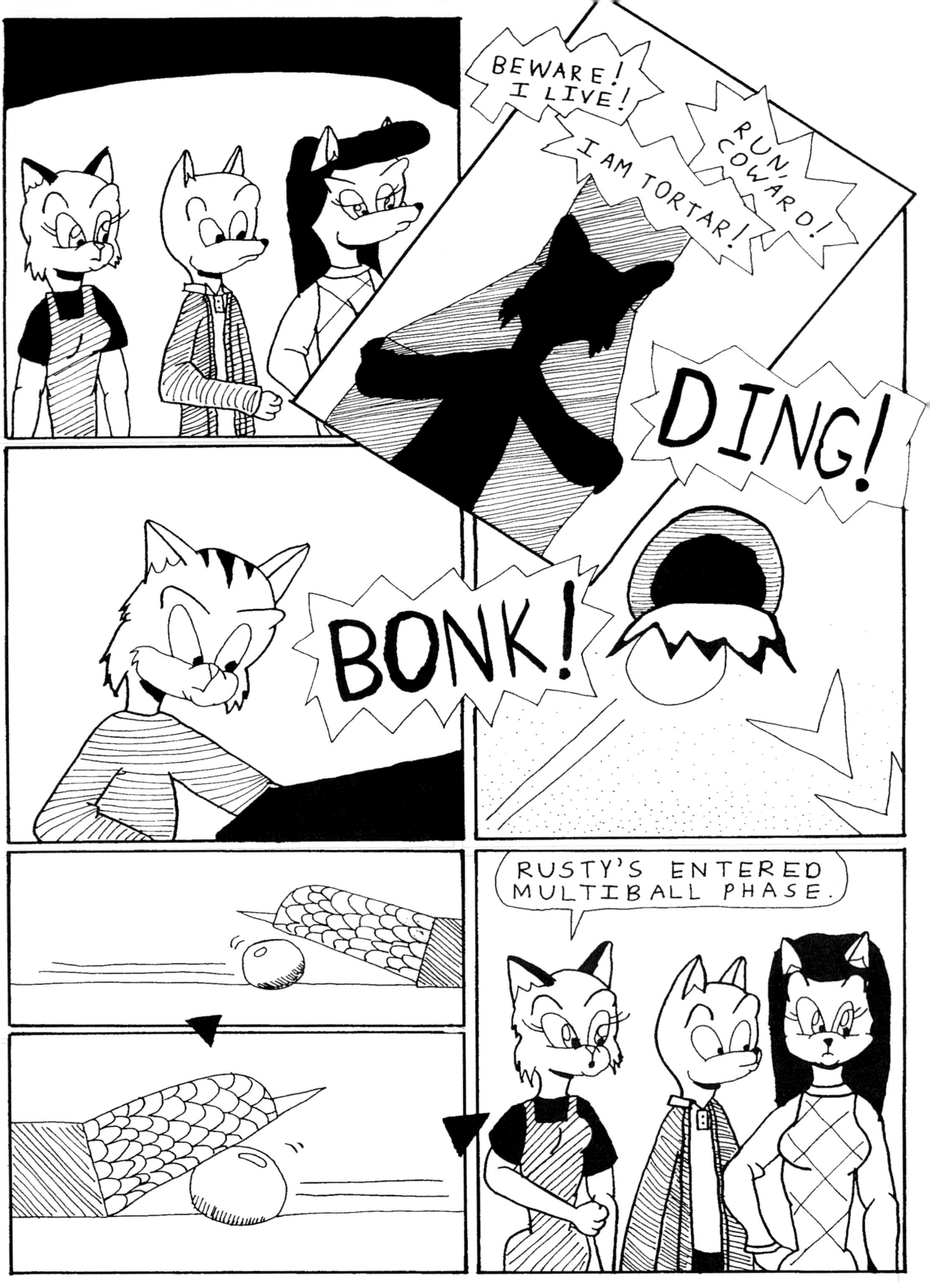
BEWARE! I LIVE!
I AM TORTAR!
RUN, COWARD!
DING!
BONK!
RUSTY'S ENTERED MULTIBALL PHASE.

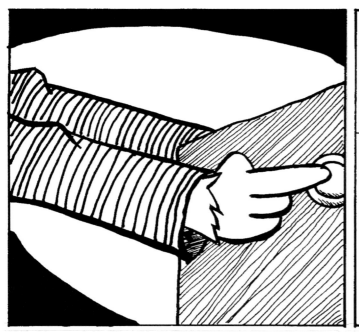

MULTIBALL
MADNESS!!

10,000,000

WHOA! I ACTUALLY GOT MULTIBALL MADNESS!

NOT EVEN ROSE HAS DONE THAT.

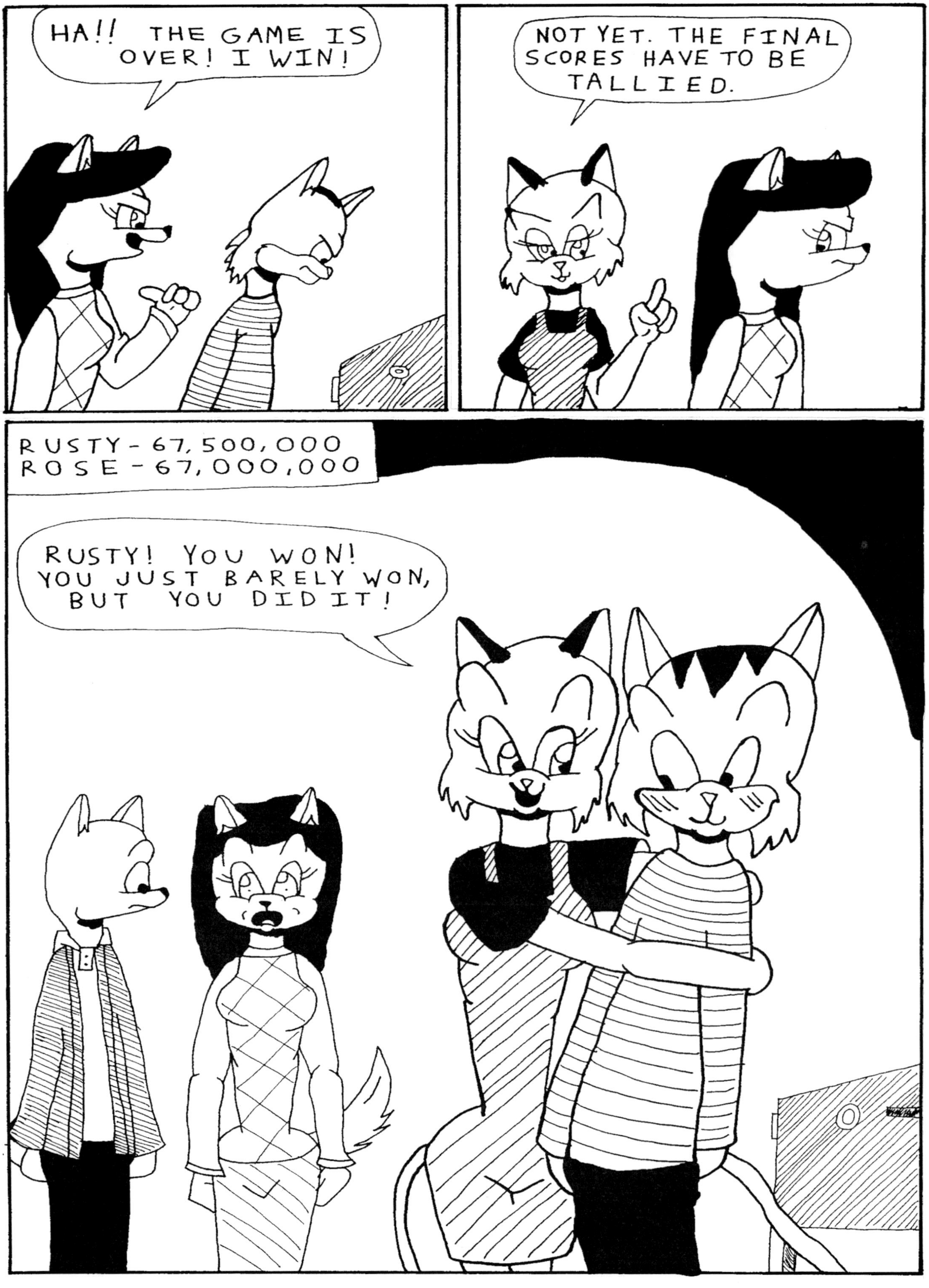
HA!! THE GAME IS OVER! I WIN!
NOT YET. THE FINAL SCORES HAVE TO BE TALLIED.
RUSTY - 67,500,000
ROSE - 67,000,000
RUSTY! YOU WON! YOU JUST BARELY WON, BUT YOU DID IT!

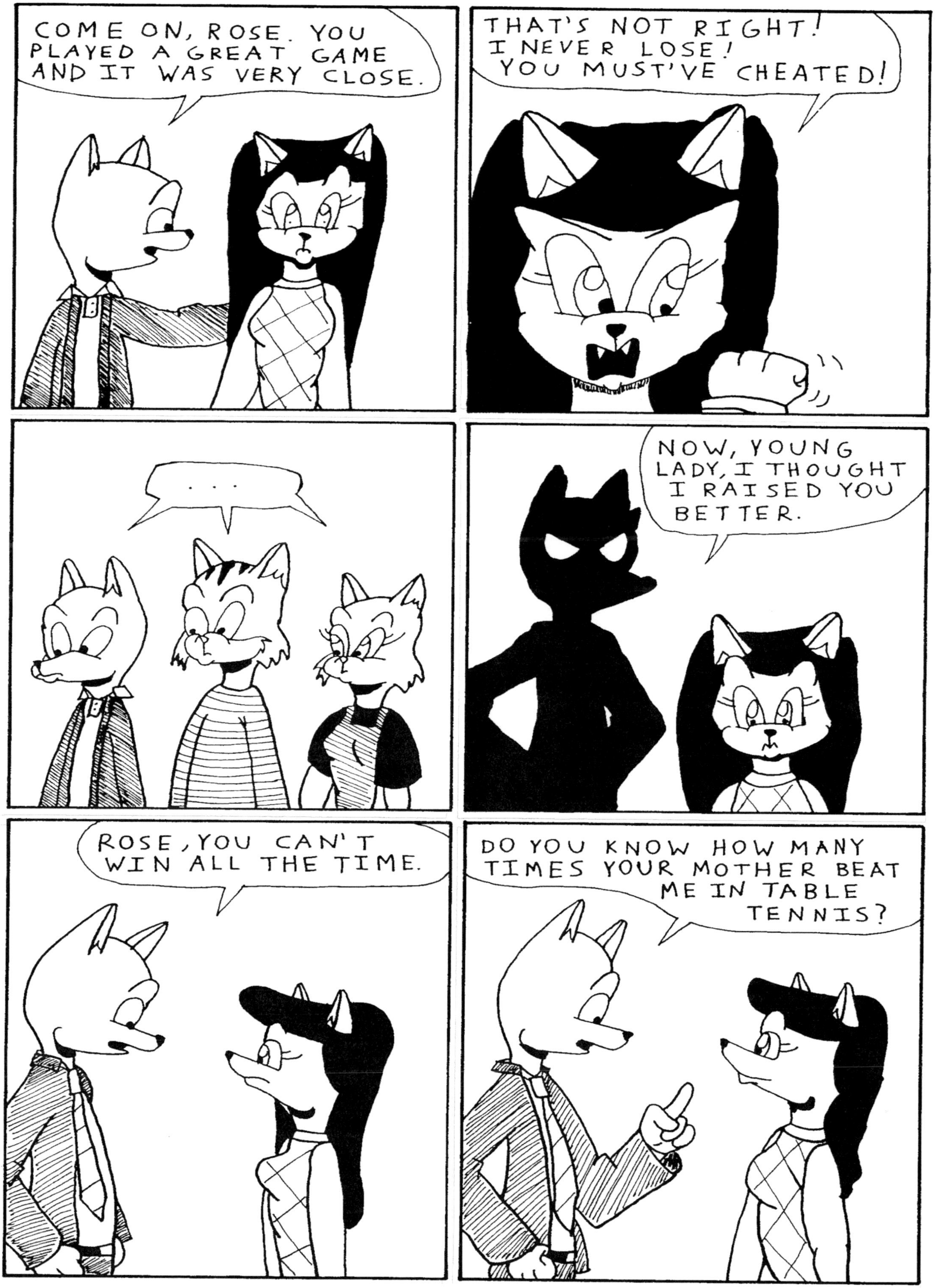
COME ON, ROSE. YOU PLAYED A GREAT GAME AND IT WAS VERY CLOSE.
THAT'S NOT RIGHT! I NEVER LOSE! YOU MUST'VE CHEATED!
...
NOW, YOUNG LADY, I THOUGHT I RAISED YOU BETTER.
ROSE, YOU CAN'T WIN ALL THE TIME.
DO YOU KNOW HOW MANY TIMES YOUR MOTHER BEAT ME IN TABLE TENNIS?

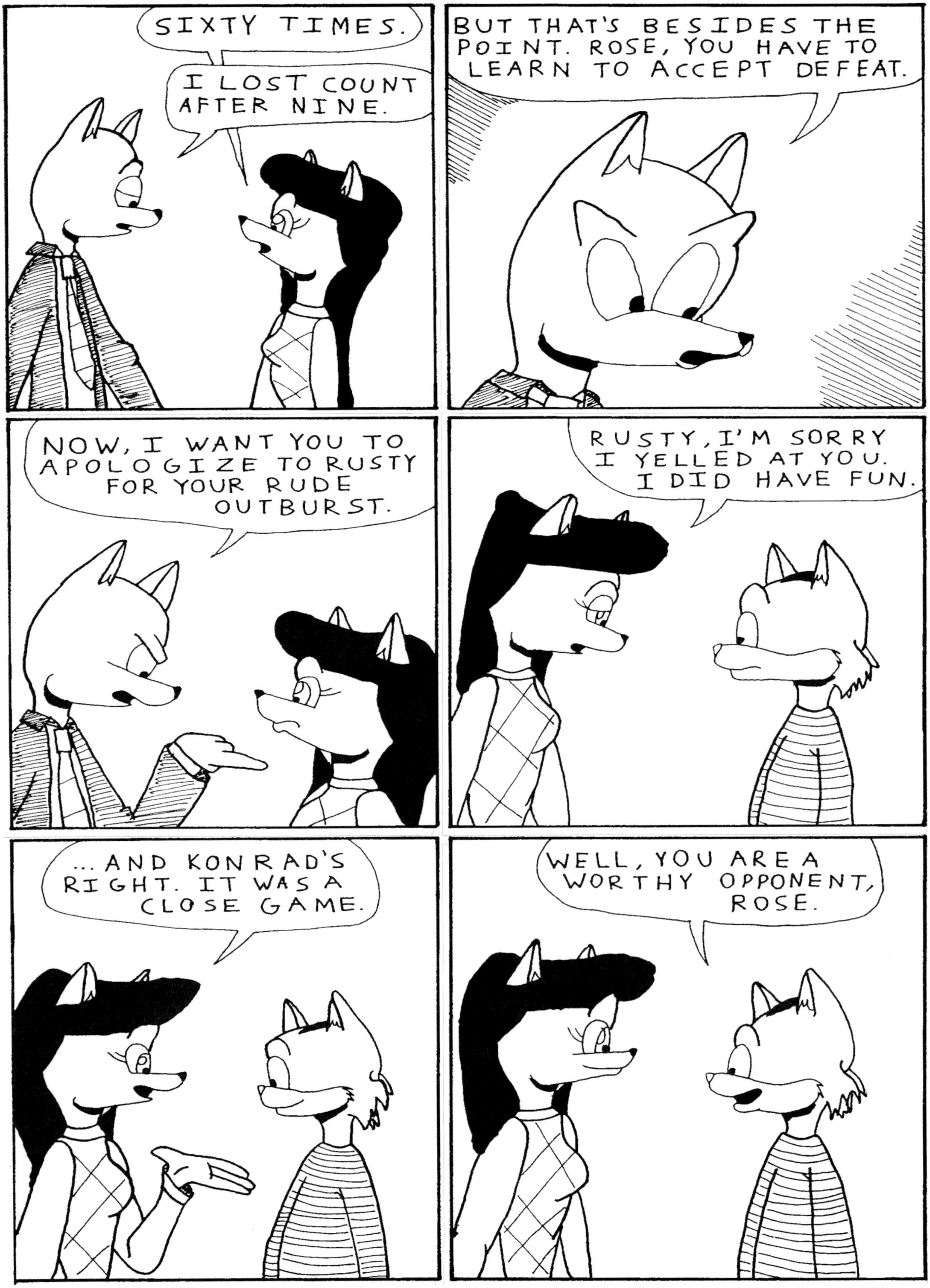
SIXTY TIMES.
I LOST COUNT AFTER NINE.
BUT THAT'S BESIDES THE POINT. ROSE, YOU HAVE TO LEARN TO ACCEPT DEFEAT.
NOW, I WANT YOU TO APOLOGIZE TO RUSTY FOR YOUR RUDE OUTBURST.
RUSTY, I'M SORRY I YELLED AT YOU. I DID HAVE FUN.
...AND KONRAD'S RIGHT. IT WAS A CLOSE GAME.
WELL, YOU ARE A WORTHY OPPONENT, ROSE.

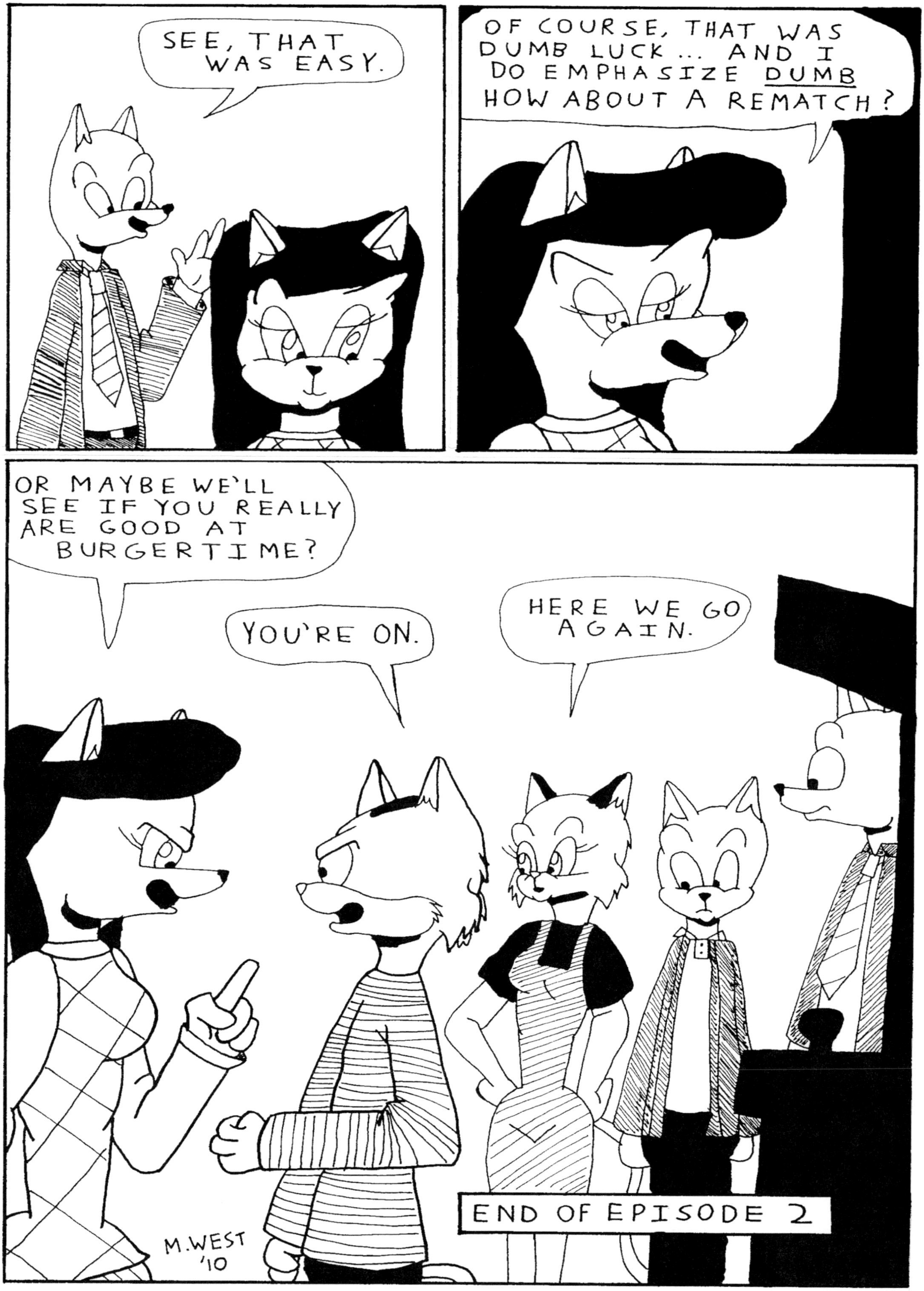
SEE, THAT WAS EASY.
OF COURSE, THAT WAS DUMB LUCK ... AND I DO EMPHASIZE DUMB
HOW ABOUT A REMATCH?
OR MAYBE WE'LL SEE IF YOU REALLY ARE GOOD AT BURGERTIME?
YOU'RE ON.
HERE WE GO AGAIN.
END OF EPISODE 2
M.WEST '10

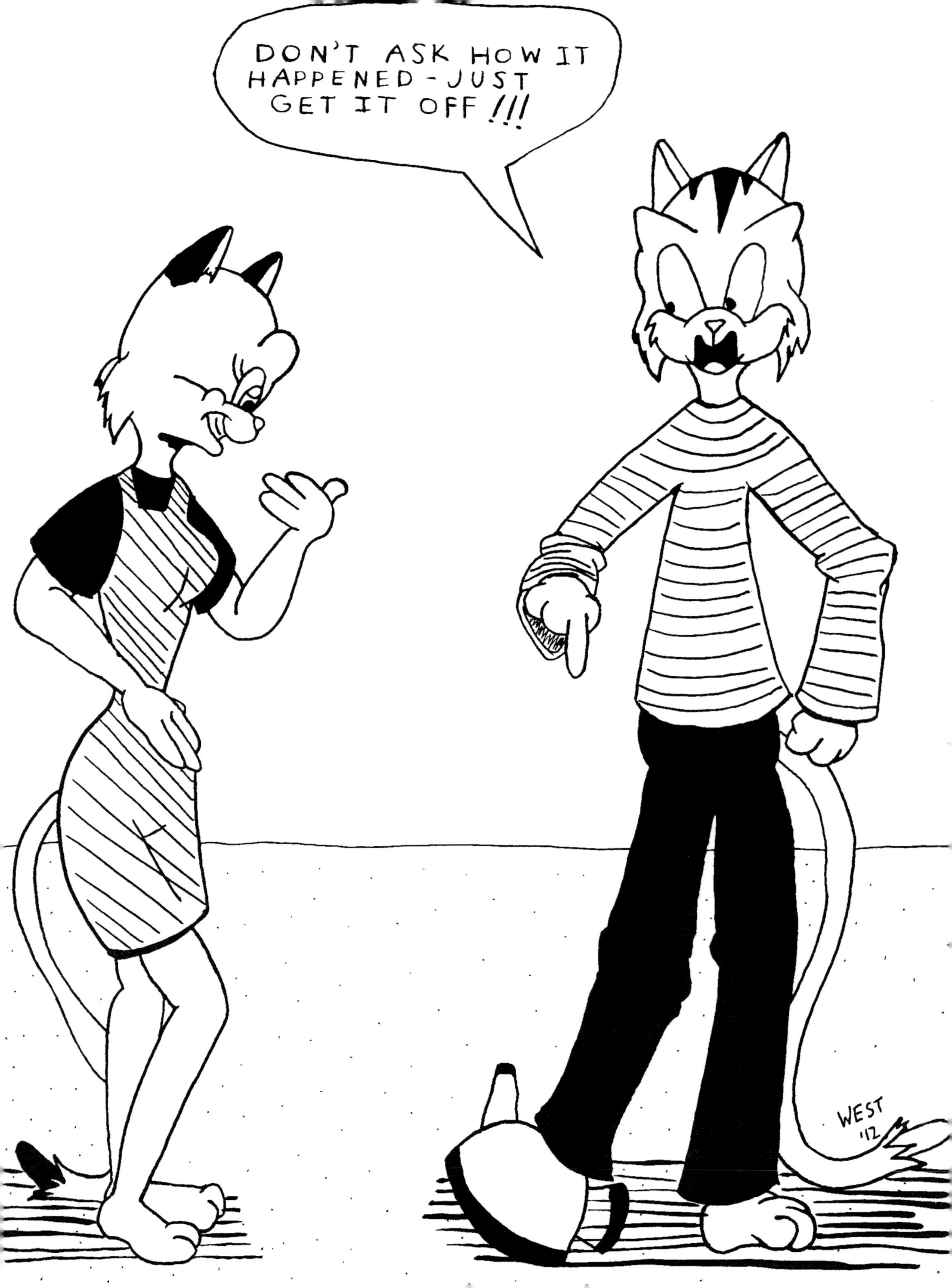
DON'T ASK HOW IT HAPPENED - JUST GET IT OFF !!!
WEST '12

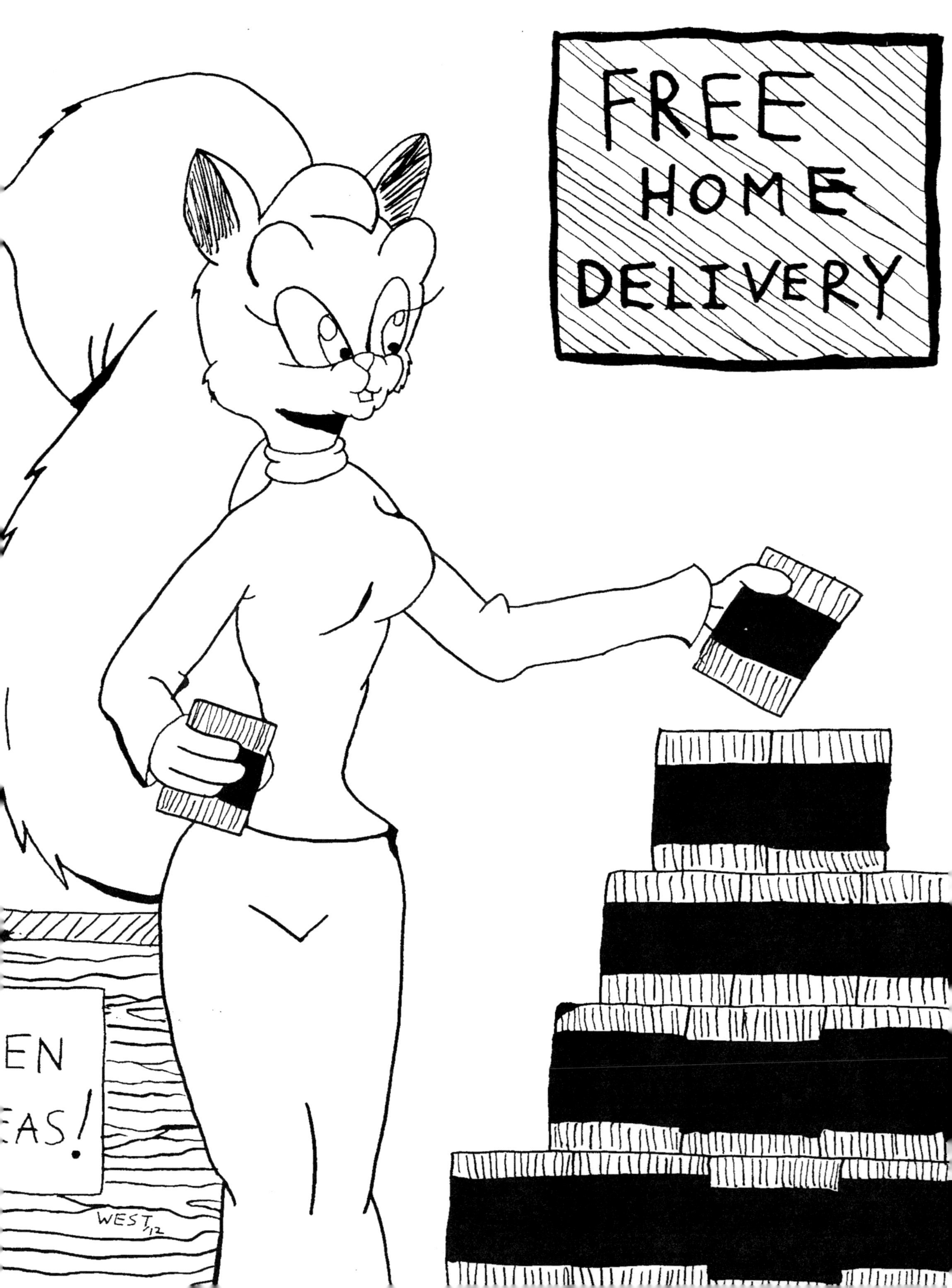
FREE HOME DELIVERY
EN
EAS!
WEST 12

Episode 3 - The Train Robbers

Written and Illustrated by
Max West

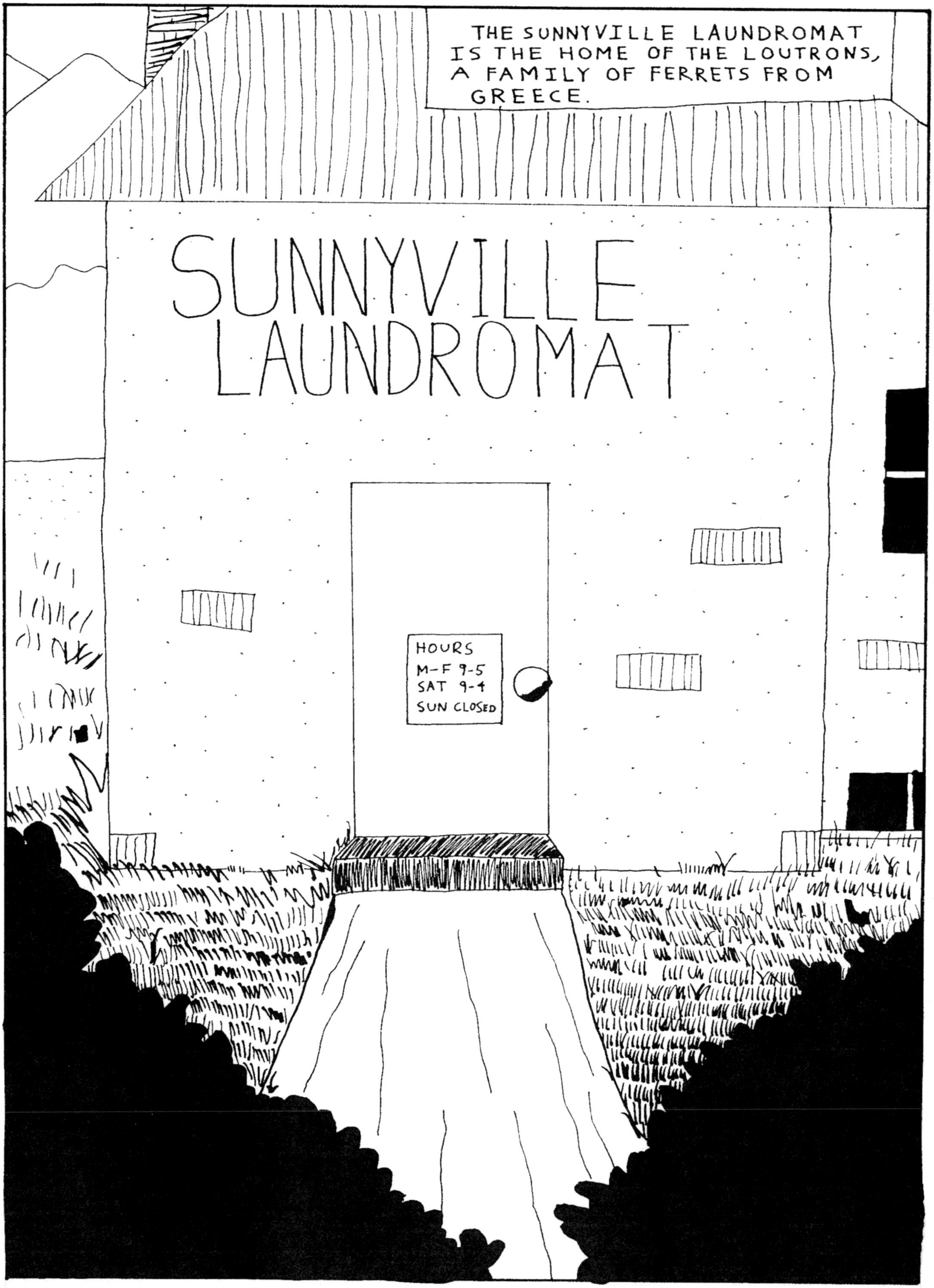
THE SUNNYVILLE LAUNDROMAT IS THE HOME OF THE LOUTRONS, A FAMILY OF FERRETS FROM GREECE.
SUNNYVILLE LAUNDROMAT
HOURS
M-F 9-5
SAT 9-4
SUN CLOSED

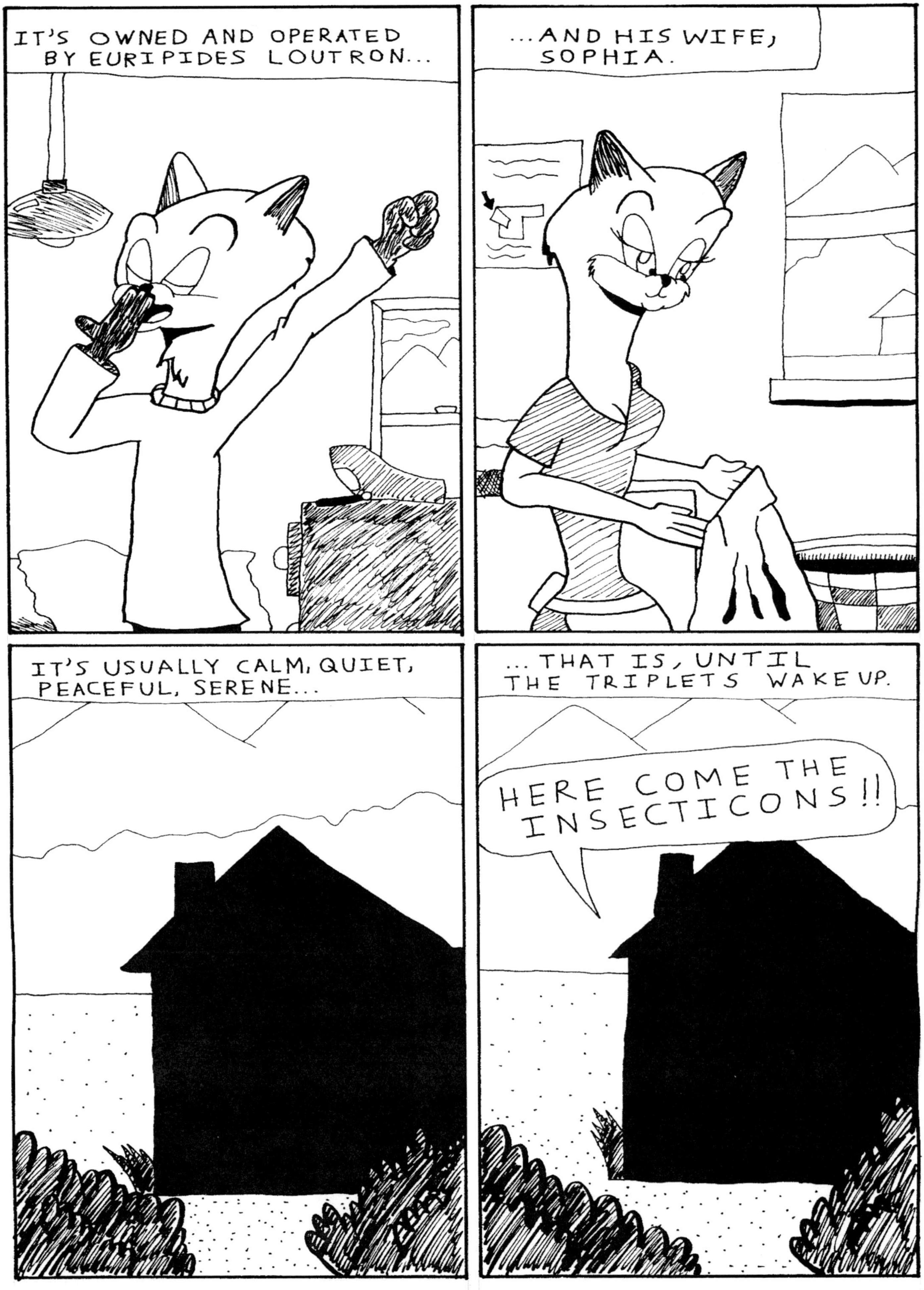
IT'S OWNED AND OPERATED BY EURIPIDES LOUTRON...
...AND HIS WIFE, SOPHIA.
IT'S USUALLY CALM, QUIET, PEACEFUL, SERENE...
...THAT IS, UNTIL THE TRIPLETS WAKE UP.
HERE COME THE INSECTICONS!!

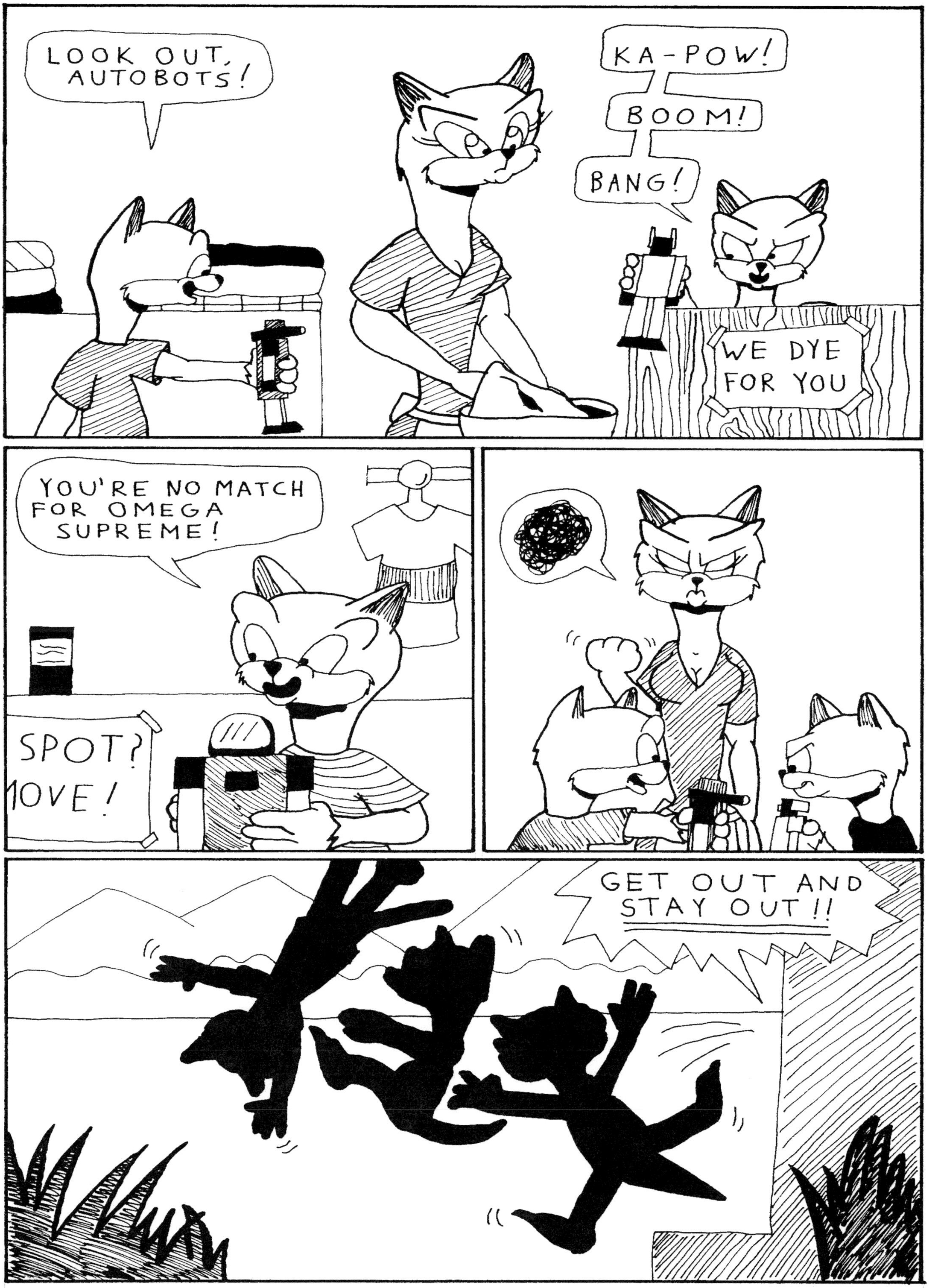
LOOK OUT, AUTOBOTS!
KA-POW!
BOOM!
BANG!
WE DYE FOR YOU
YOU'RE NO MATCH FOR OMEGA SUPREME!
SPOT?
IOVE!
GET OUT AND STAY OUT!!

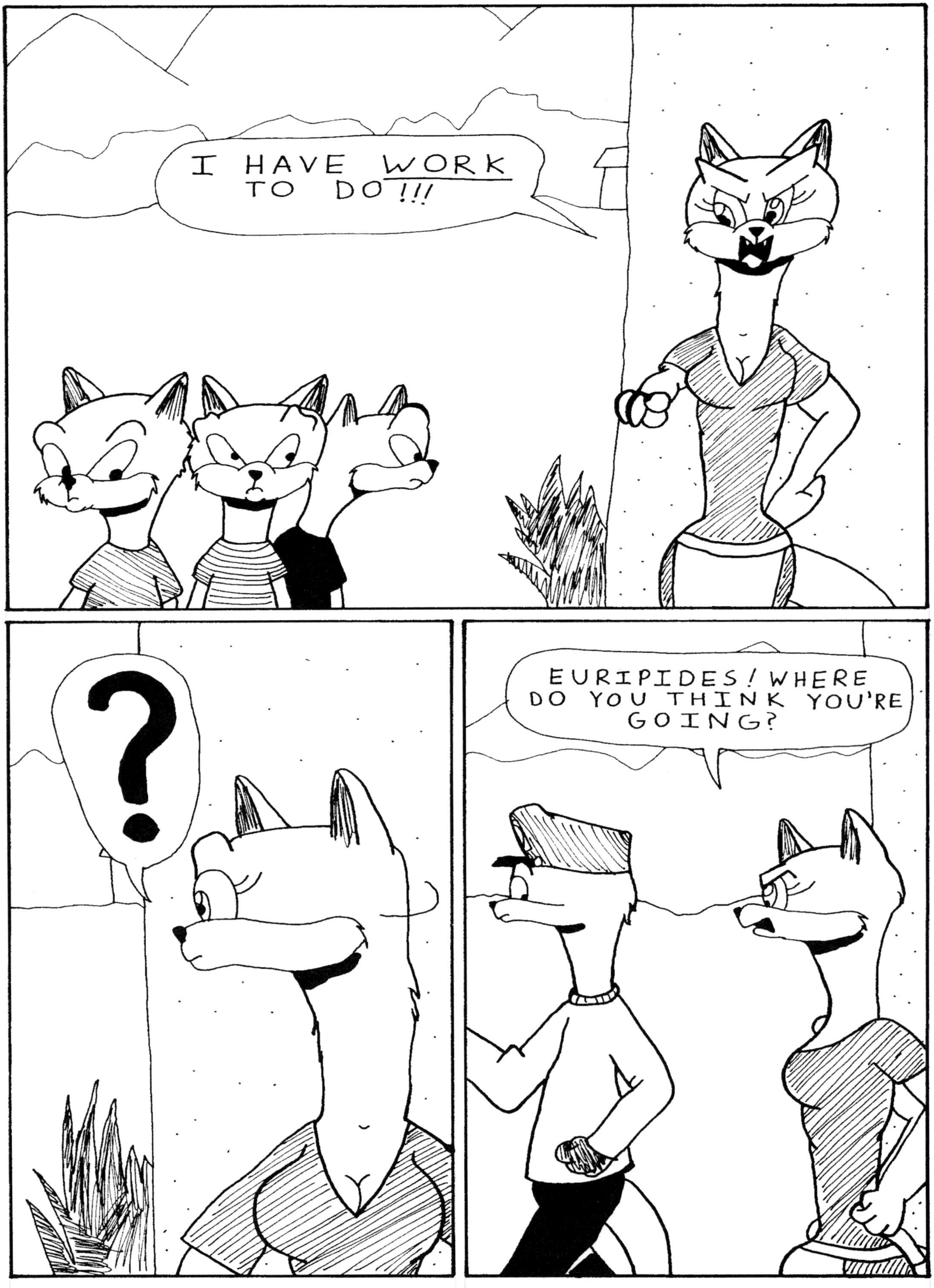
I HAVE WORK TO DO!!!
?
EURIPIDES! WHERE DO YOU THINK YOU'RE GOING?

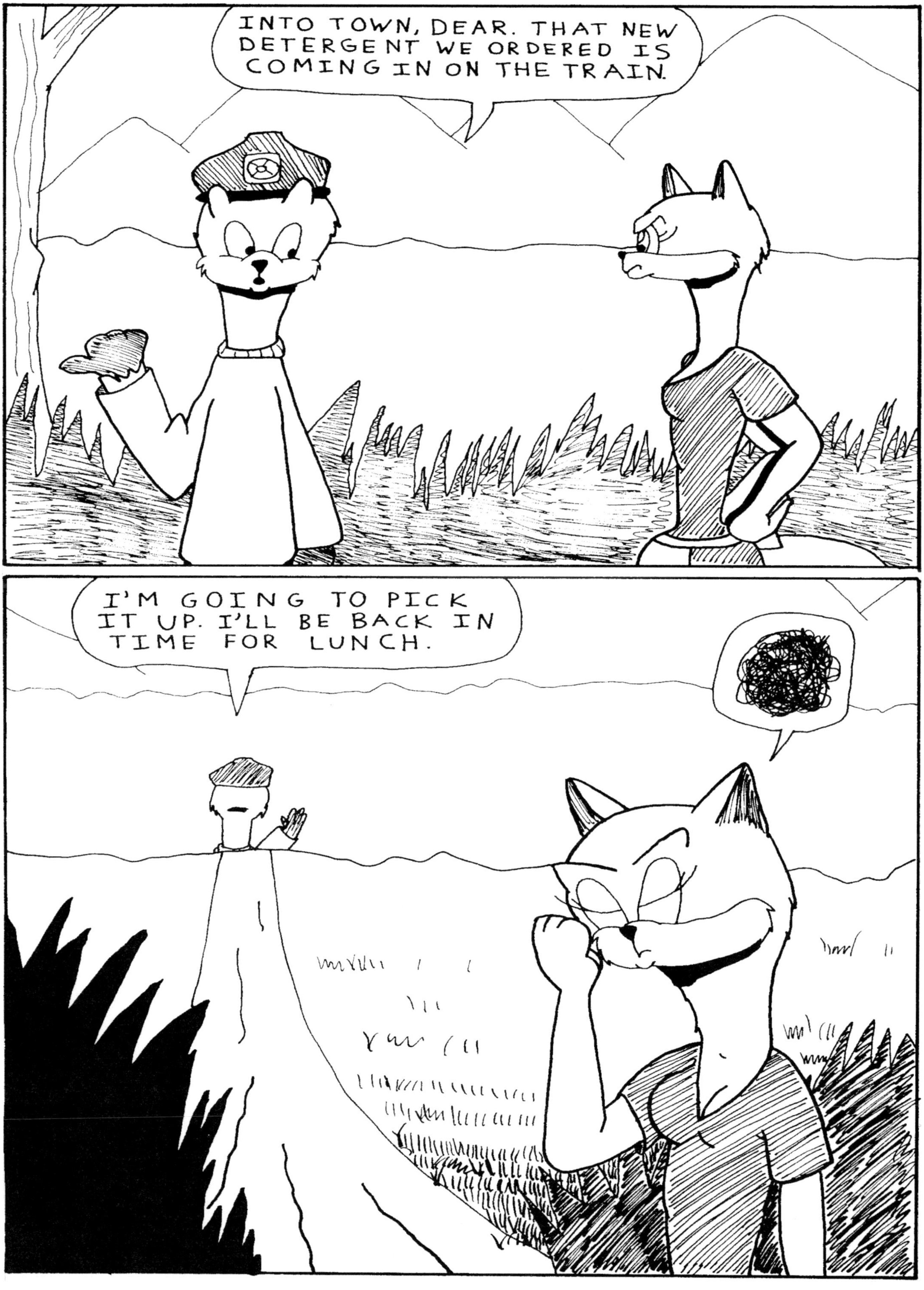
INTO TOWN, DEAR. THAT NEW DETERGENT WE ORDERED IS COMING IN ON THE TRAIN.
I'M GOING TO PICK IT UP. I'LL BE BACK IN TIME FOR LUNCH.

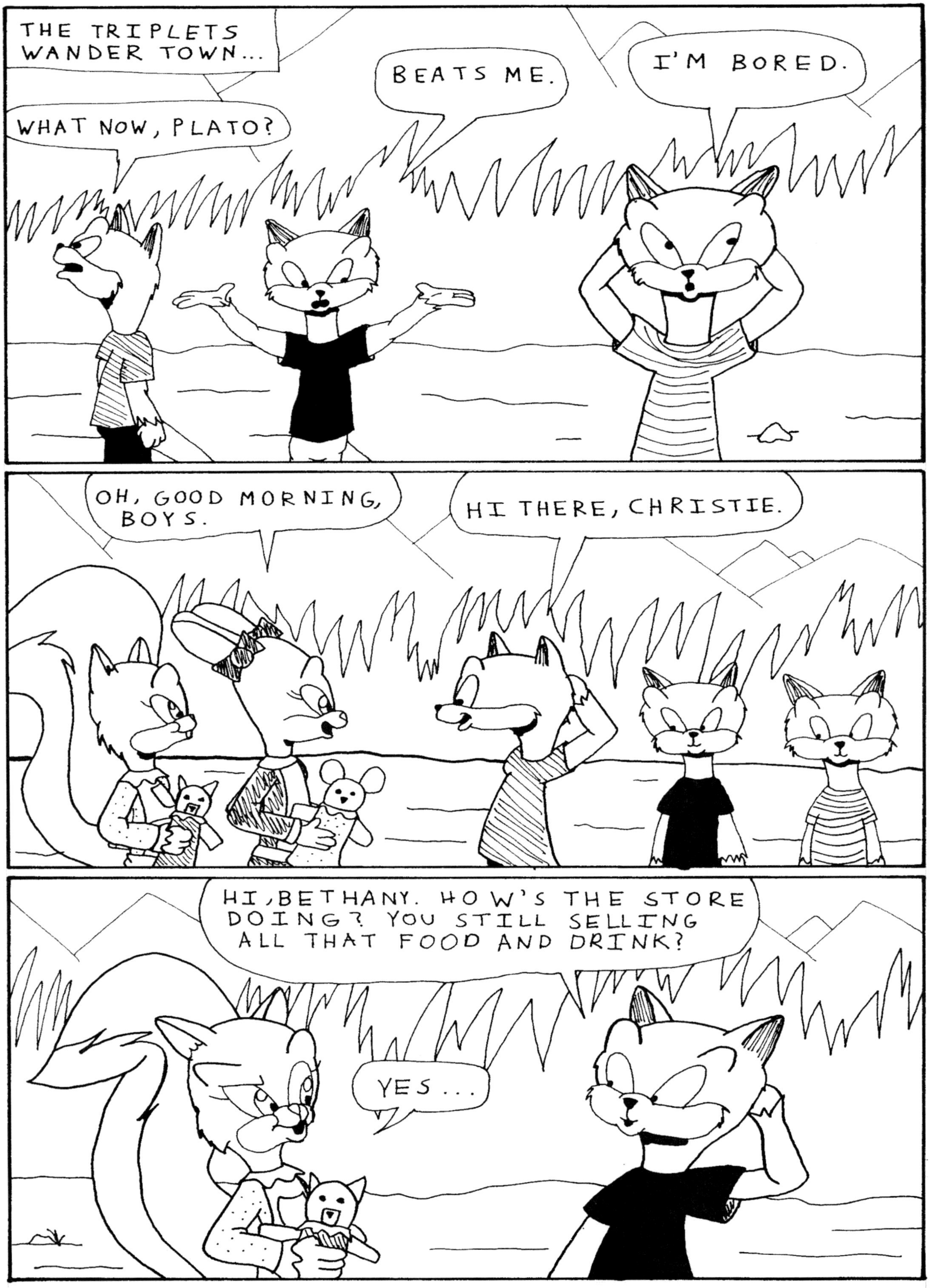
THE TRIPLETS WANDER TOWN...
WHAT NOW, PLATO?
BEATS ME.
I'M BORED.
OH, GOOD MORNING, BOYS.
HI THERE, CHRISTIE.
HI, BETHANY. HOW'S THE STORE DOING? YOU STILL SELLING ALL THAT FOOD AND DRINK?
YES...

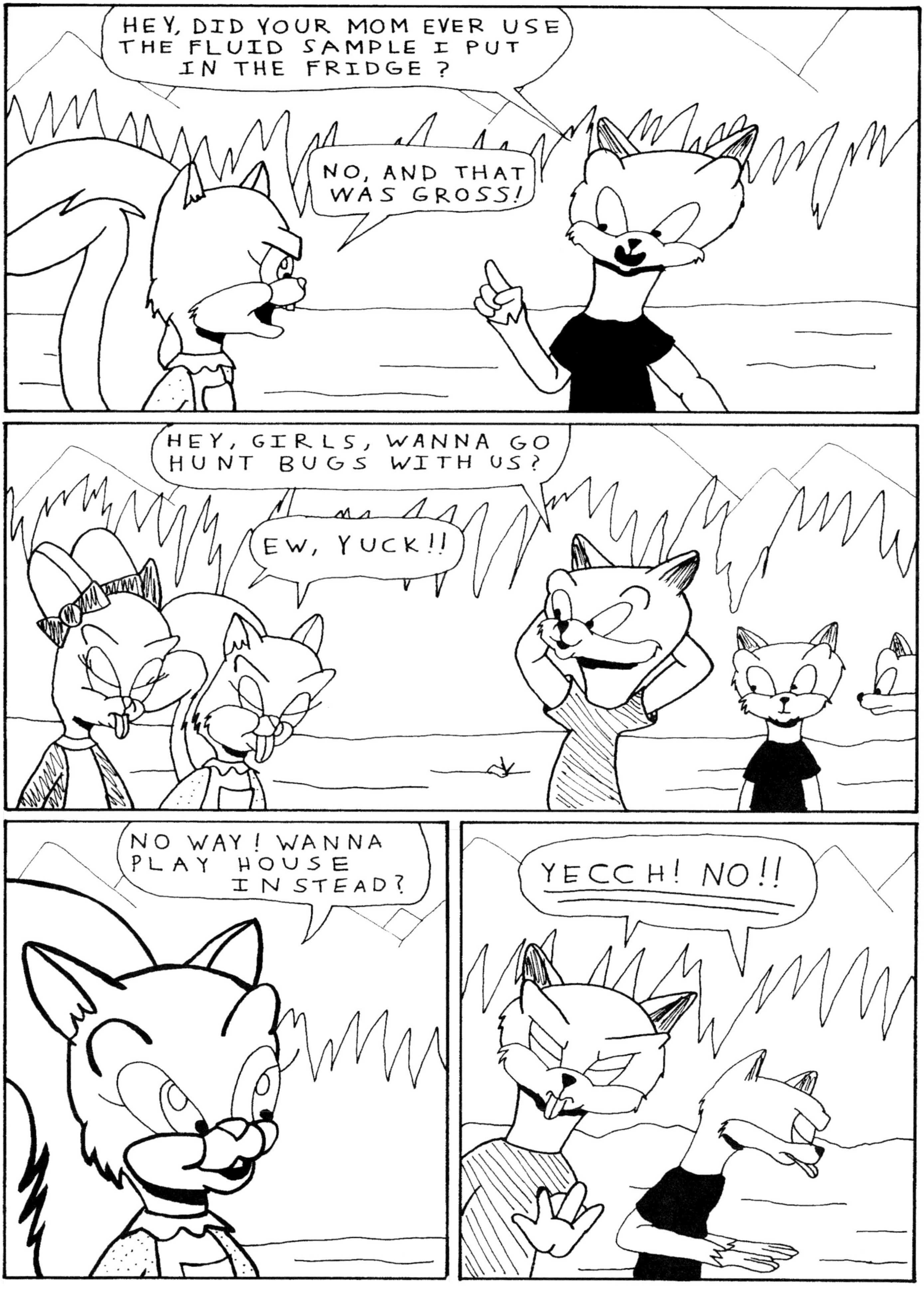
HEY, DID YOUR MOM EVER USE THE FLUID SAMPLE I PUT IN THE FRIDGE?
NO, AND THAT WAS GROSS!
HEY, GIRLS, WANNA GO HUNT BUGS WITH US?
EW, YUCK!!
NO WAY! WANNA PLAY HOUSE INSTEAD?
YECCH! NO!!

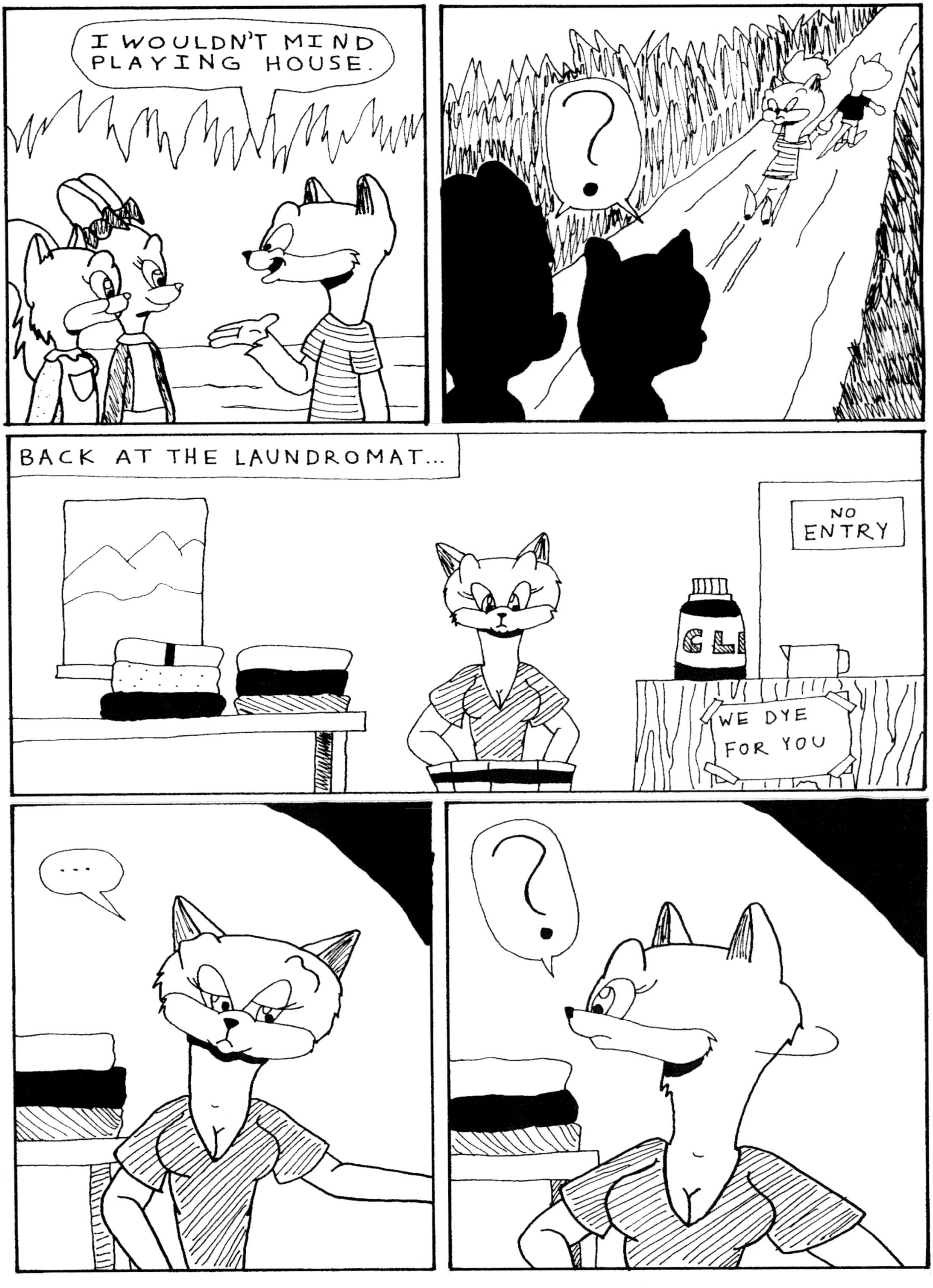
I WOULDN'T MIND PLAYING HOUSE.
?
BACK AT THE LAUNDROMAT...
NO ENTRY
WE DYE FOR YOU
...
?

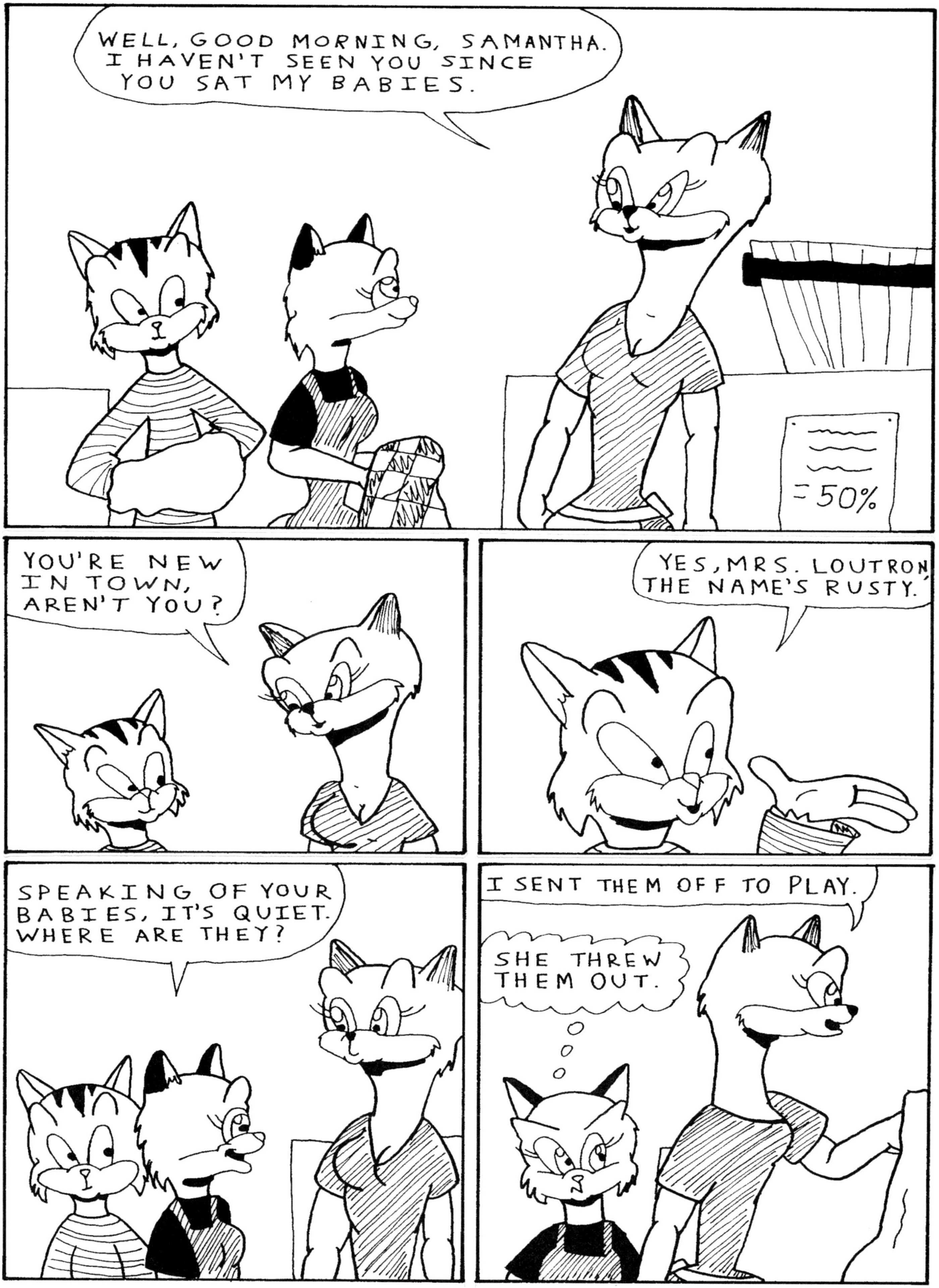
WELL, GOOD MORNING, SAMANTHA. I HAVEN'T SEEN YOU SINCE YOU SAT MY BABIES.
=50%
YOU'RE NEW IN TOWN, AREN'T YOU?
YES, MRS. LOUTRON. THE NAME'S RUSTY.
SPEAKING OF YOUR BABIES, IT'S QUIET. WHERE ARE THEY?
I SENT THEM OFF TO PLAY.
SHE THREW THEM OUT.

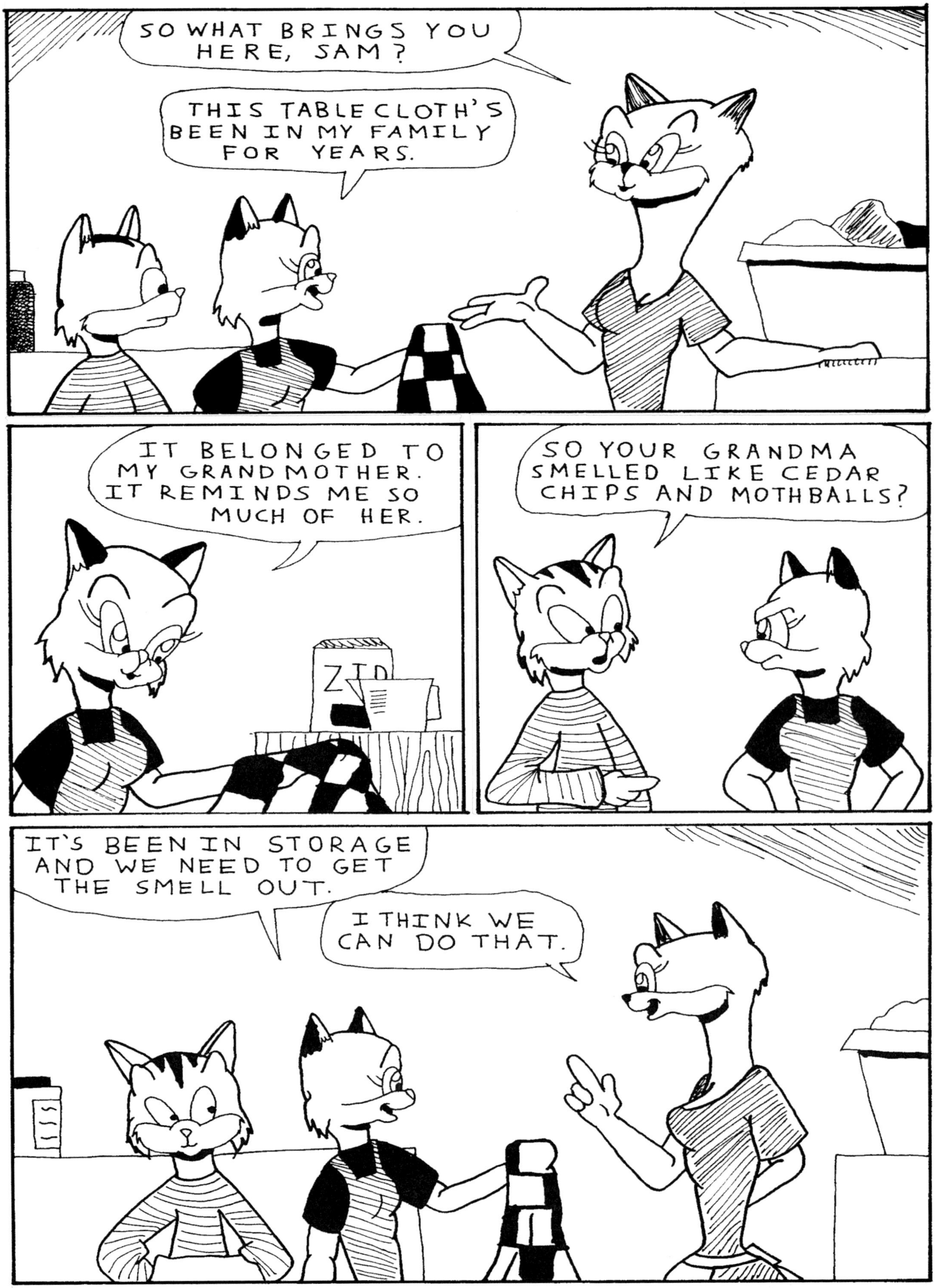
SO WHAT BRINGS YOU HERE, SAM?
THIS TABLECLOTH'S BEEN IN MY FAMILY FOR YEARS.
IT BELONGED TO MY GRANDMOTHER. IT REMINDS ME SO MUCH OF HER.
SO YOUR GRANDMA SMELLED LIKE CEDAR CHIPS AND MOTHBALLS?
IT'S BEEN IN STORAGE AND WE NEED TO GET THE SMELL OUT.
I THINK WE CAN DO THAT.

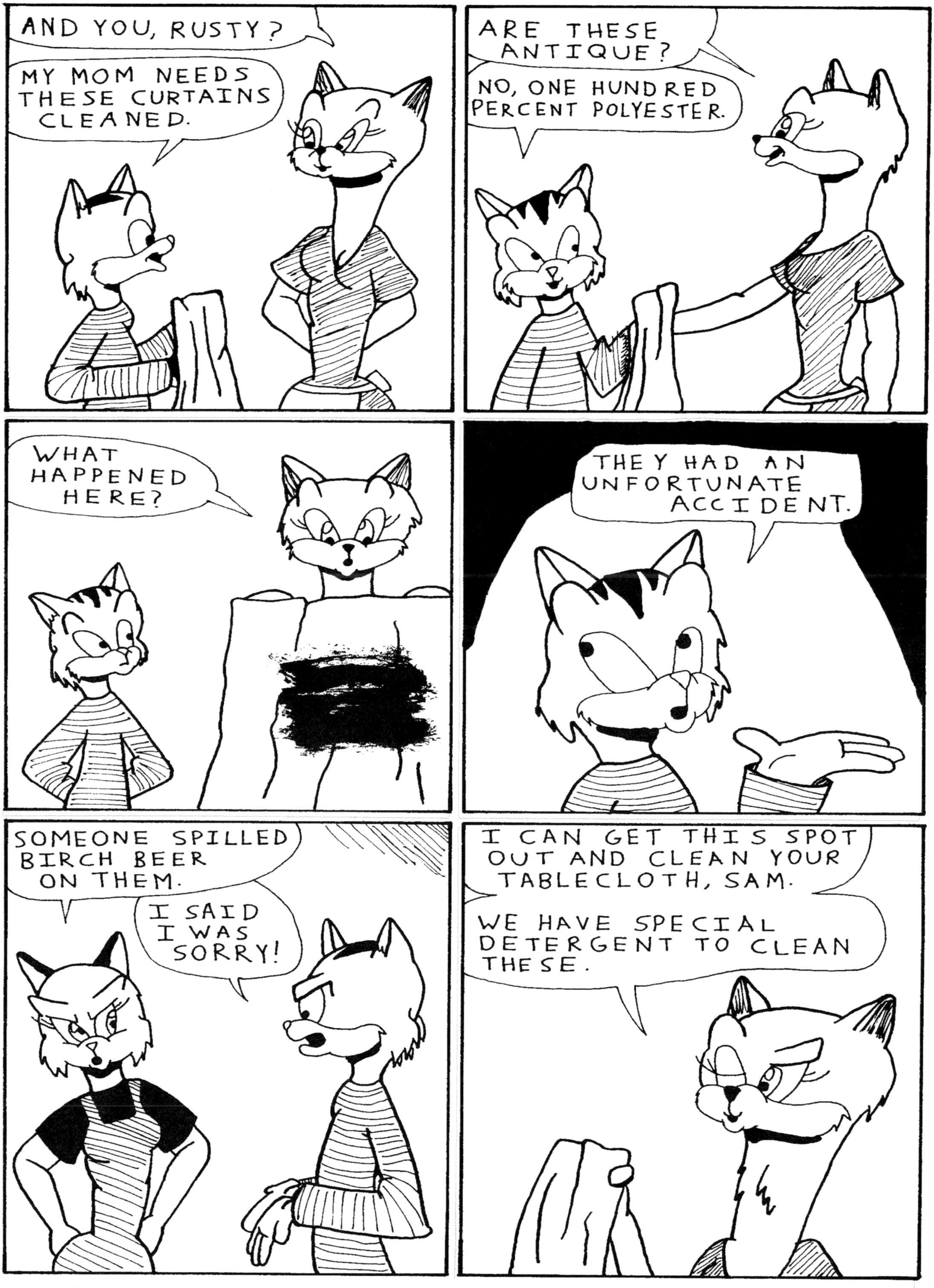
AND YOU, RUSTY?
MY MOM NEEDS THESE CURTAINS CLEANED.
ARE THESE ANTIQUE?
NO, ONE HUNDRED PERCENT POLYESTER.
WHAT HAPPENED HERE?
THEY HAD AN UNFORTUNATE ACCIDENT.
SOMEONE SPILLED BIRCH BEER ON THEM.
I SAID I WAS SORRY!
I CAN GET THIS SPOT OUT AND CLEAN YOUR TABLECLOTH, SAM.
WE HAVE SPECIAL DETERGENT TO CLEAN THESE.

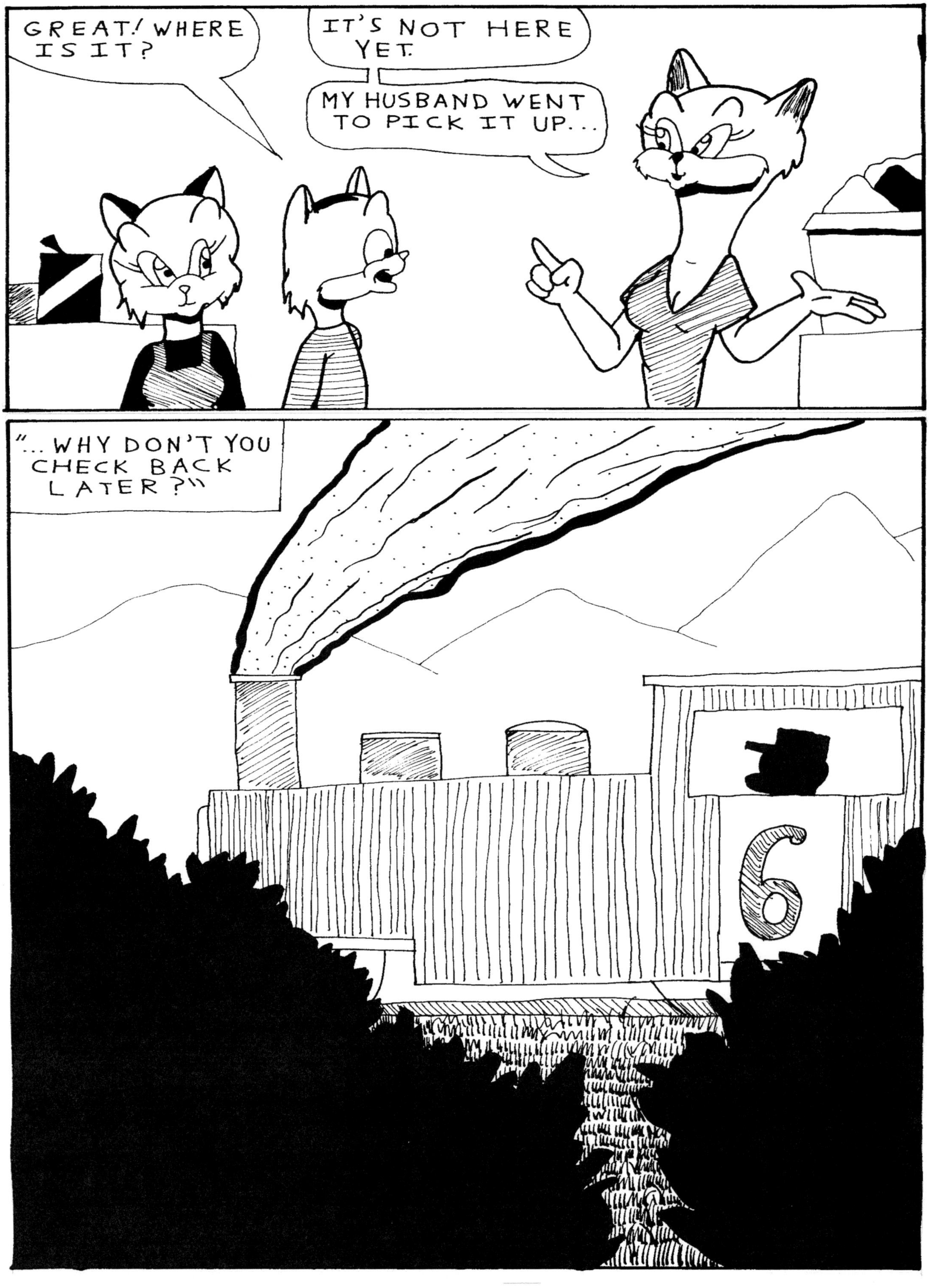
GREAT! WHERE IS IT?
IT'S NOT HERE YET.
MY HUSBAND WENT TO PICK IT UP...
"...WHY DON'T YOU CHECK BACK LATER?"
6

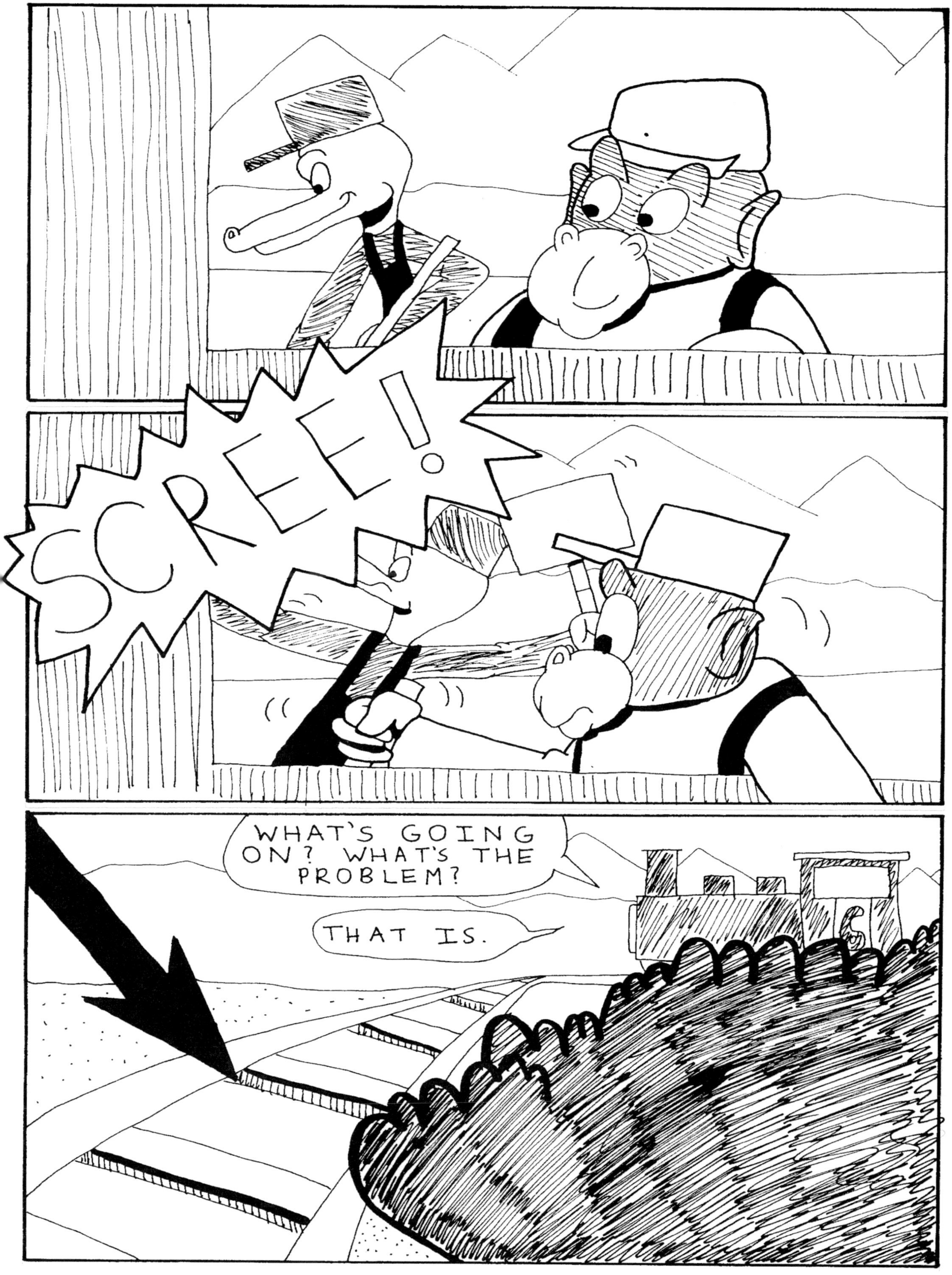
SCREE!
WHAT'S GOING ON? WHAT'S THE PROBLEM?
THAT IS.

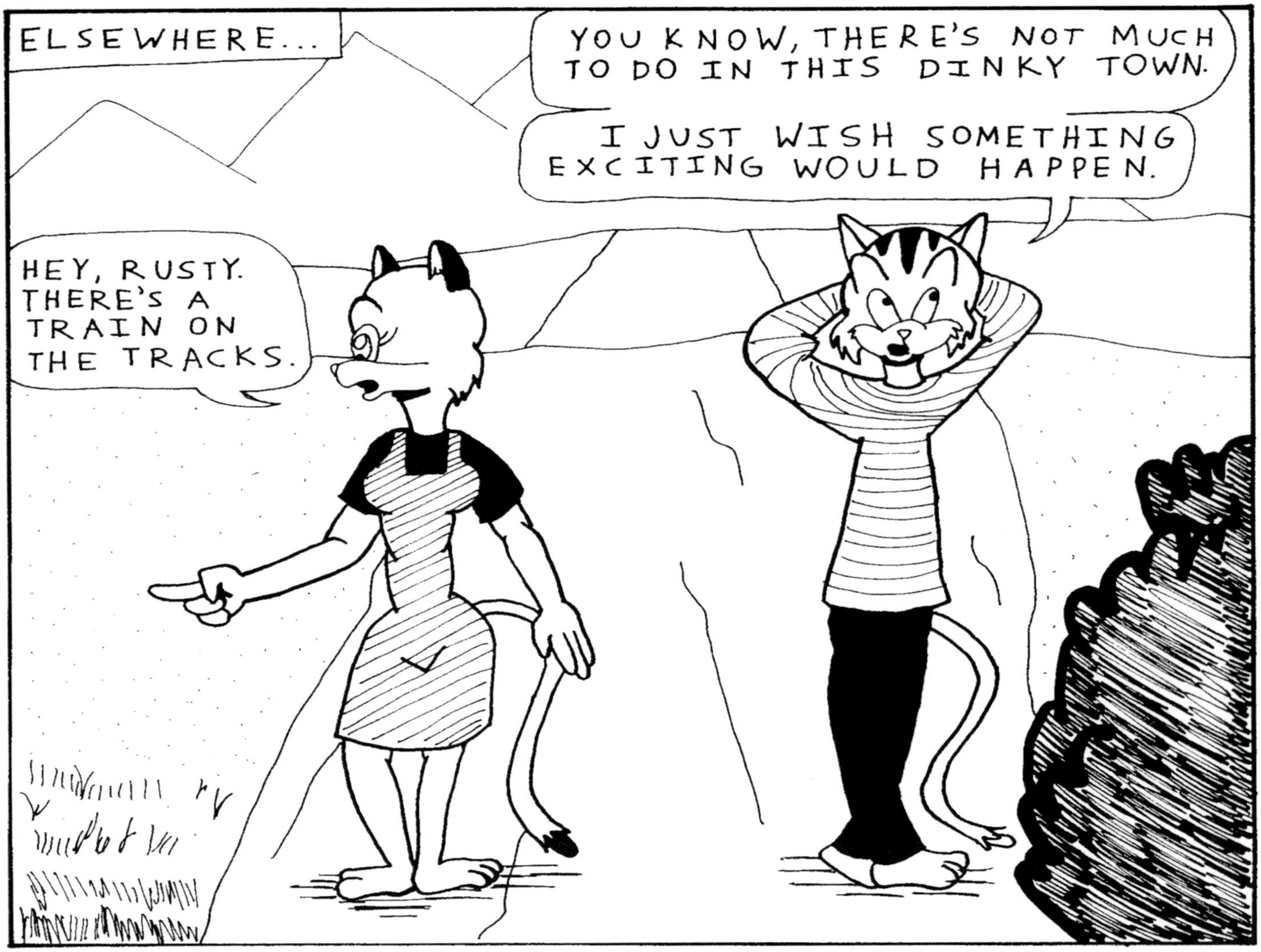
ELSEWHERE...
YOU KNOW, THERE'S NOT MUCH TO DO IN THIS DINKY TOWN.
I JUST WISH SOMETHING EXCITING WOULD HAPPEN.
HEY, RUSTY. THERE'S A TRAIN ON THE TRACKS.

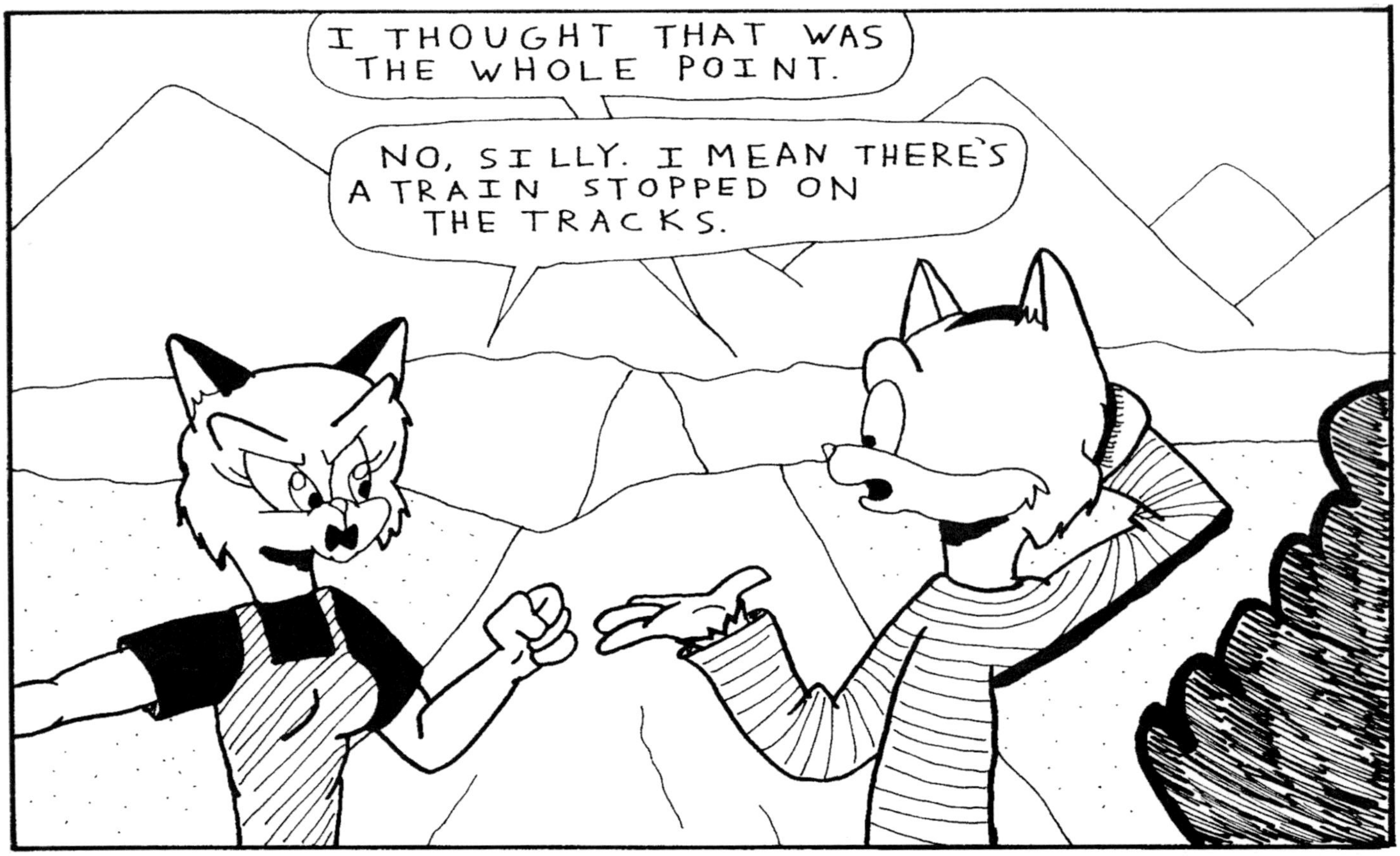
I THOUGHT THAT WAS THE WHOLE POINT.
NO, SILLY. I MEAN THERE'S A TRAIN STOPPED ON THE TRACKS.

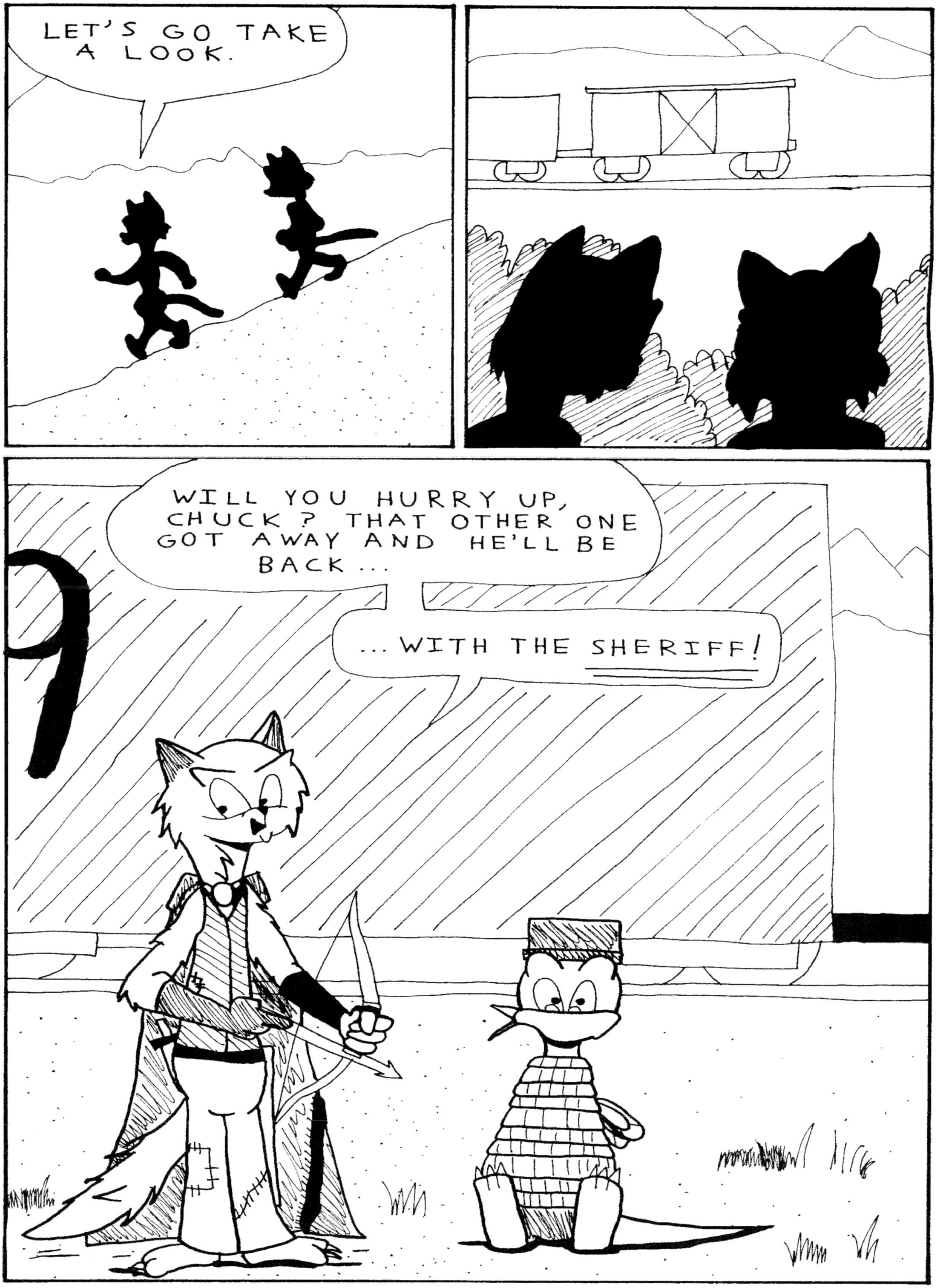
LET'S GO TAKE A LOOK.
WILL YOU HURRY UP, CHUCK? THAT OTHER ONE GOT AWAY AND HE'LL BE BACK...
...WITH THE SHERIFF!

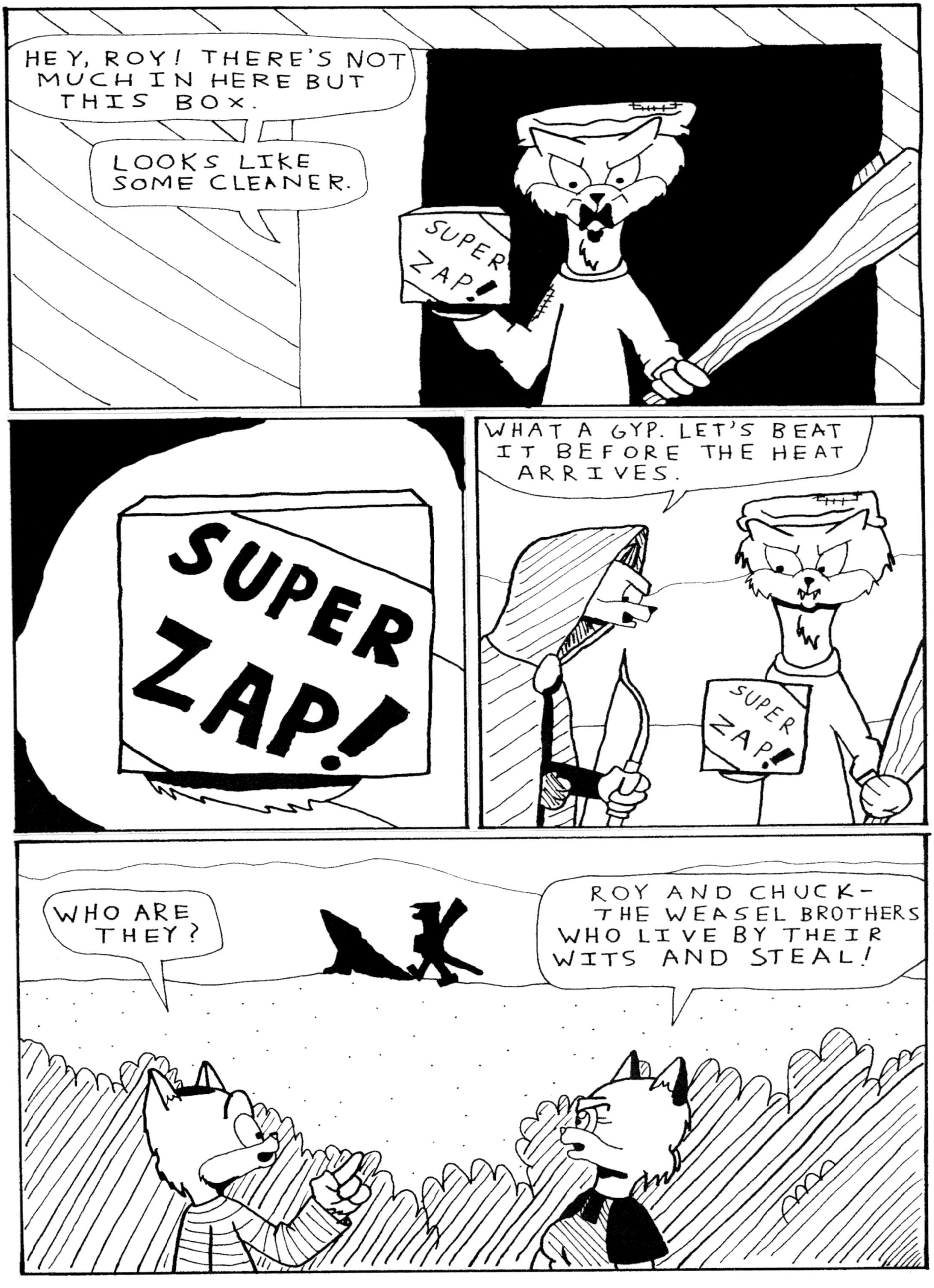
HEY, ROY! THERE'S NOT MUCH IN HERE BUT THIS BOX.
LOOKS LIKE SOME CLEANER.
SUPER ZAP!
SUPER ZAP!
WHAT A GYP. LET'S BEAT IT BEFORE THE HEAT ARRIVES.
SUPER ZAP!
WHO ARE THEY?
ROY AND CHUCK- THE WEASEL BROTHERS WHO LIVE BY THEIR WITS AND STEAL!

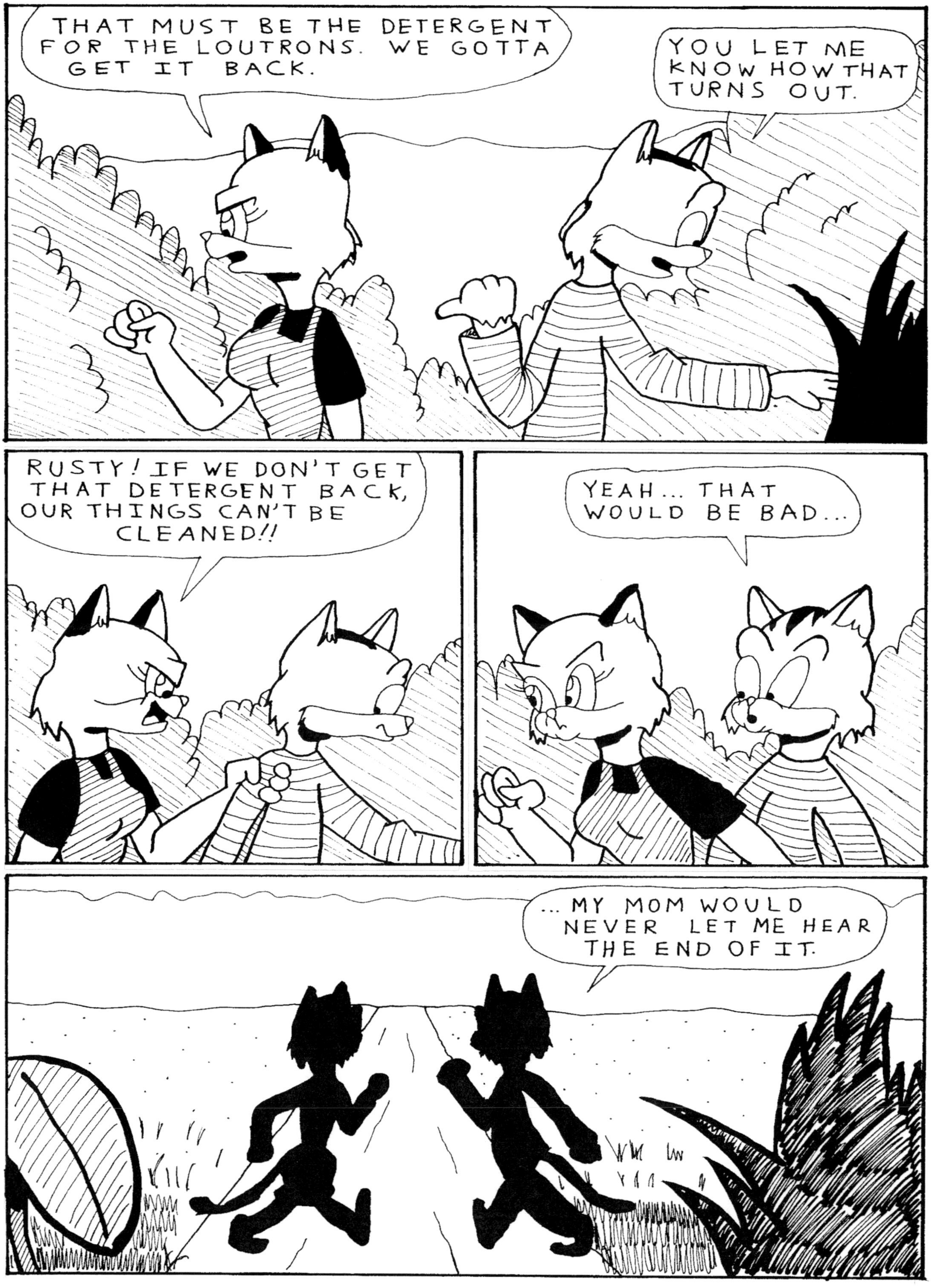
THAT MUST BE THE DETERGENT FOR THE LOUTRONS. WE GOTTA GET IT BACK.
YOU LET ME KNOW HOW THAT TURNS OUT.
RUSTY! IF WE DON'T GET THAT DETERGENT BACK, OUR THINGS CAN'T BE CLEANED!!
YEAH... THAT WOULD BE BAD...
...MY MOM WOULD NEVER LET ME HEAR THE END OF IT.

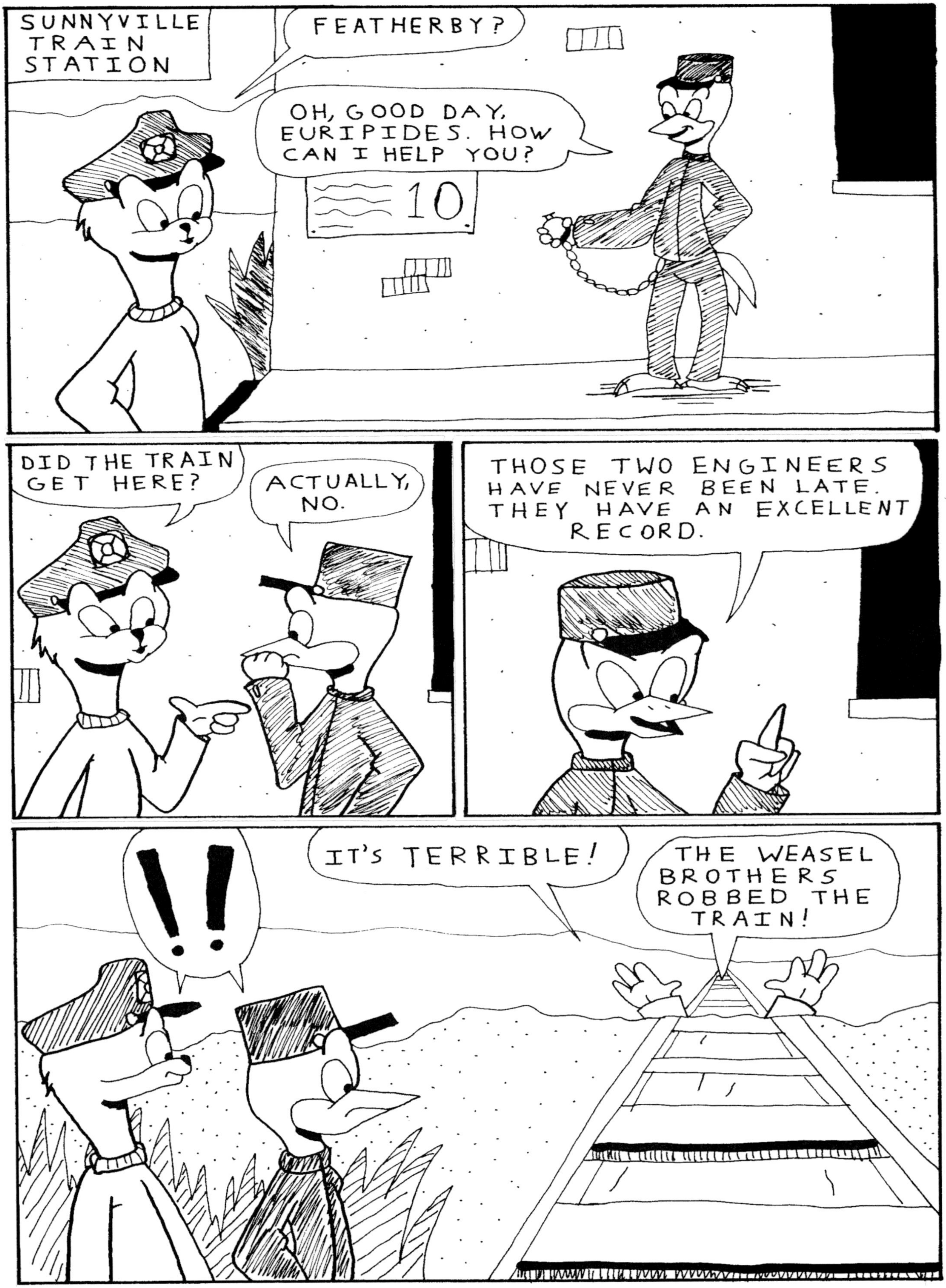

SUNNYVILLE TRAIN STATION
FEATHERBY?
OH, GOOD DAY, EURIPIDES. HOW CAN I HELP YOU?
10
DID THE TRAIN GET HERE?
ACTUALLY, NO.
THOSE TWO ENGINEERS HAVE NEVER BEEN LATE. THEY HAVE AN EXCELLENT RECORD.
!!
IT'S TERRIBLE!
THE WEASEL BROTHERS ROBBED THE TRAIN!

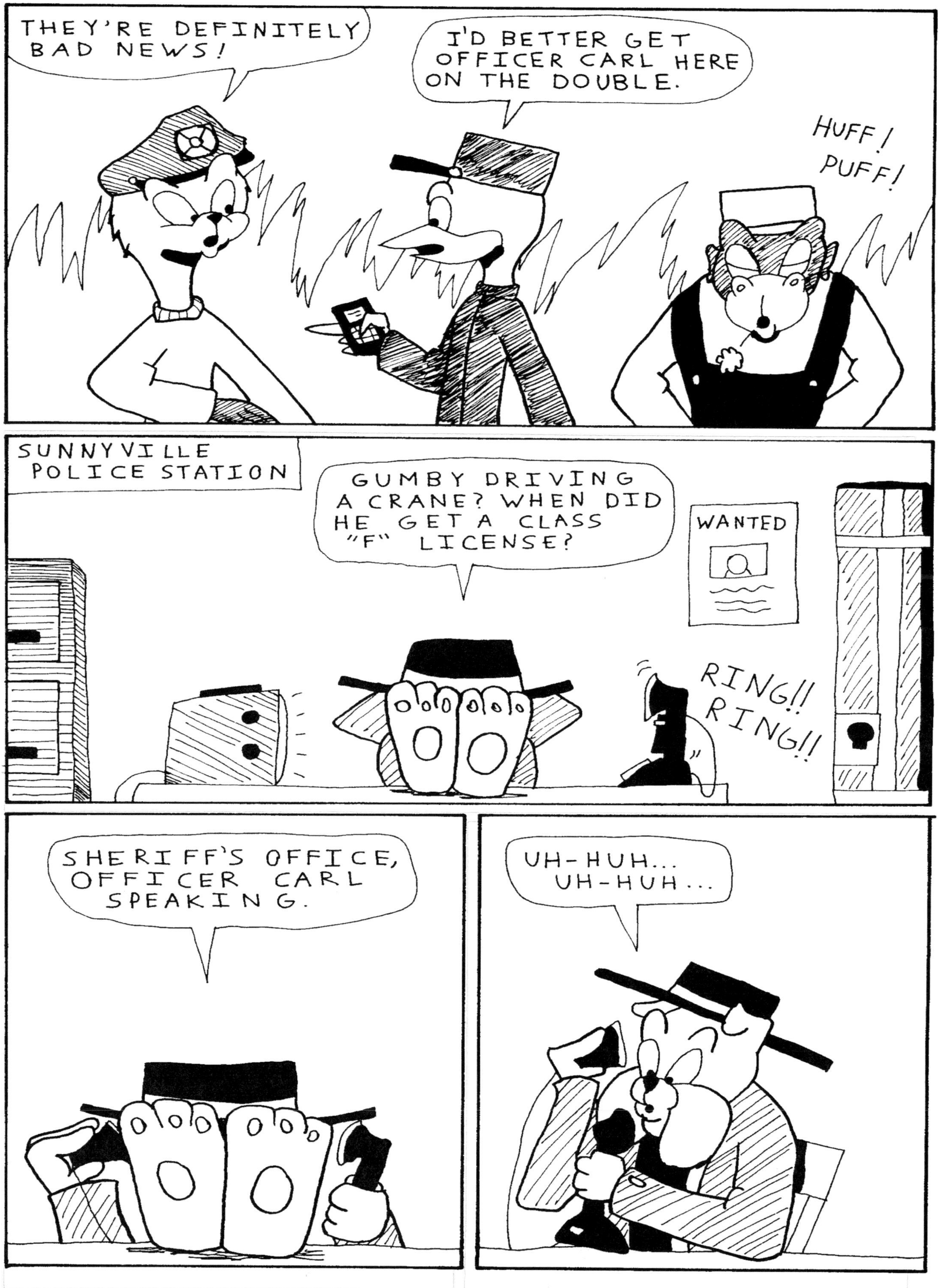
THEY'RE DEFINITELY BAD NEWS!
I'D BETTER GET OFFICER CARL HERE ON THE DOUBLE.
HUFF! PUFF!
SUNNYVILLE POLICE STATION
GUMBY DRIVING A CRANE? WHEN DID HE GET A CLASS "F" LICENSE?
WANTED
RING!! RING!!
SHERIFF'S OFFICE, OFFICER CARL SPEAKING.
UH-HUH... UH-HUH...

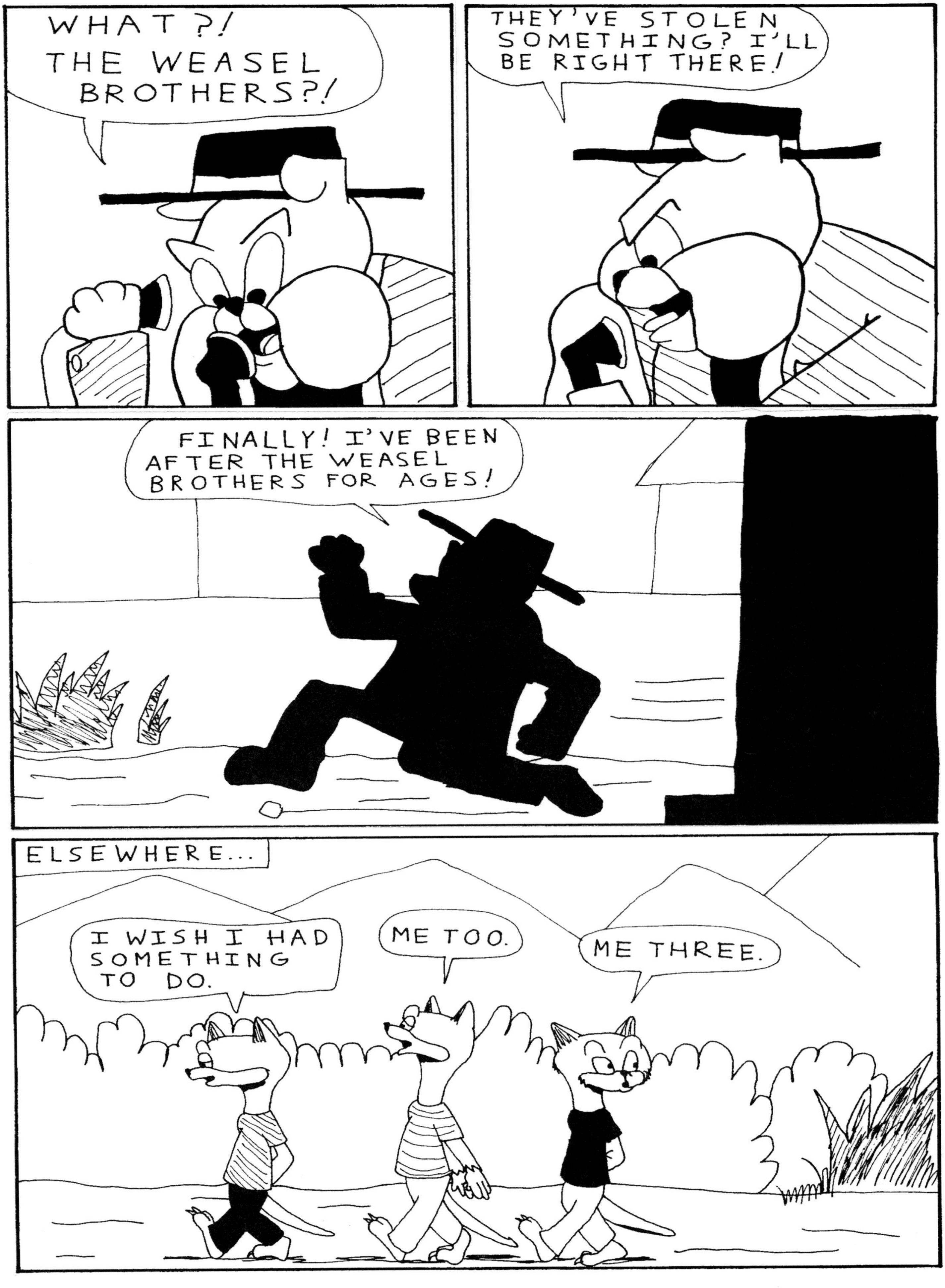
WHAT?! THE WEASEL BROTHERS?!
THEY'VE STOLEN SOMETHING? I'LL BE RIGHT THERE!
FINALLY! I'VE BEEN AFTER THE WEASEL BROTHERS FOR AGES!
ELSEWHERE...
I WISH I HAD SOMETHING TO DO.
ME TOO.
ME THREE.

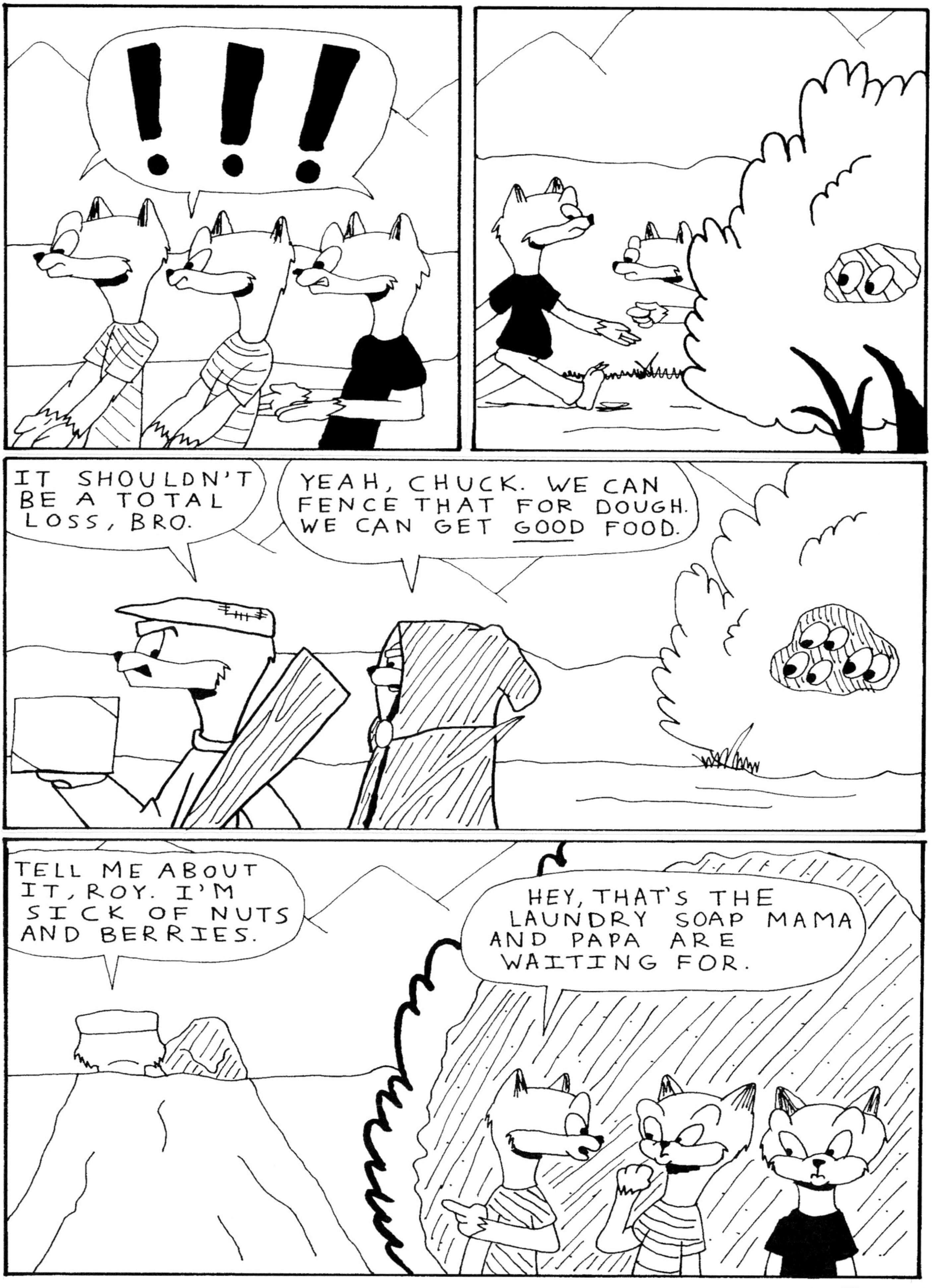
!!!
IT SHOULDN'T BE A TOTAL LOSS, BRO.
YEAH, CHUCK. WE CAN FENCE THAT FOR DOUGH. WE CAN GET GOOD FOOD.
TELL ME ABOUT IT, ROY. I'M SICK OF NUTS AND BERRIES.
HEY, THAT'S THE LAUNDRY SOAP MAMA AND PAPA ARE WAITING FOR.

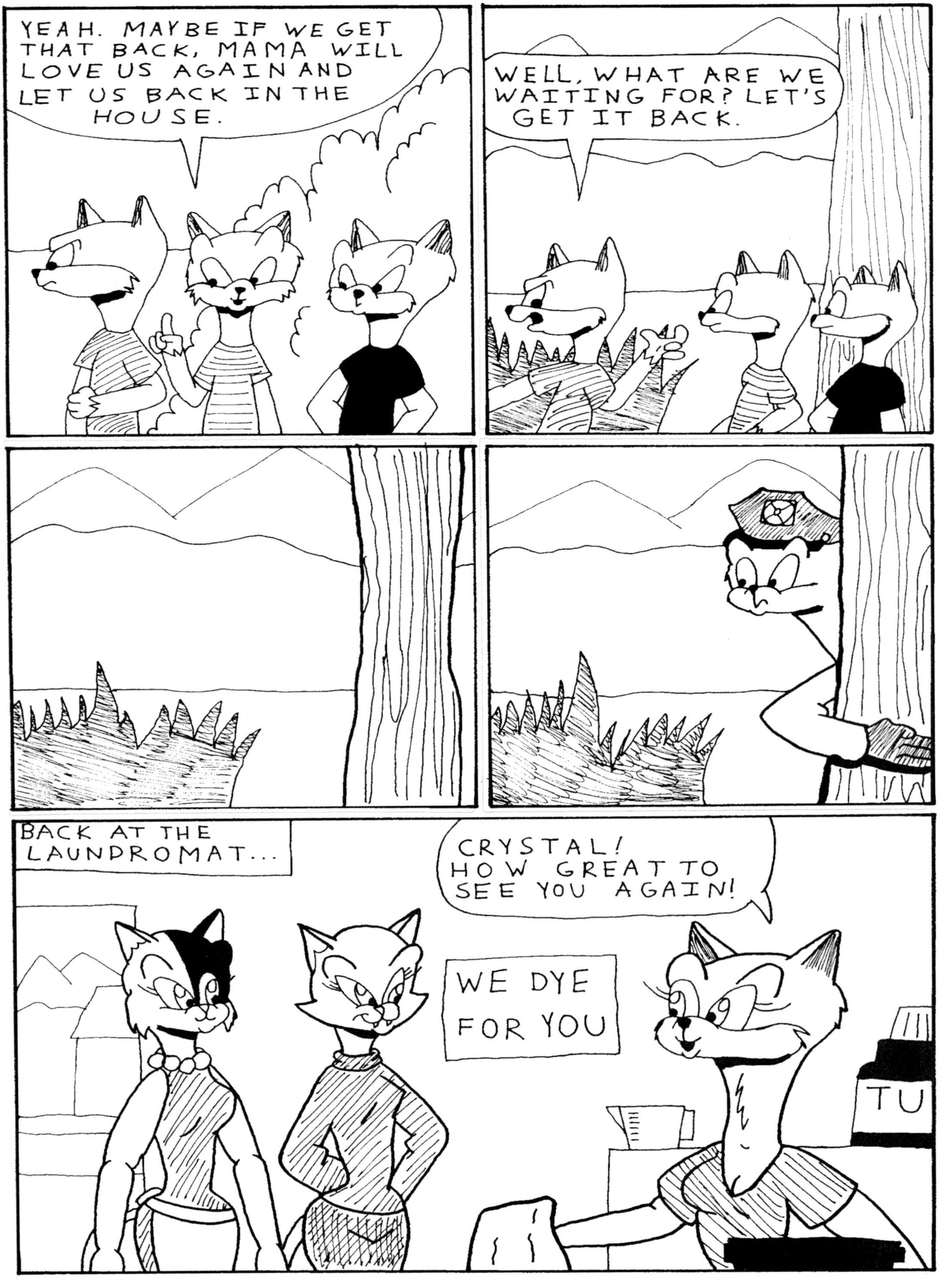
YEAH. MAYBE IF WE GET THAT BACK, MAMA WILL LOVE US AGAIN AND LET US BACK IN THE HOUSE.
WELL, WHAT ARE WE WAITING FOR? LET'S GET IT BACK.
BACK AT THE LAUNDROMAT...
CRYSTAL! HOW GREAT TO SEE YOU AGAIN!
WE DYE FOR YOU
TU

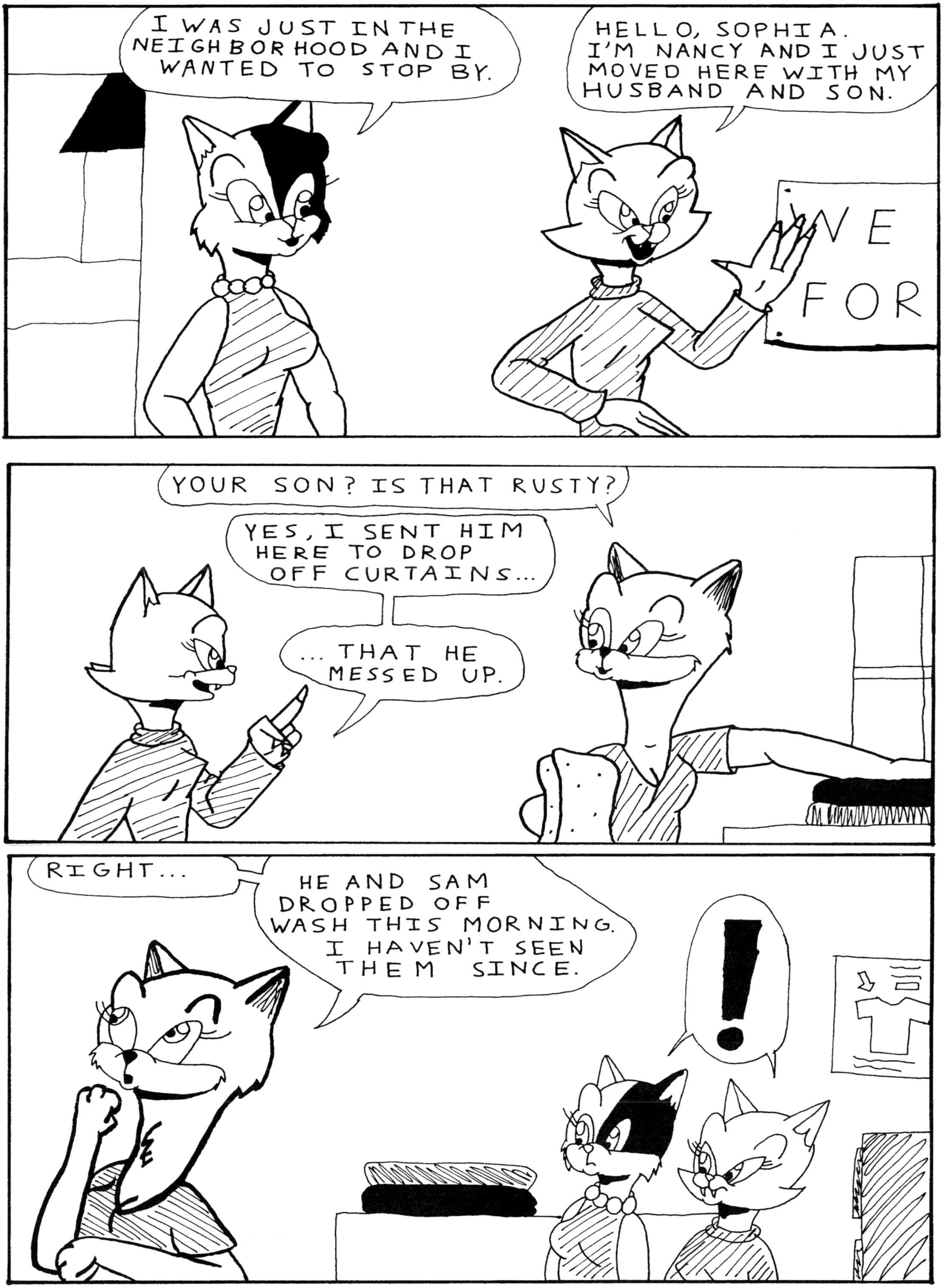
I WAS JUST IN THE NEIGHBORHOOD AND I WANTED TO STOP BY.
HELLO, SOPHIA. I'M NANCY AND I JUST MOVED HERE WITH MY HUSBAND AND SON.
YOUR SON? IS THAT RUSTY?
YES, I SENT HIM HERE TO DROP OFF CURTAINS...
... THAT HE MESSED UP.
RIGHT...
HE AND SAM DROPPED OFF WASH THIS MORNING. I HAVEN'T SEEN THEM SINCE.
!

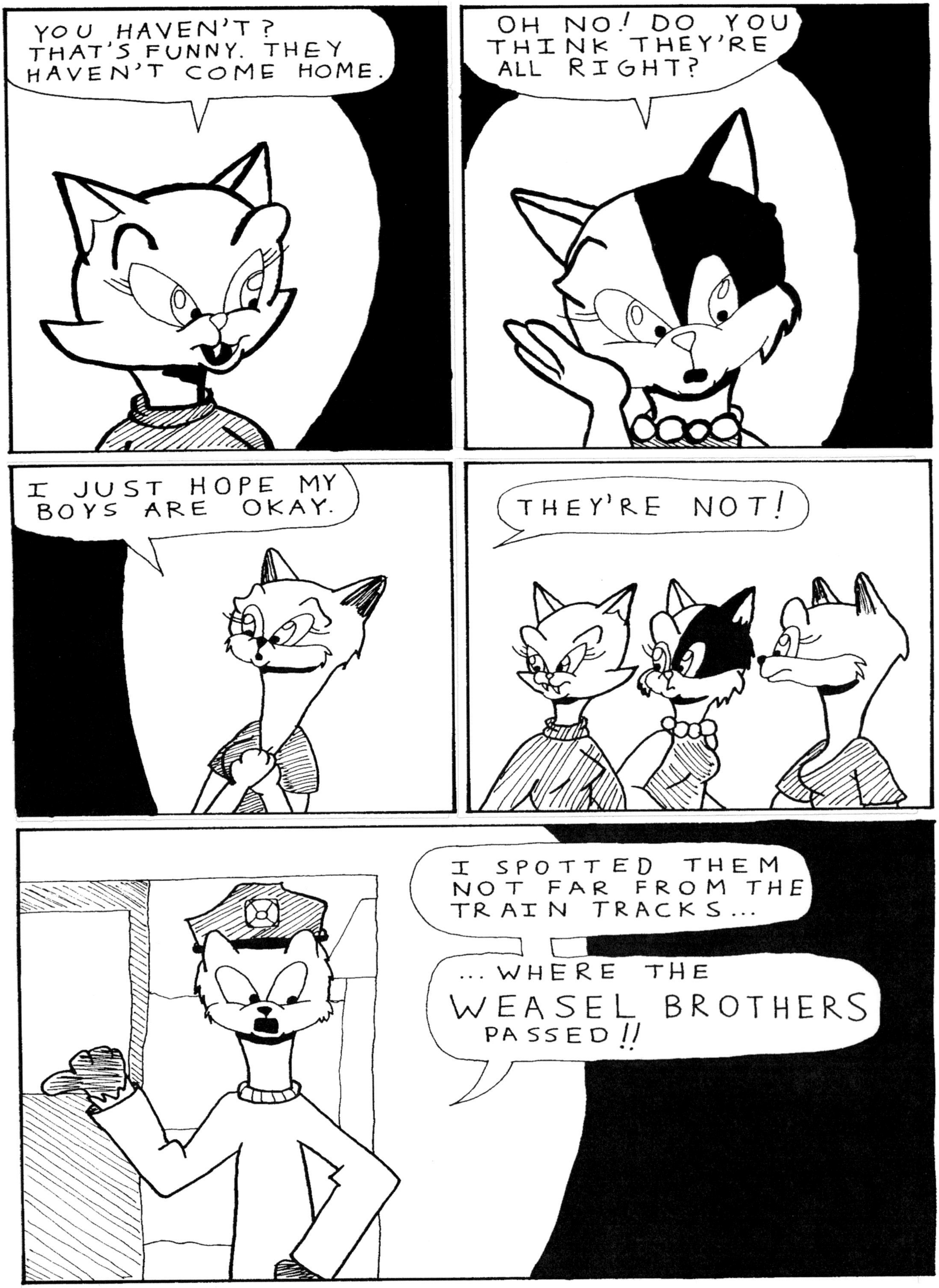
YOU HAVEN'T? THAT'S FUNNY. THEY HAVEN'T COME HOME.
OH NO! DO YOU THINK THEY'RE ALL RIGHT?
I JUST HOPE MY BOYS ARE OKAY.
THEY'RE NOT!
I SPOTTED THEM NOT FAR FROM THE TRAIN TRACKS...
...WHERE THE WEASEL BROTHERS PASSED!!

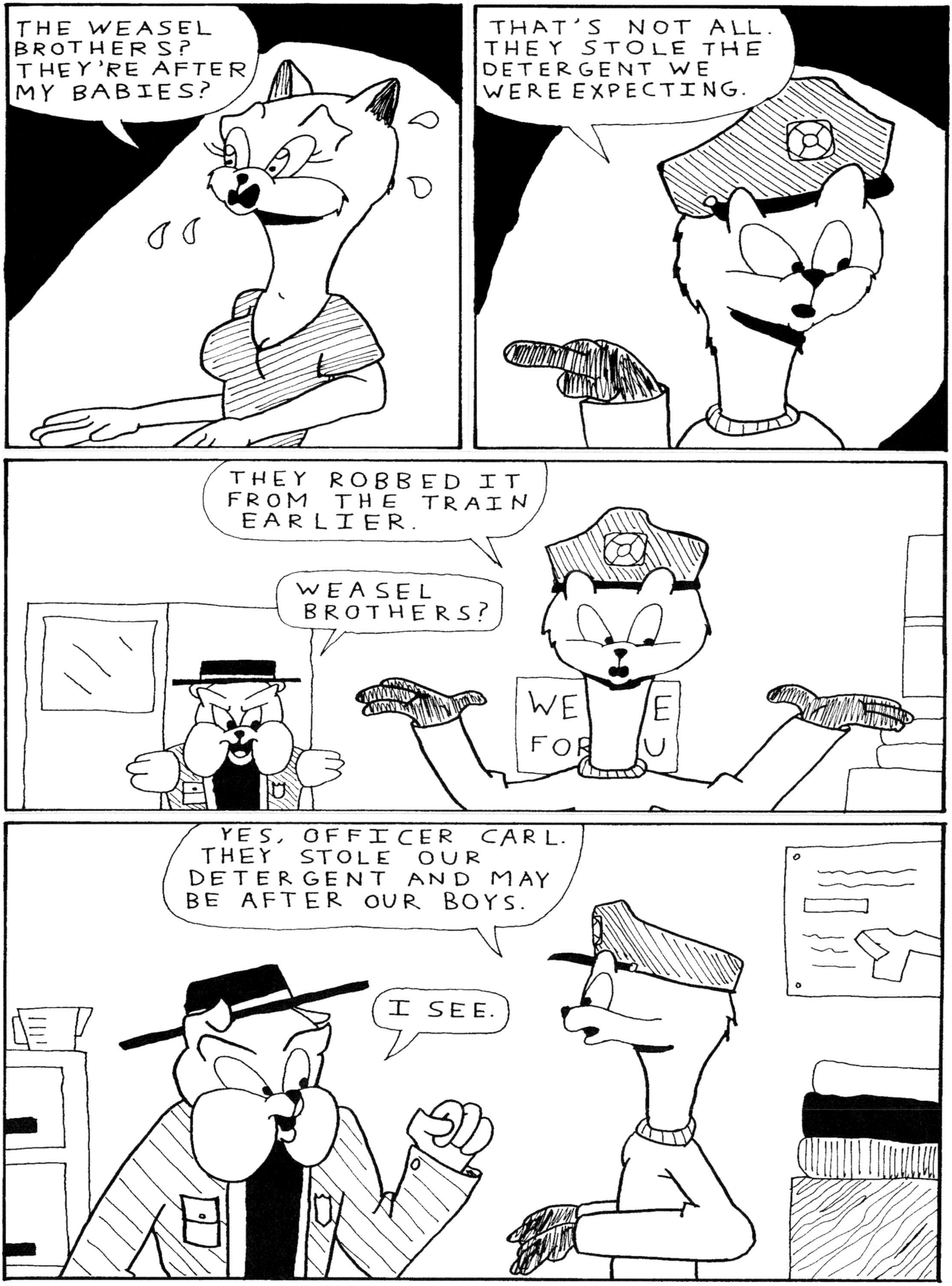
THE WEASEL BROTHERS? THEY'RE AFTER MY BABIES?
THAT'S NOT ALL. THEY STOLE THE DETERGENT WE WERE EXPECTING.
THEY ROBBED IT FROM THE TRAIN EARLIER.
WEASEL BROTHERS?
YES, OFFICER CARL. THEY STOLE OUR DETERGENT AND MAY BE AFTER OUR BOYS.
I SEE.

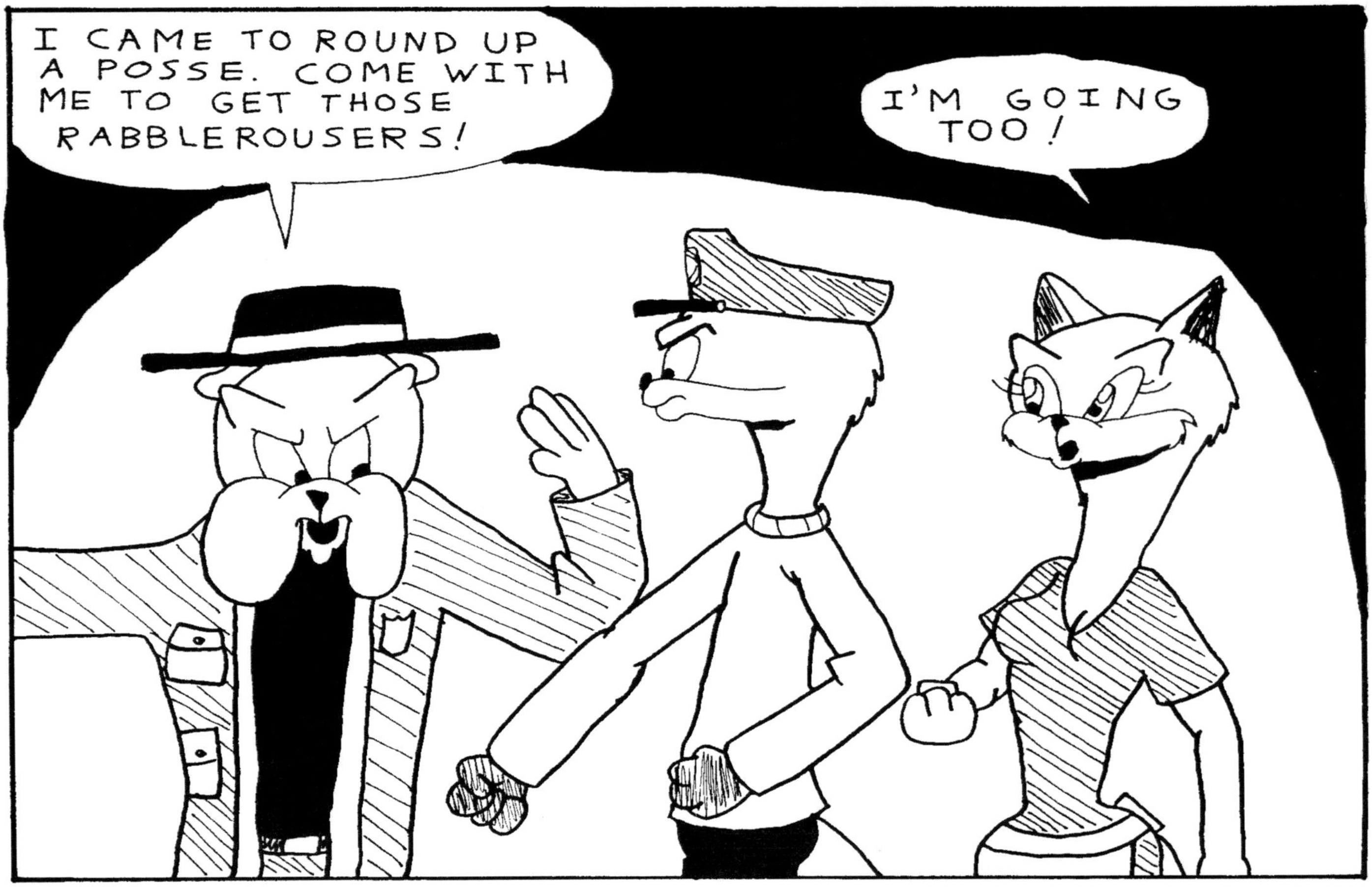
I CAME TO ROUND UP A POSSE. COME WITH ME TO GET THOSE RABBLEROUSERS!
I'M GOING TOO!

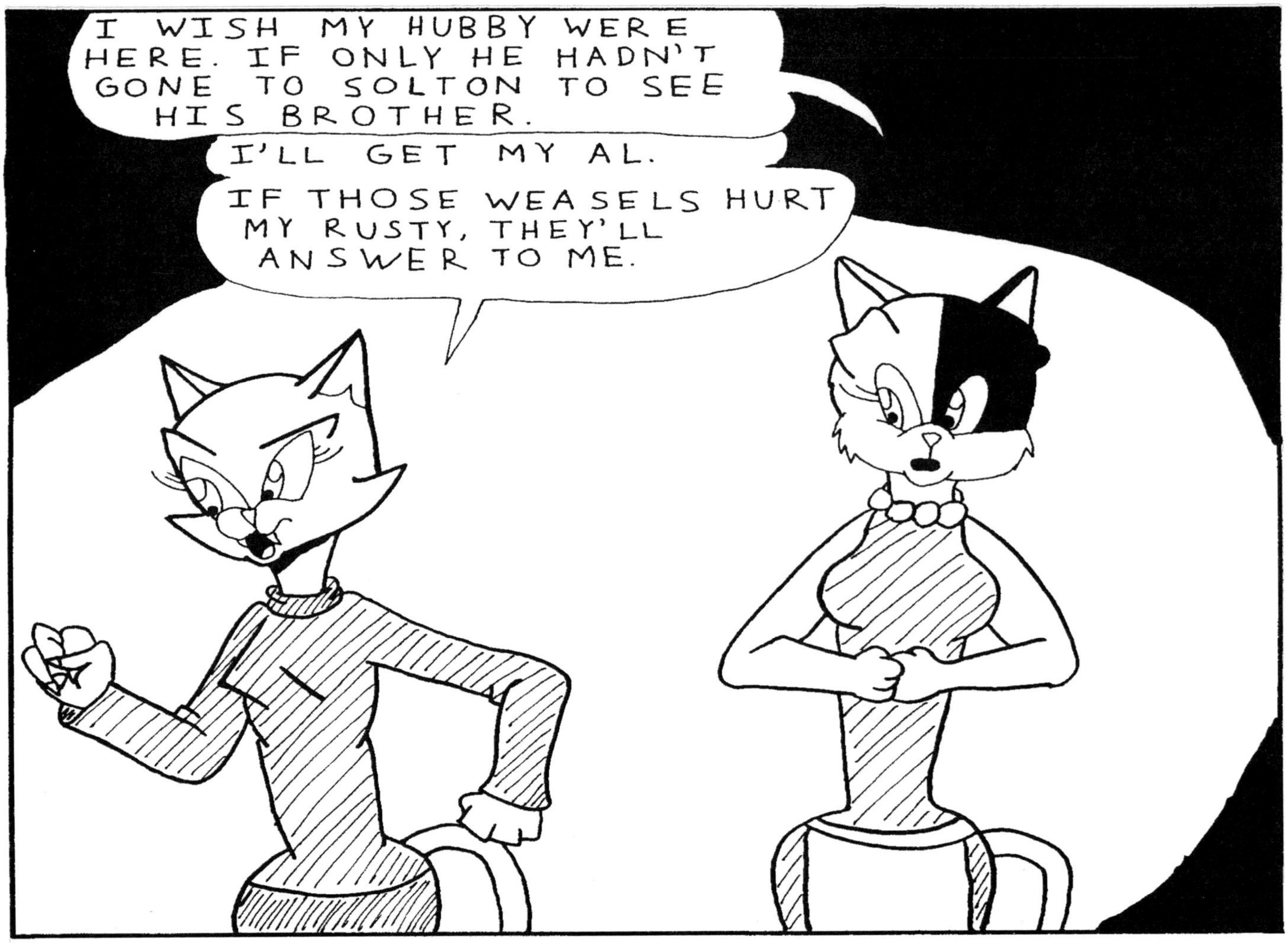
I WISH MY HUBBY WERE HERE. IF ONLY HE HADN'T GONE TO SOLTON TO SEE HIS BROTHER.
I'LL GET MY AL.
IF THOSE WEASELS HURT MY RUSTY, THEY'LL ANSWER TO ME.

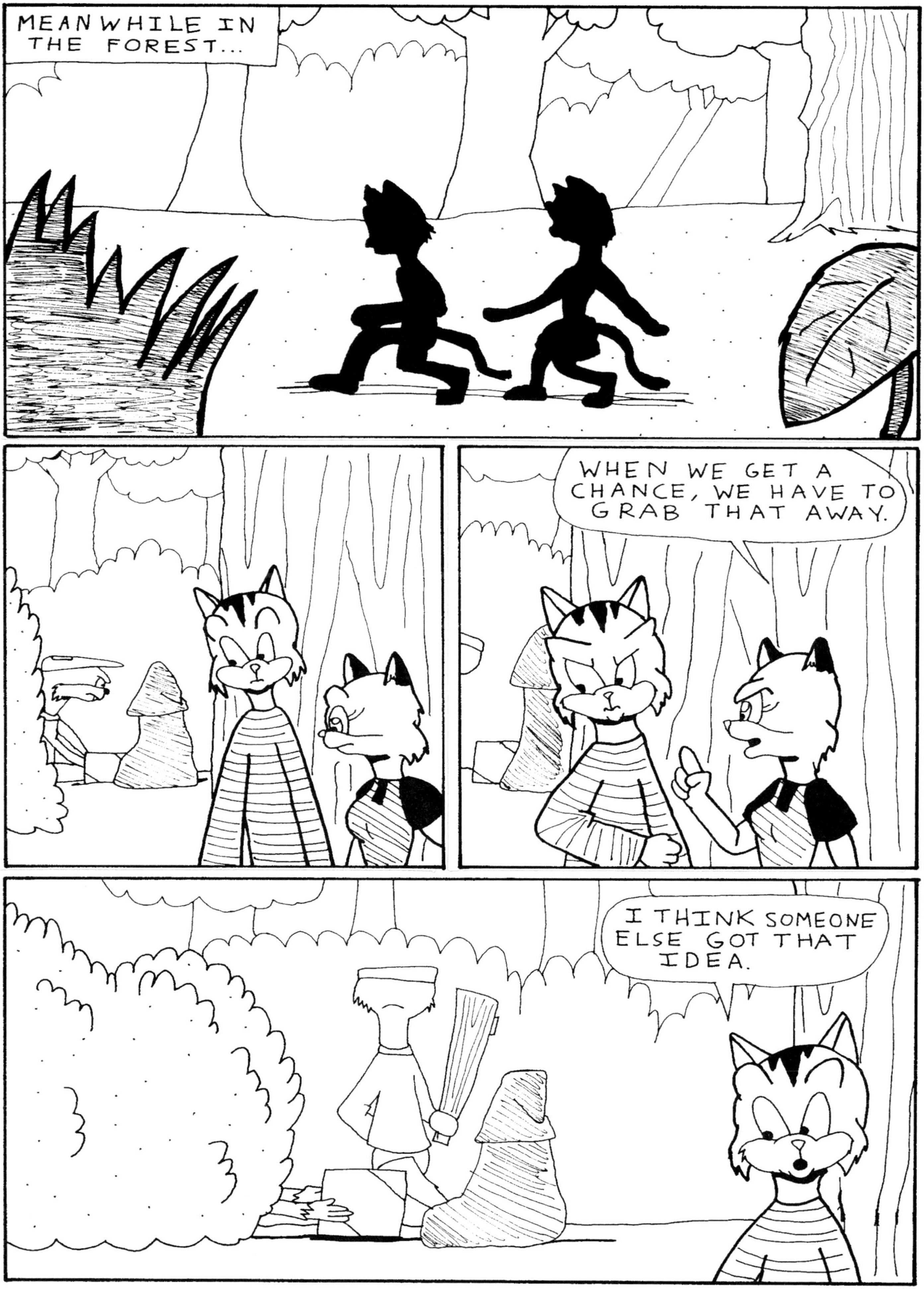
MEANWHILE IN THE FOREST...
WHEN WE GET A CHANCE, WE HAVE TO GRAB THAT AWAY.
I THINK SOMEONE ELSE GOT THAT IDEA.

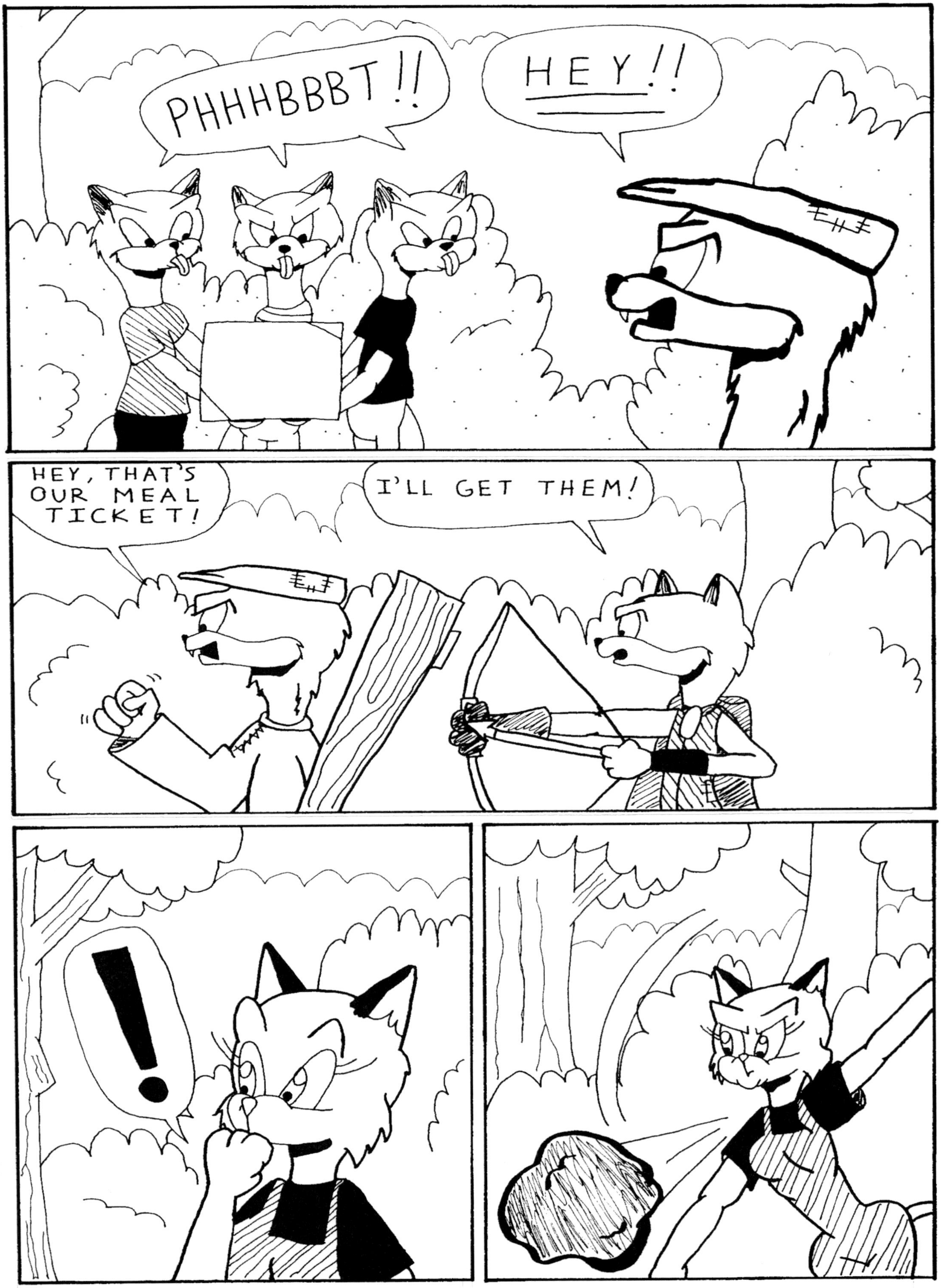
PHHHBBBT!!
HEY!!
HEY, THAT'S OUR MEAL TICKET!
I'LL GET THEM!
!

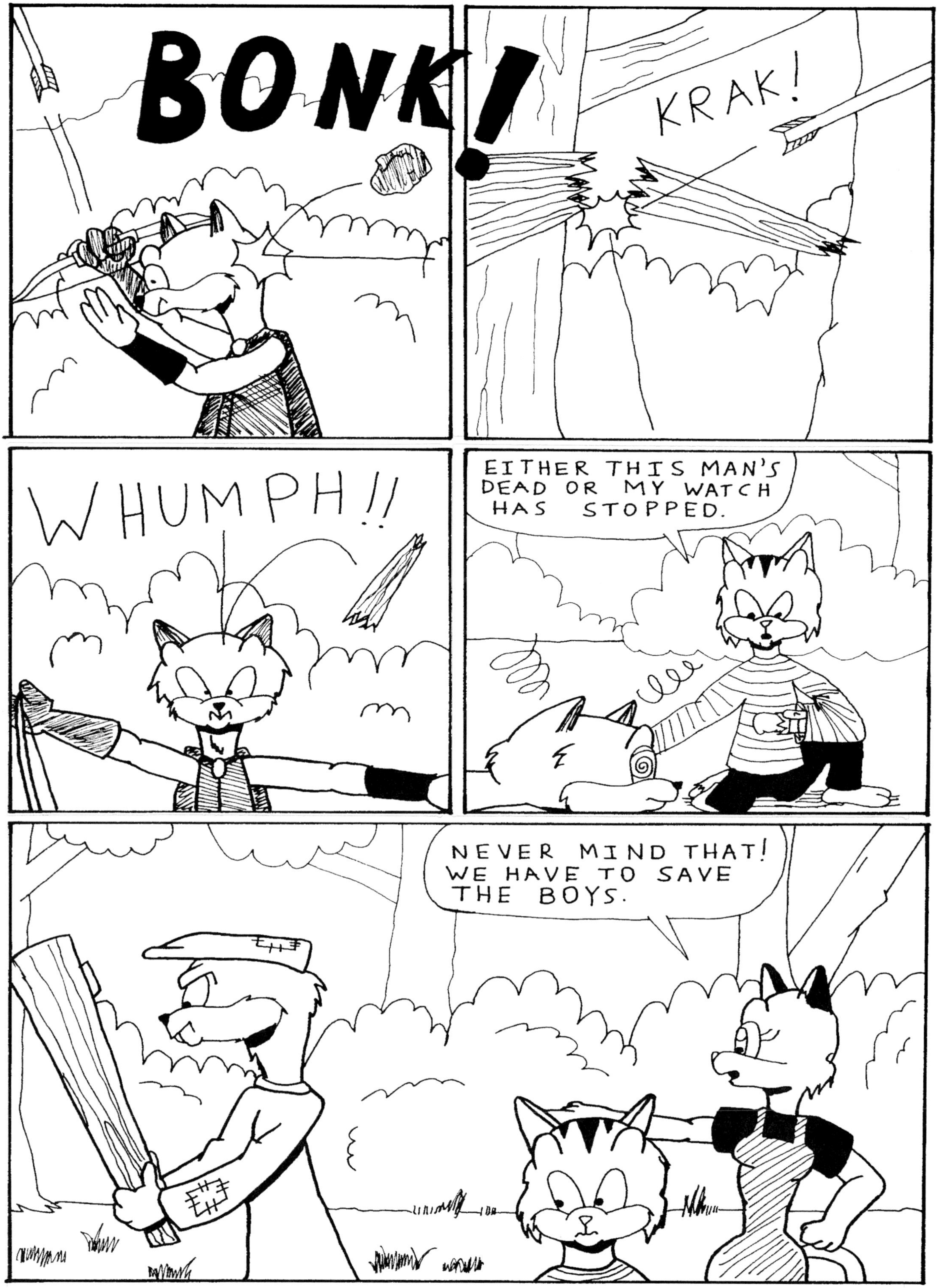
BONK!
KRAK!
WHUMPH!!
EITHER THIS MAN'S DEAD OR MY WATCH HAS STOPPED.
NEVER MIND THAT! WE HAVE TO SAVE THE BOYS.

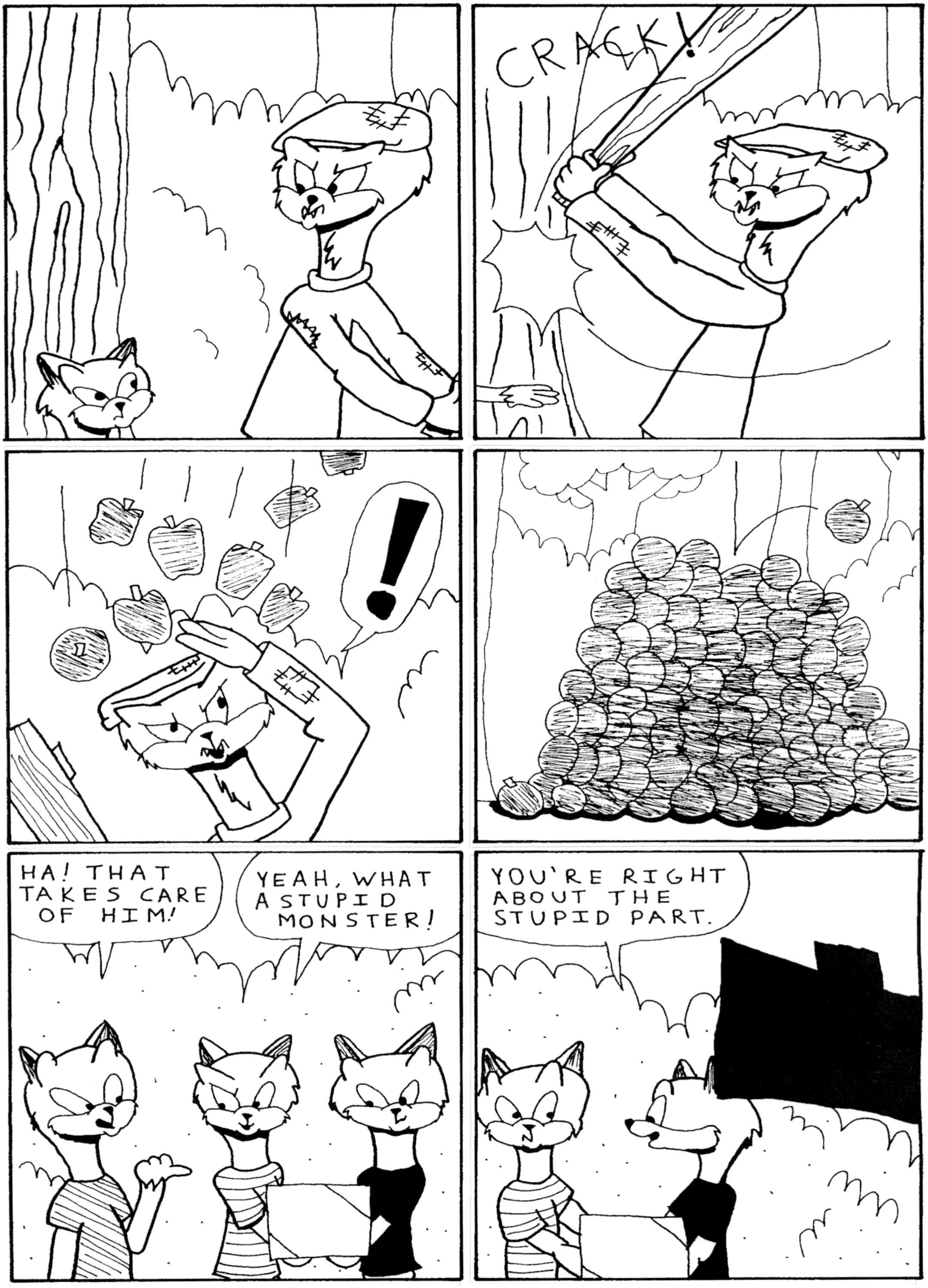
CRACK!
!
HA! THAT TAKES CARE OF HIM!
YEAH, WHAT A STUPID MONSTER!
YOU'RE RIGHT ABOUT THE STUPID PART.

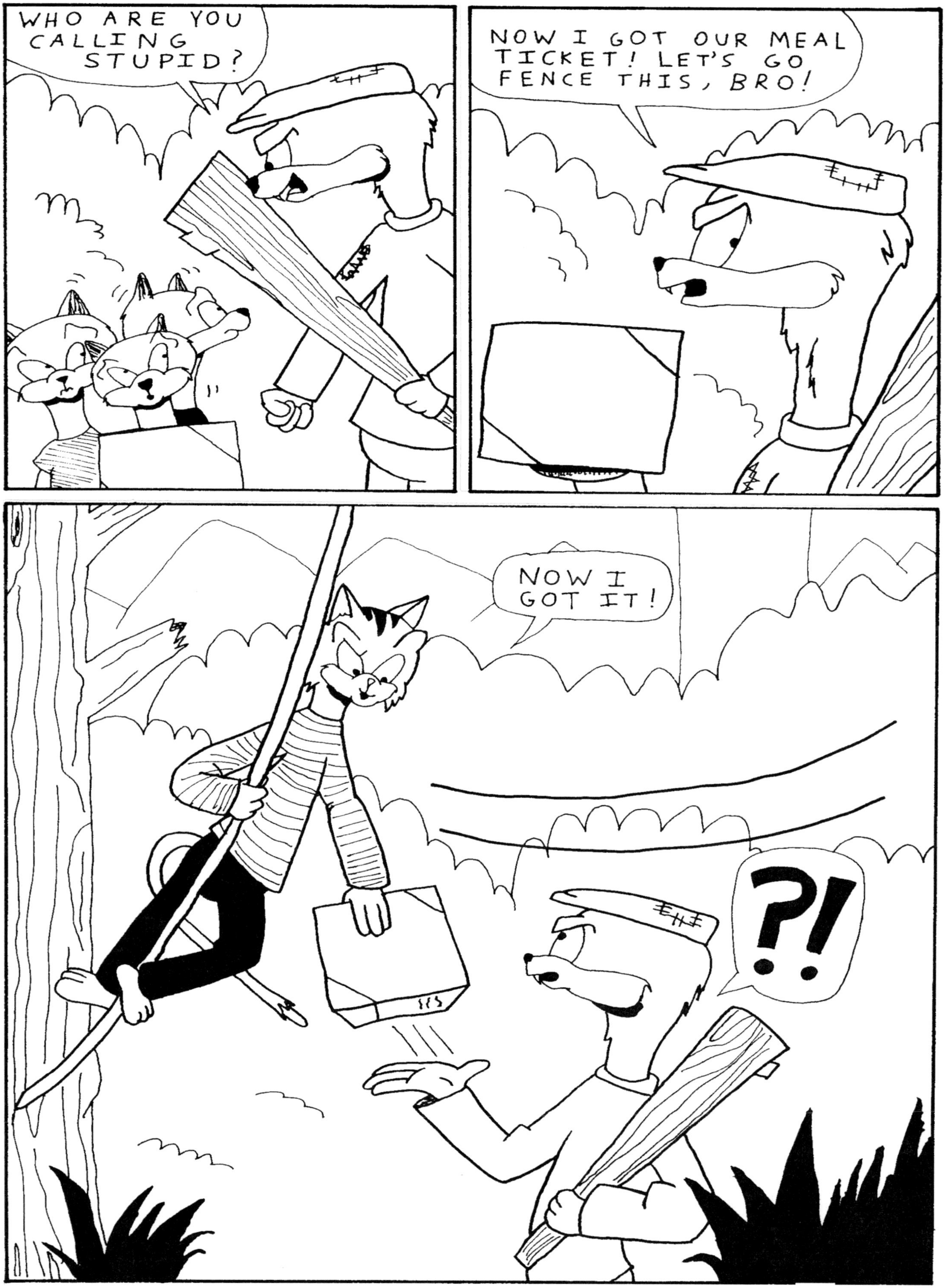
WHO ARE YOU CALLING STUPID?
NOW I GOT OUR MEAL TICKET! LET'S GO FENCE THIS, BRO!
NOW I GOT IT!
?!

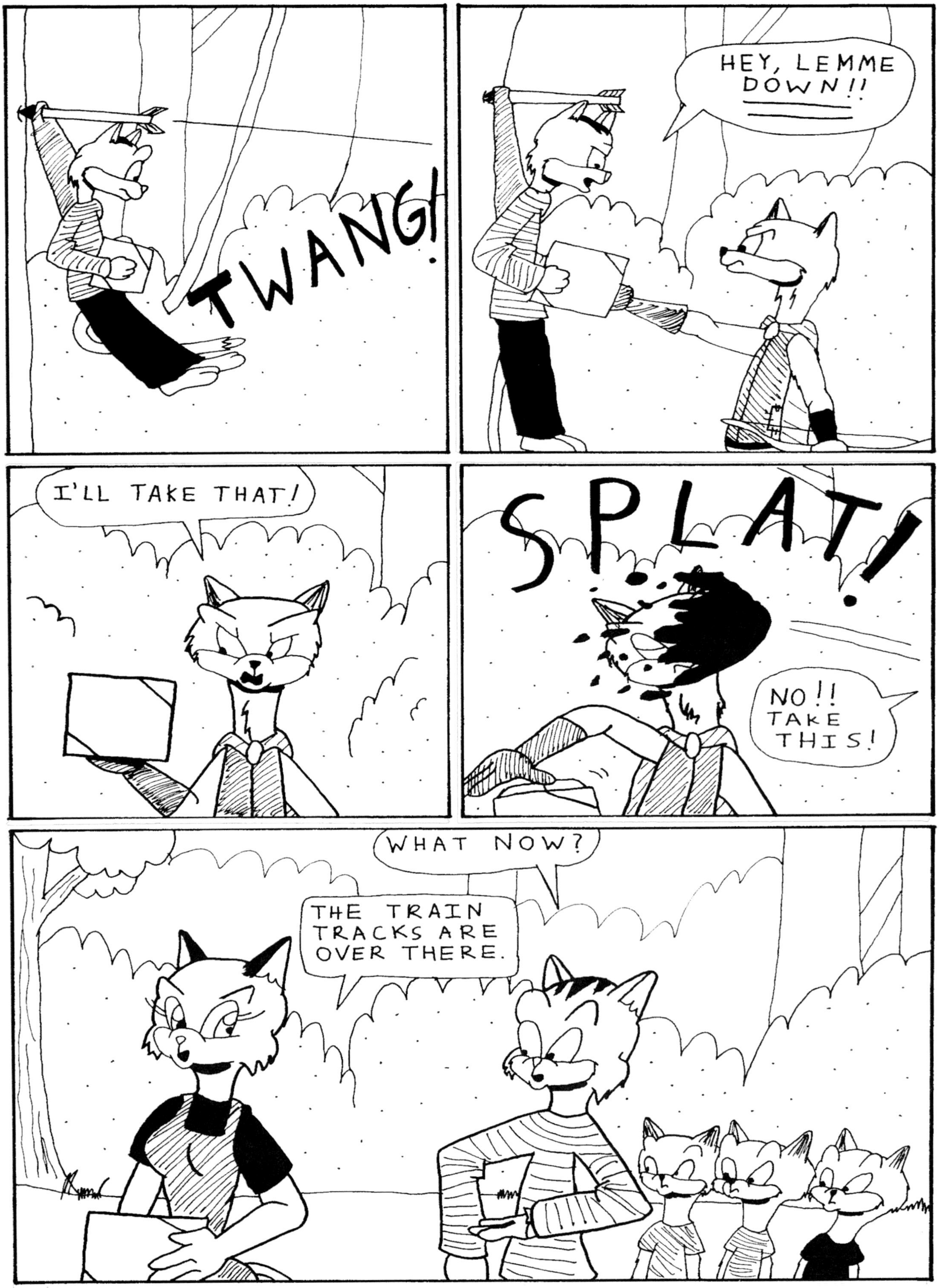
TWANG!
HEY, LEMME DOWN!!
I'LL TAKE THAT!
SPLAT!
NO!! TAKE THIS!
WHAT NOW?
THE TRAIN TRACKS ARE OVER THERE.

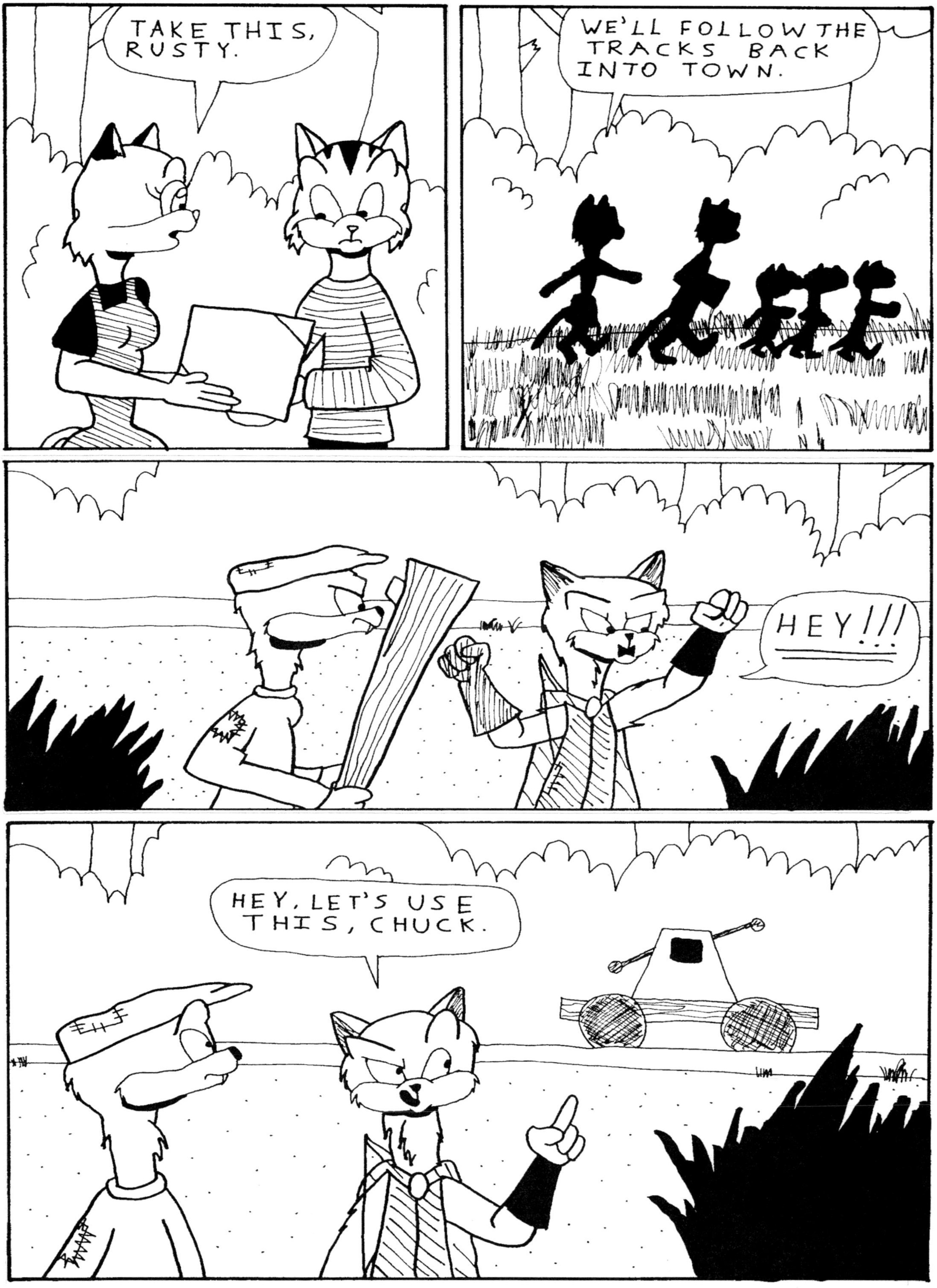
TAKE THIS, RUSTY.
WE'LL FOLLOW THE TRACKS BACK INTO TOWN.
HEY!!!
HEY, LET'S USE THIS, CHUCK.

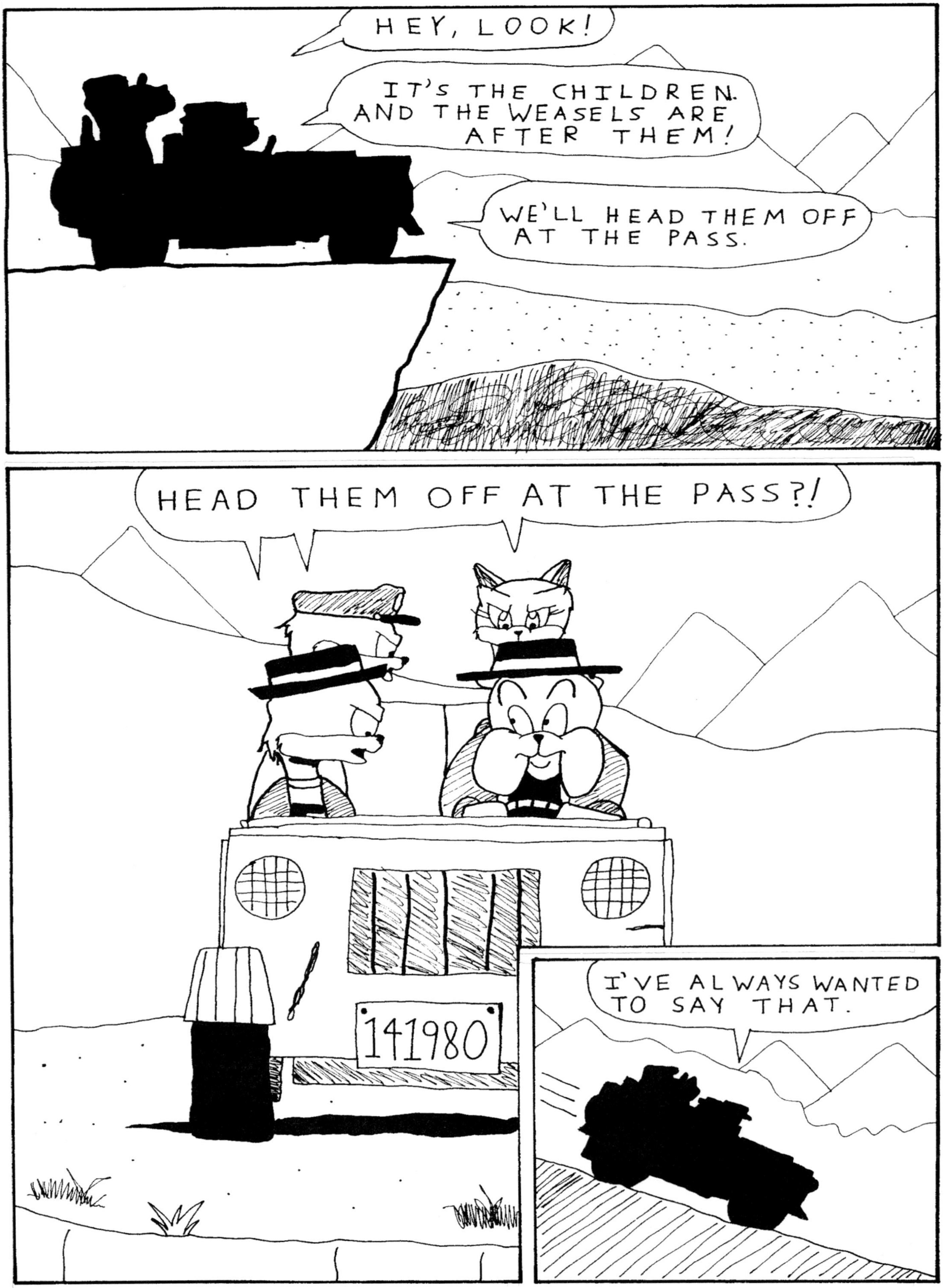
HEY, LOOK!
IT'S THE CHILDREN. AND THE WEASELS ARE AFTER THEM!
WE'LL HEAD THEM OFF AT THE PASS.
HEAD THEM OFF AT THE PASS?!
141980
I'VE ALWAYS WANTED TO SAY THAT.

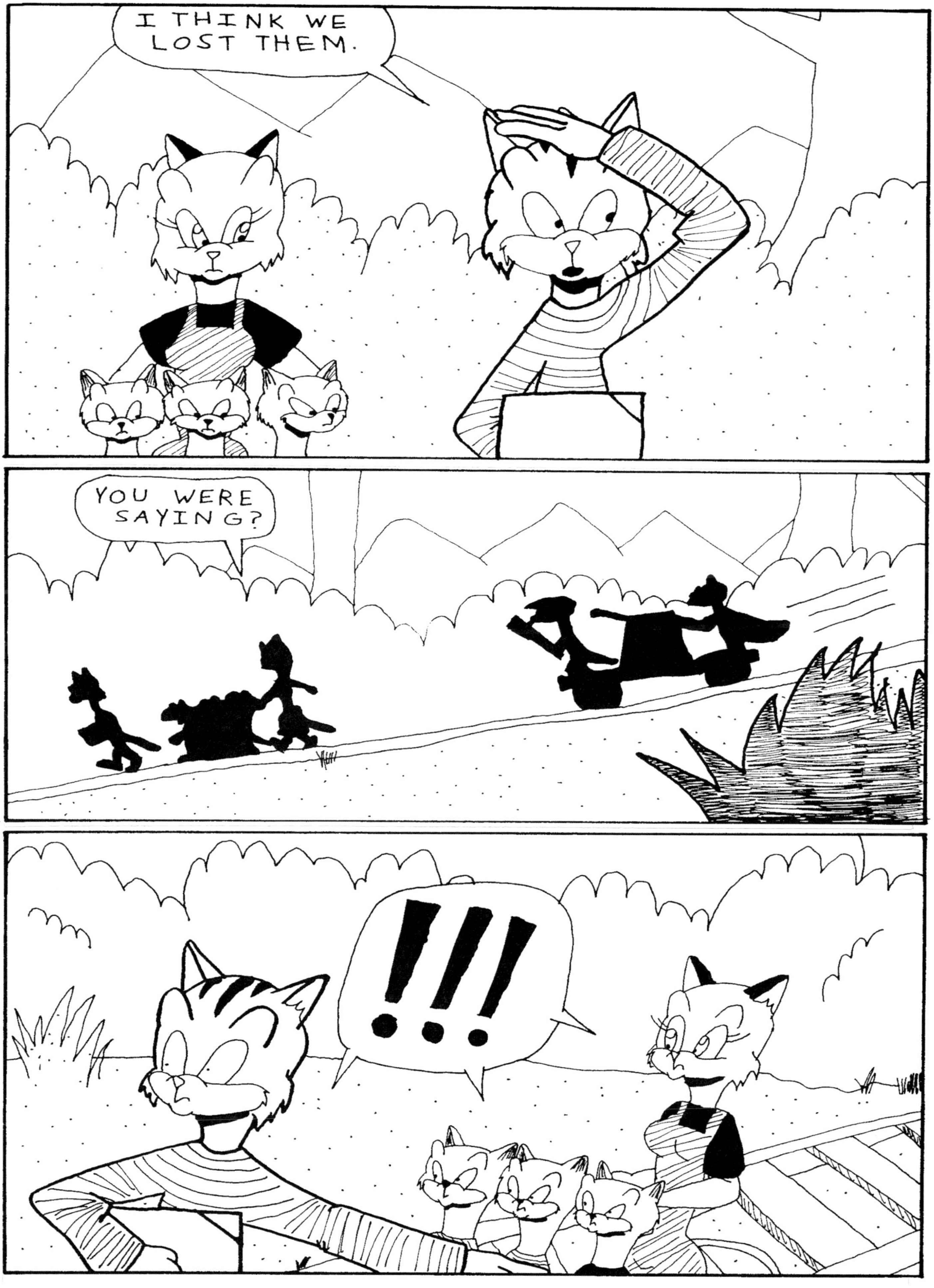
I THINK WE LOST THEM.
YOU WERE SAYING?
!!!

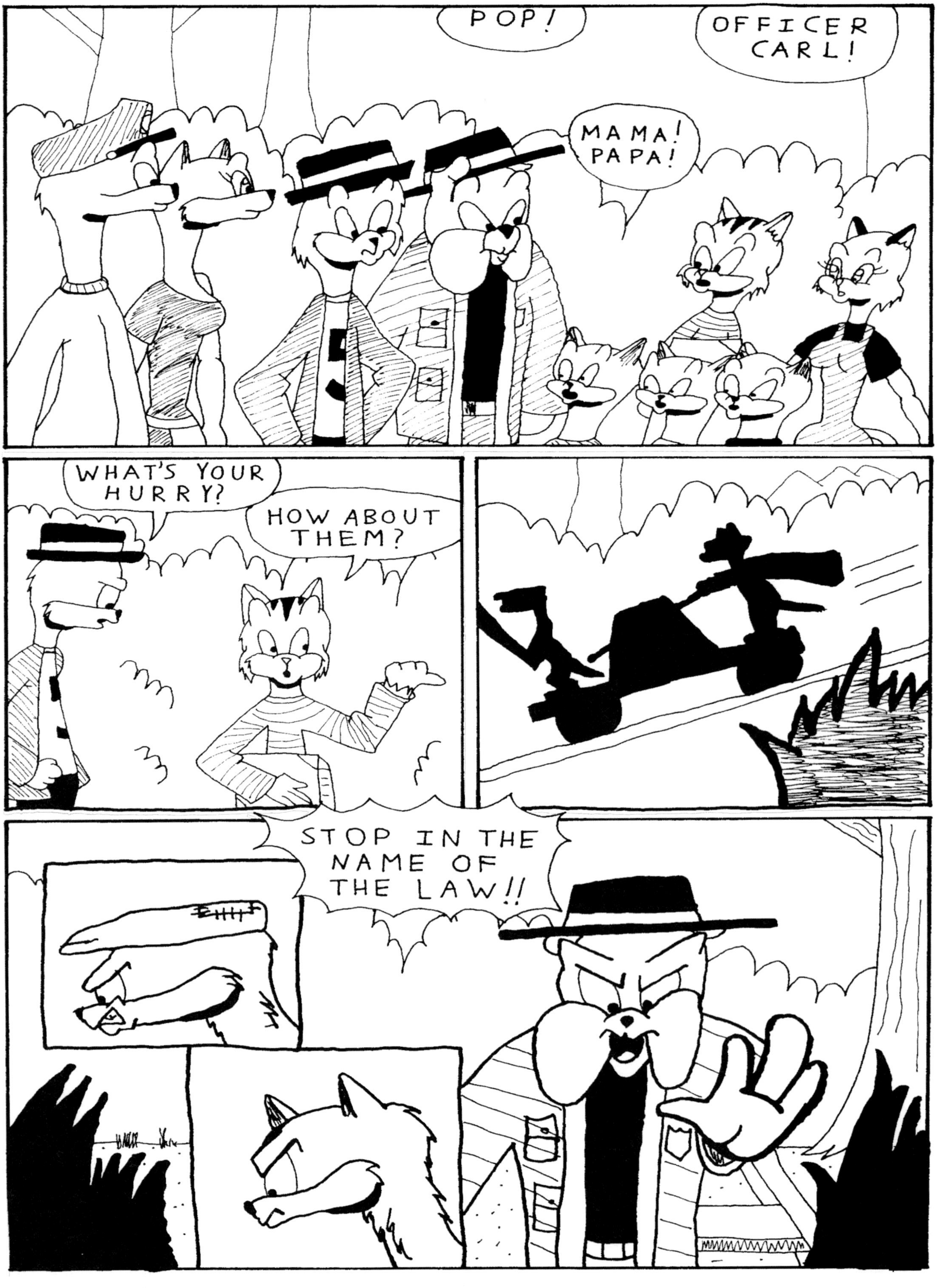
POP!
OFFICER CARL!
MAMA! PAPA!
WHAT'S YOUR HURRY?
HOW ABOUT THEM?
STOP IN THE NAME OF THE LAW!!

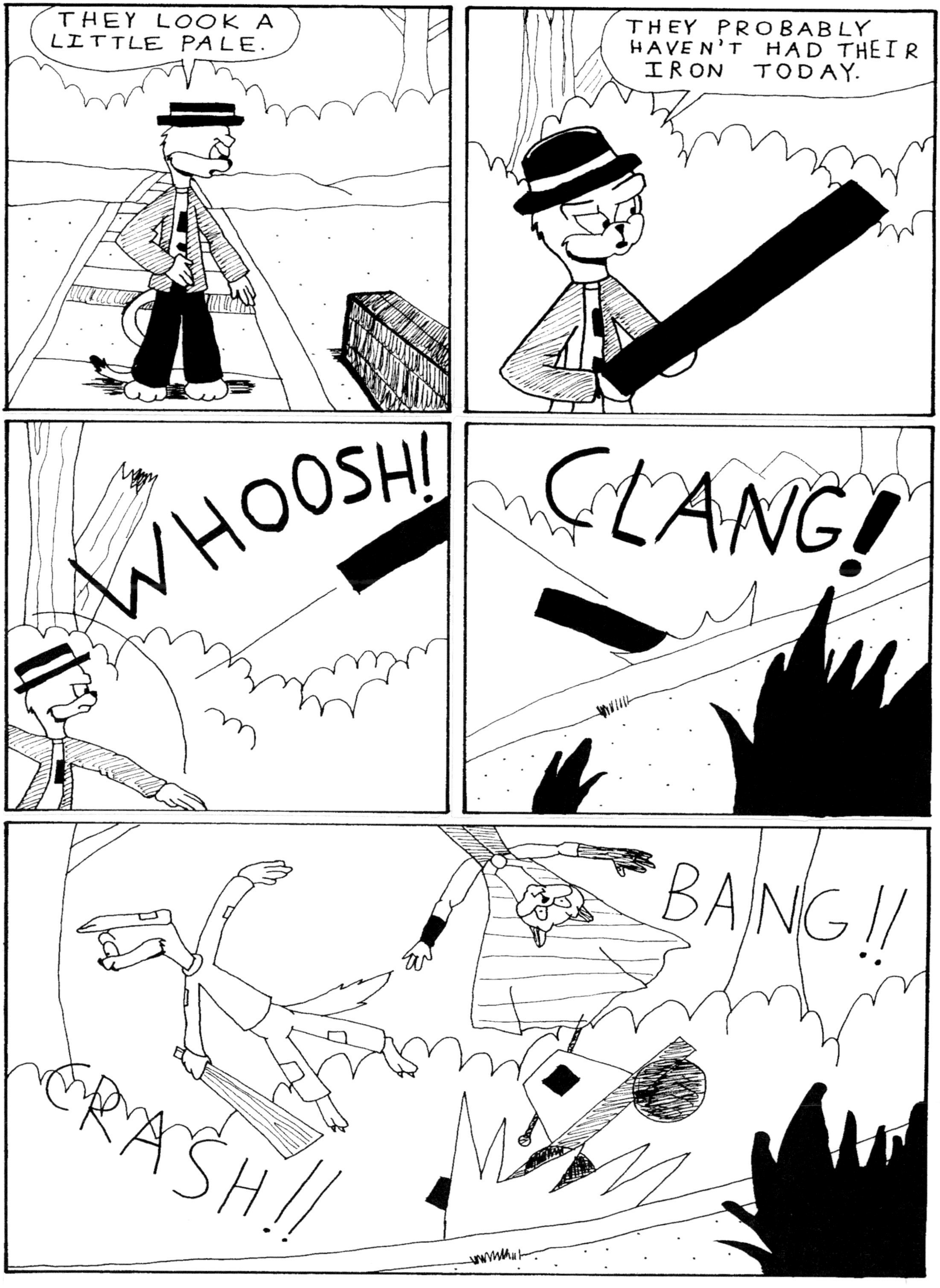
THEY LOOK A LITTLE PALE.
THEY PROBABLY HAVEN'T HAD THEIR IRON TODAY.
WHOOSH!
CLANG!
BANG!!
CRASH!!!

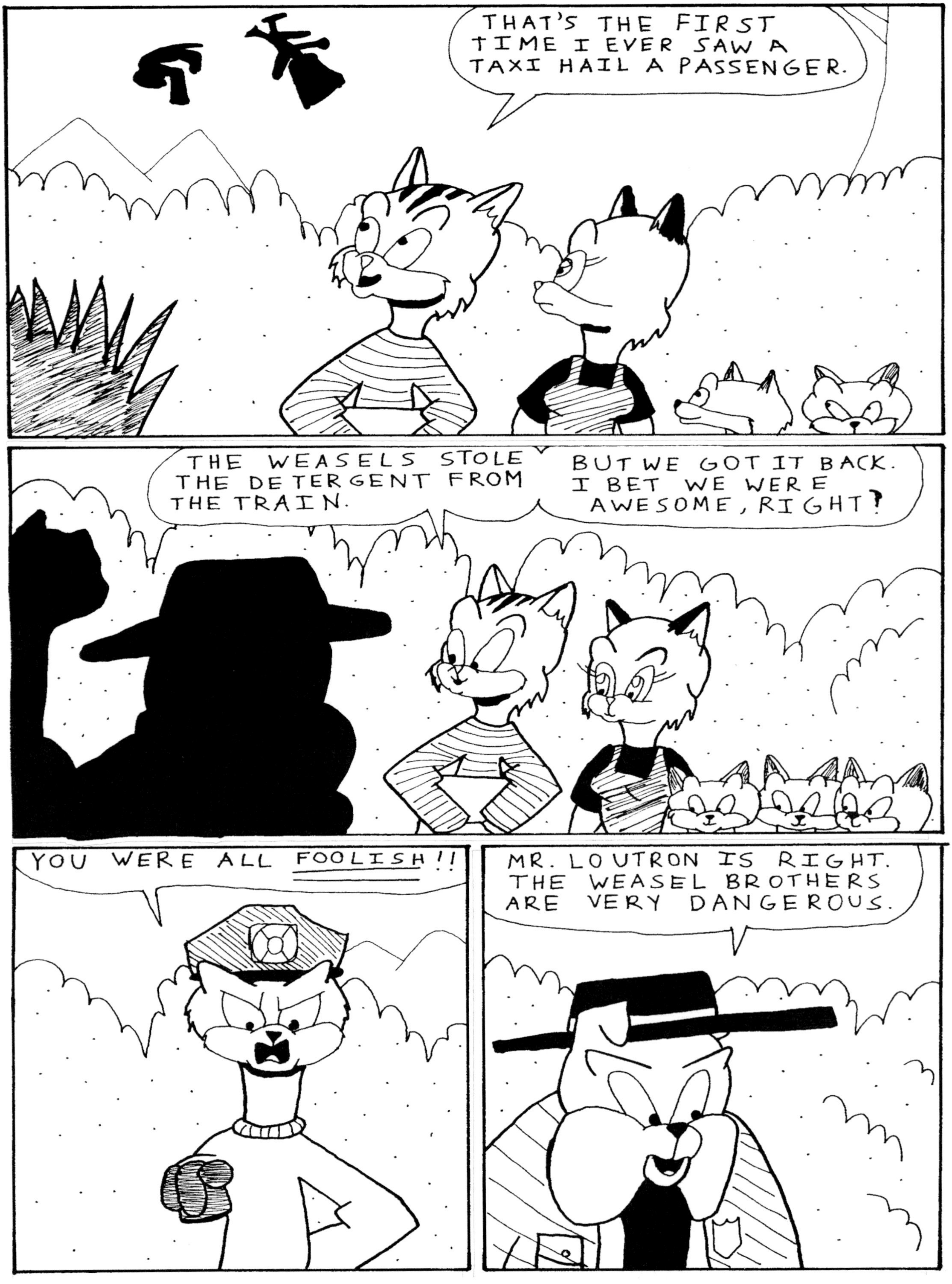
THAT'S THE FIRST TIME I EVER SAW A TAXI HAIL A PASSENGER.
THE WEASELS STOLE THE DETERGENT FROM THE TRAIN.
BUT WE GOT IT BACK. I BET WE WERE AWESOME, RIGHT?
YOU WERE ALL FOOLISH!!
MR. LOUTRON IS RIGHT. THE WEASEL BROTHERS ARE VERY DANGEROUS.

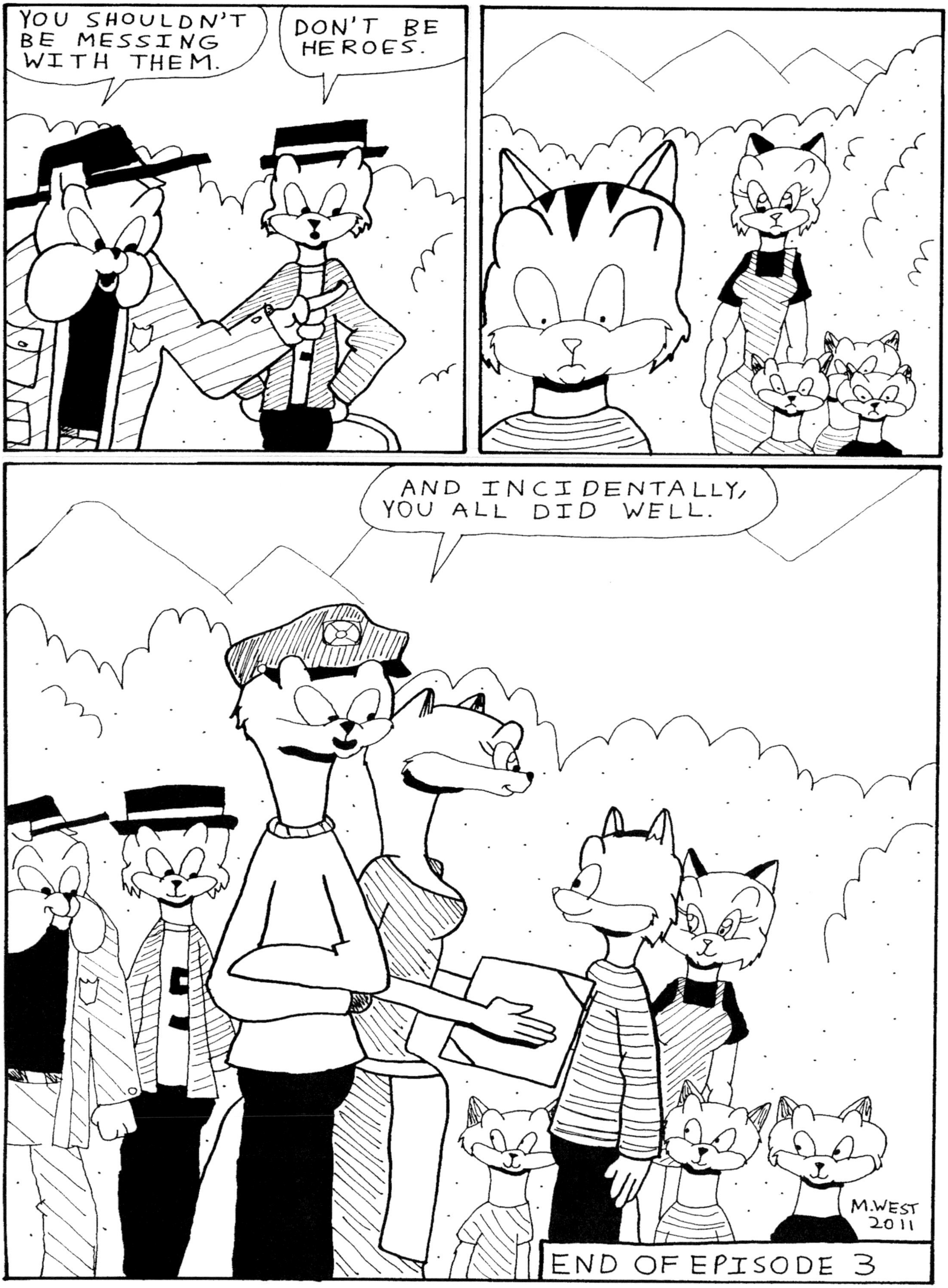

YOU SHOULDN'T BE MESSING WITH THEM.
DON'T BE HEROES.
AND INCIDENTALLY, YOU ALL DID WELL.
M.WEST 2011
END OF EPISODE 3

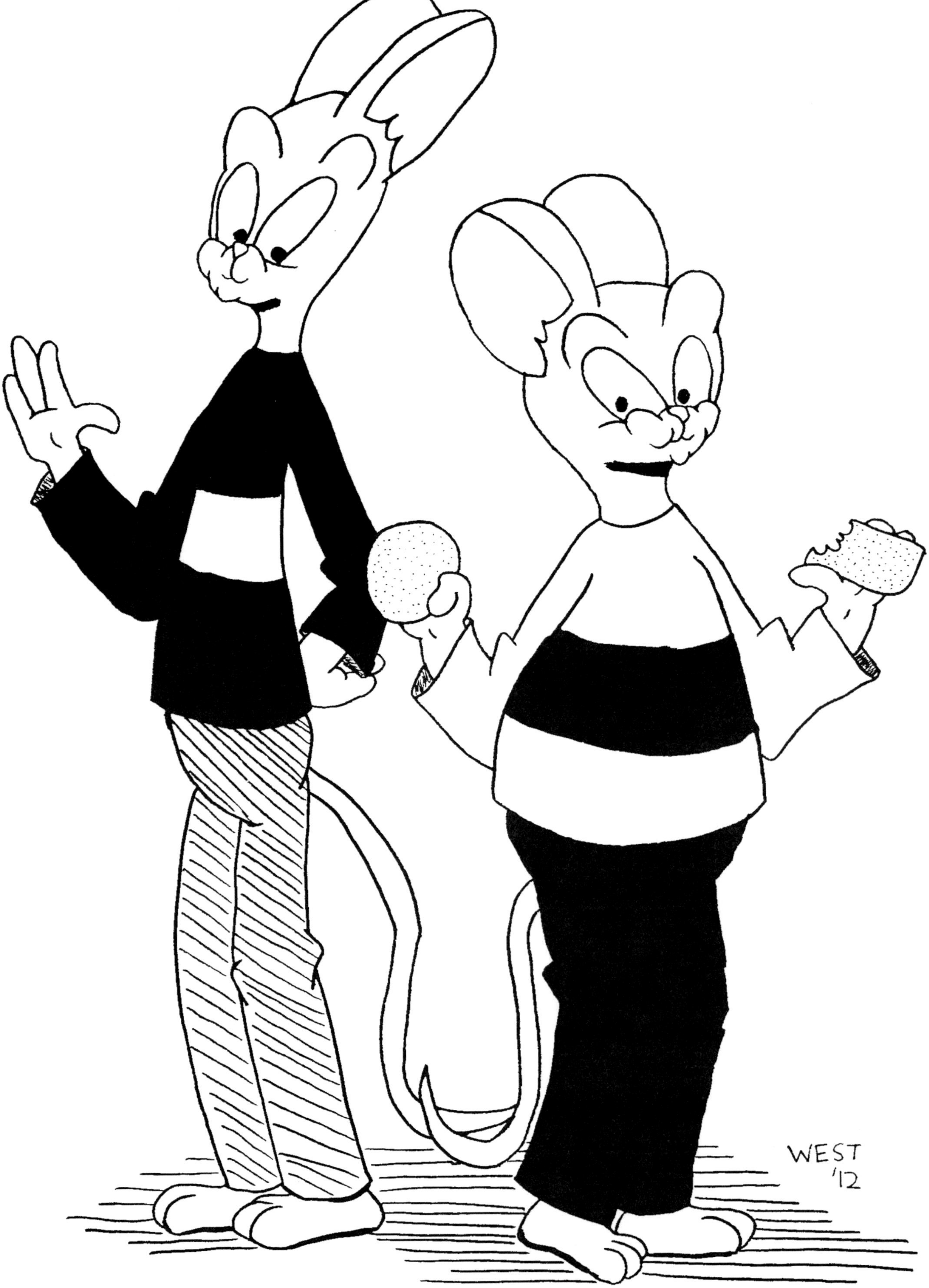
WEST
'12

And now for a...

BONUS FEATURE!!!!

Rusty & Sam #1

AUTHOR'S NOTE: The following pages are from a short
mini-comic that was done in the spring of 2009. This was
a final project for the "Cartooning Basics" continuing
education course at the School of Visual Arts. This story
marks the debut of Rusty and Sam, albeit in an early form.

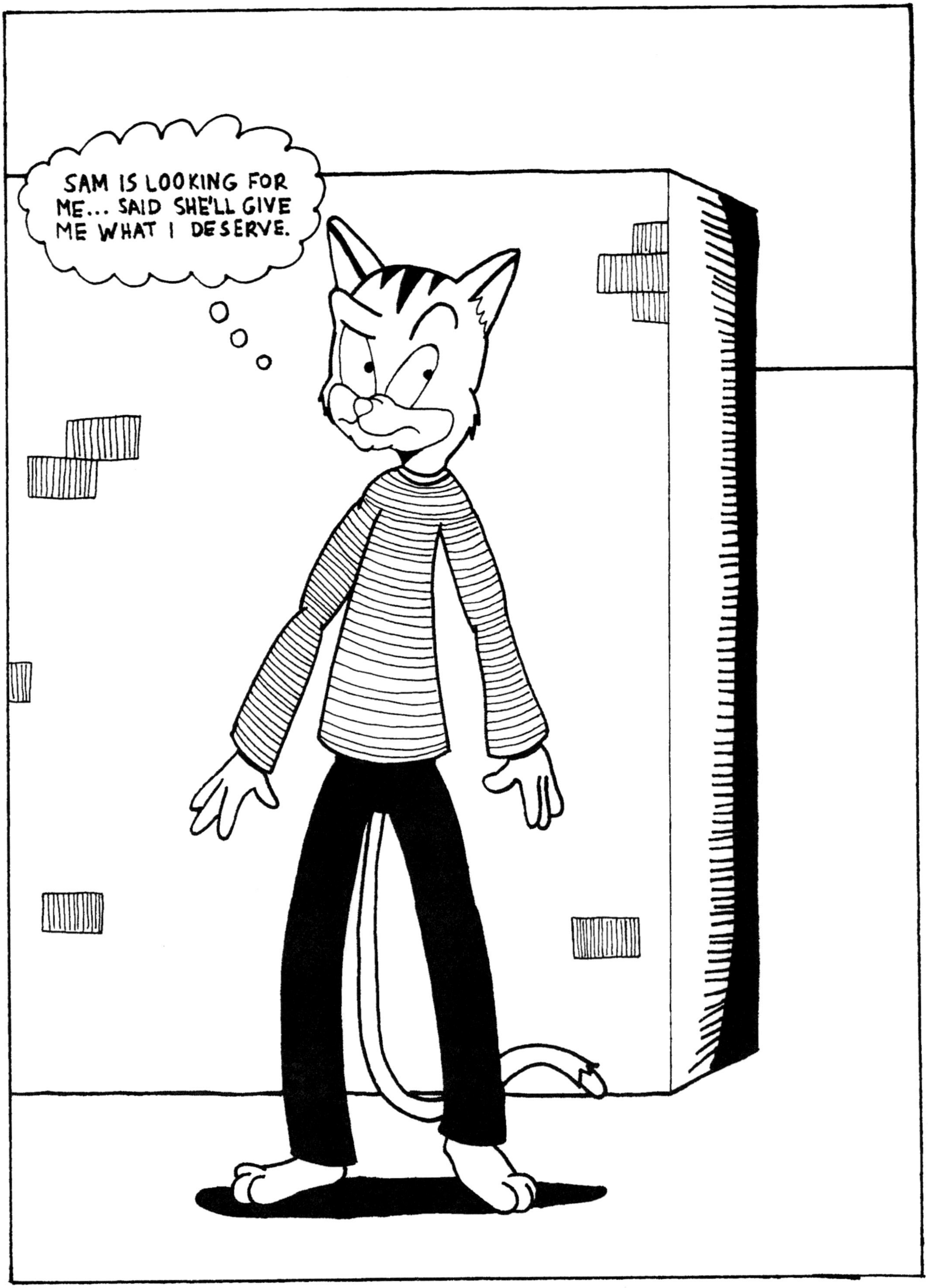
SAM IS LOOKING FOR ME... SAID SHE'LL GIVE ME WHAT I DESERVE.

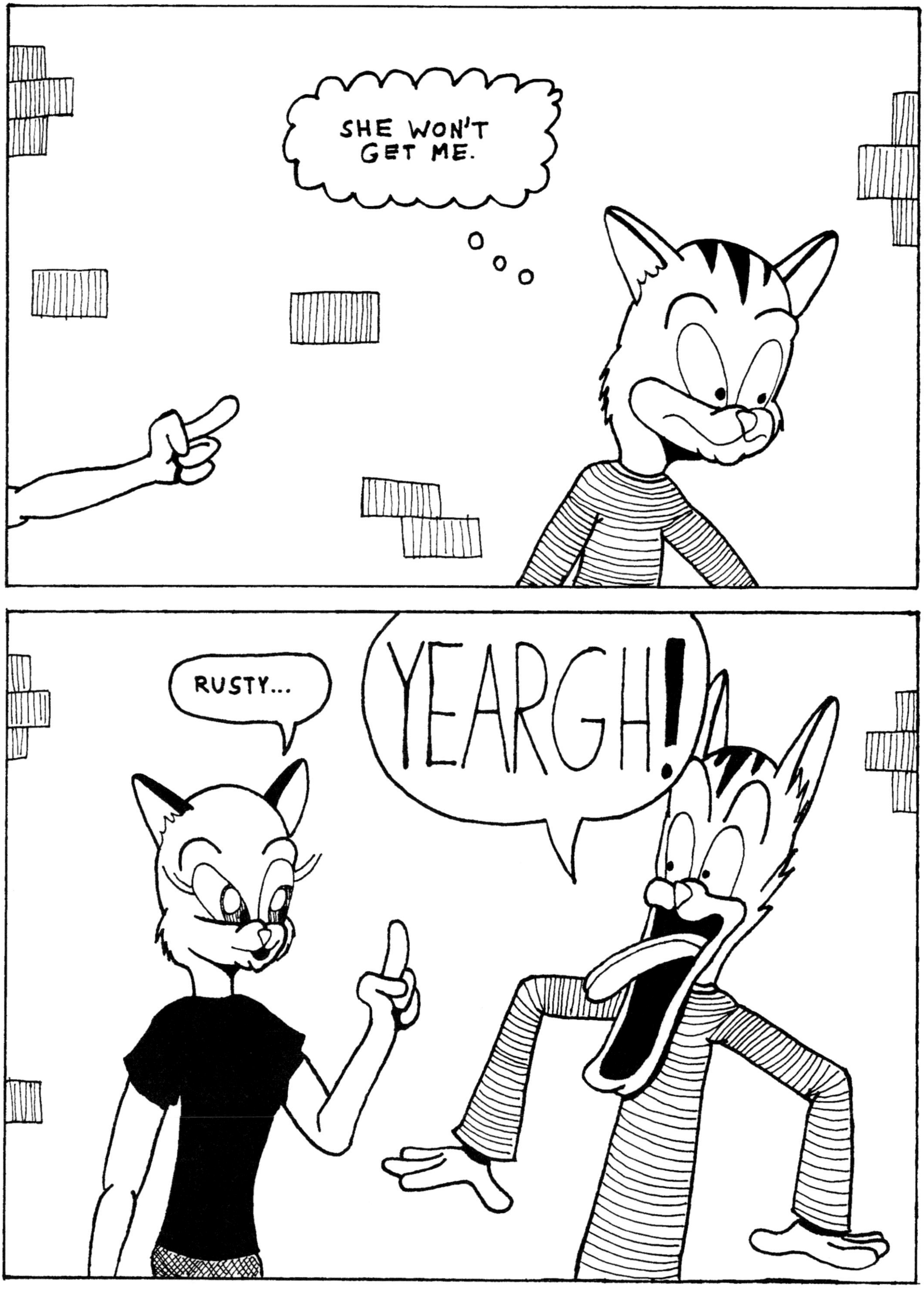
SHE WON'T GET ME.
RUSTY...
YEARGH!

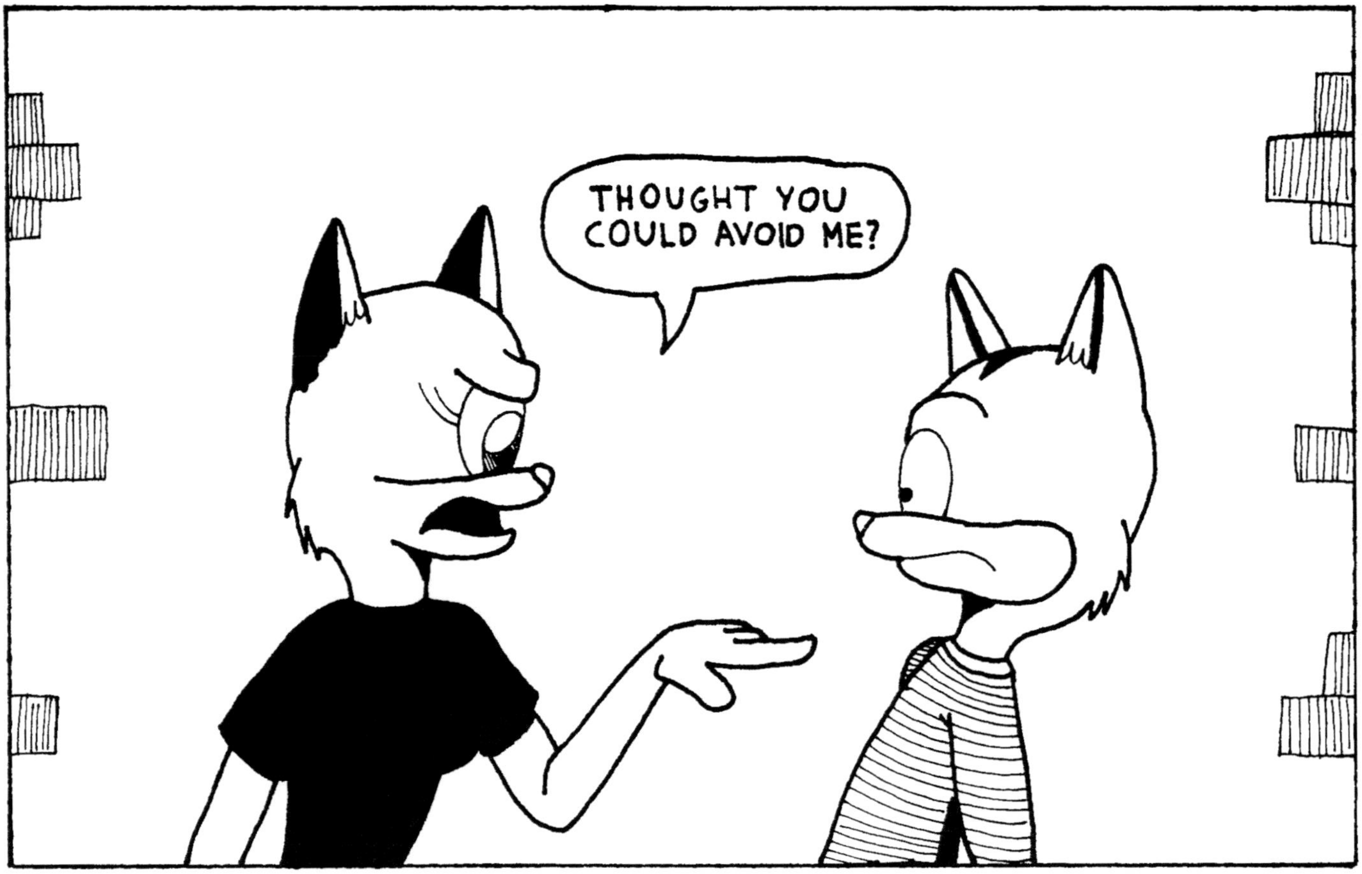
THOUGHT YOU COULD AVOID ME?

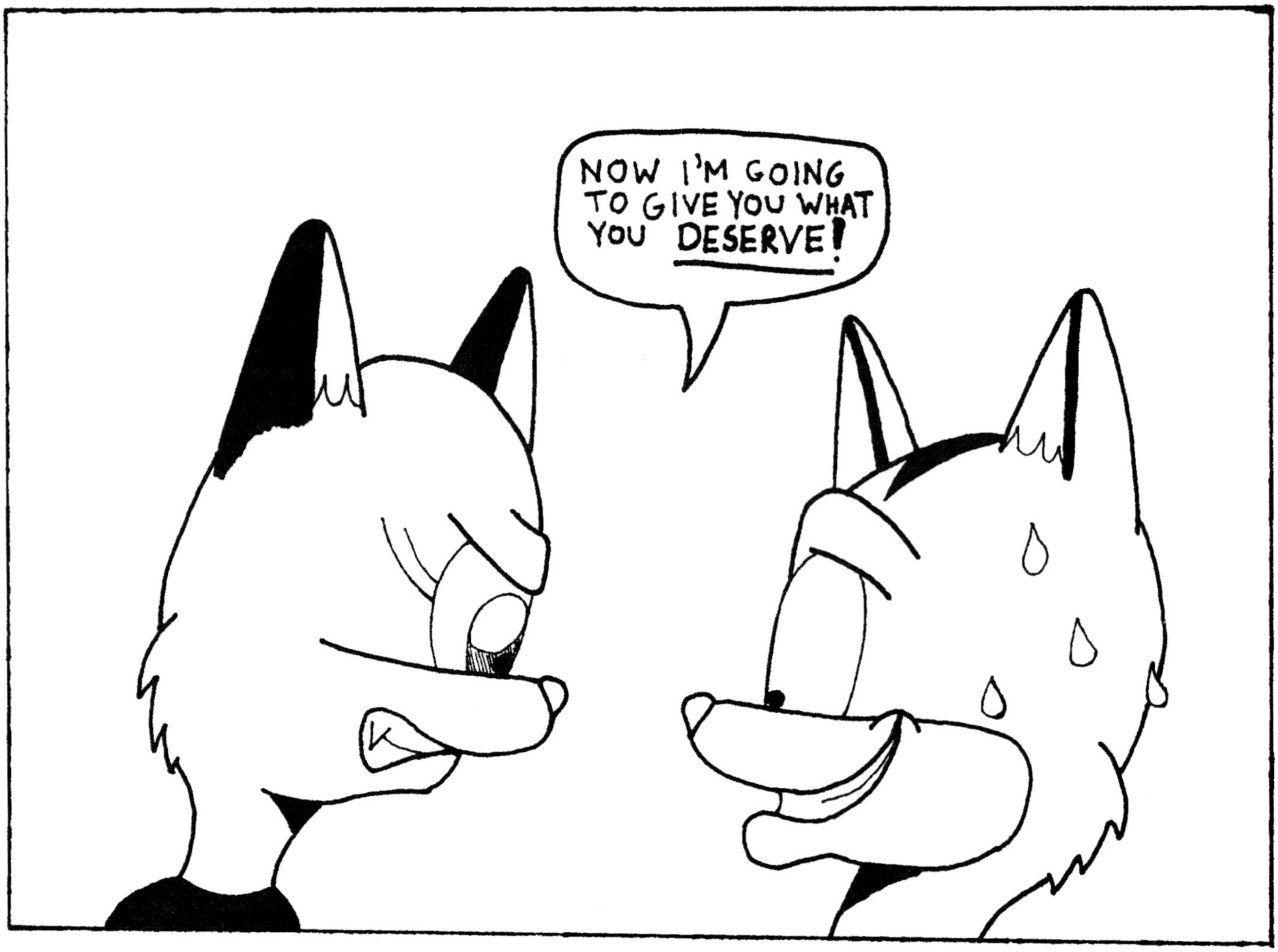
NOW I'M GOING TO GIVE YOU WHAT YOU DESERVE!

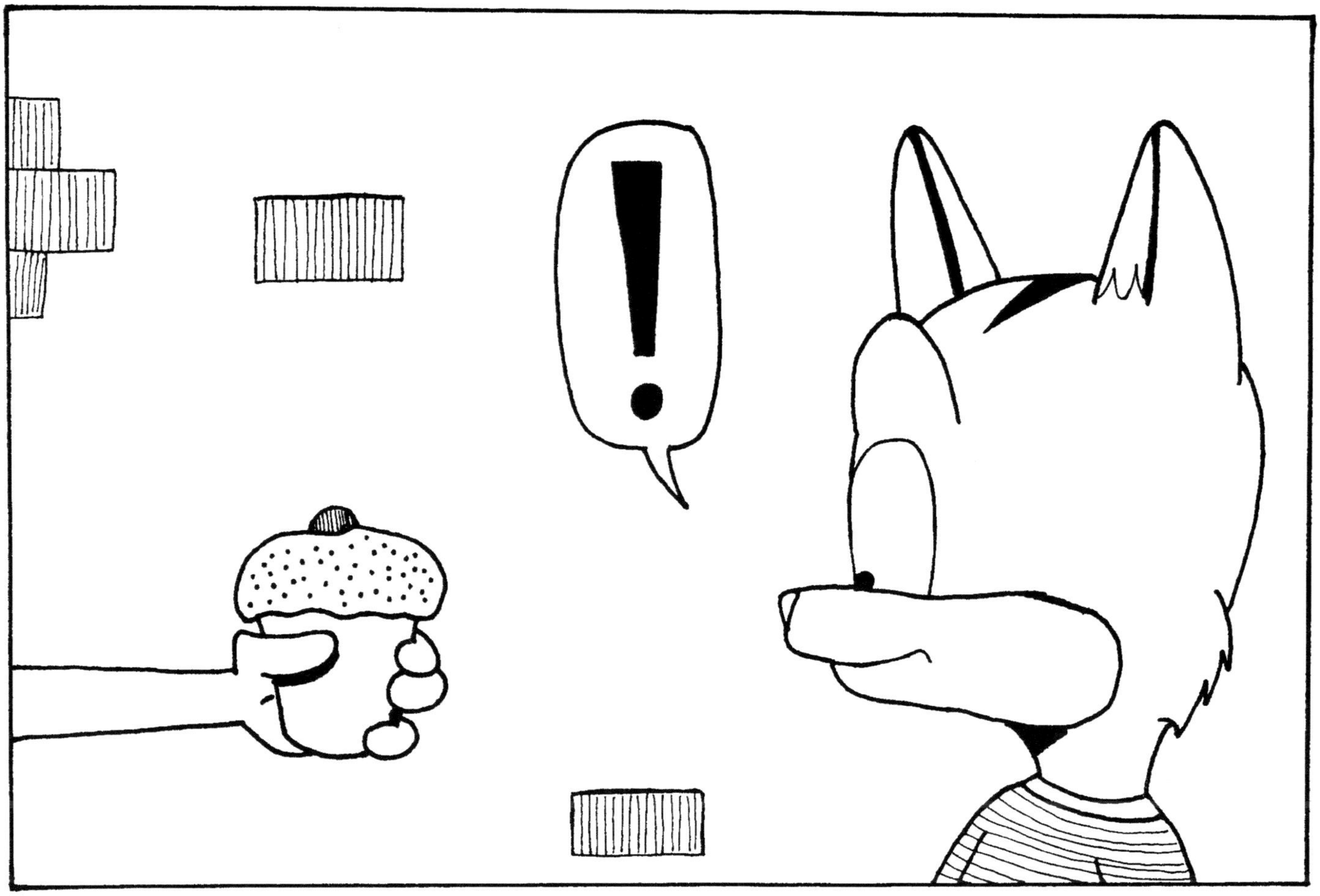
!

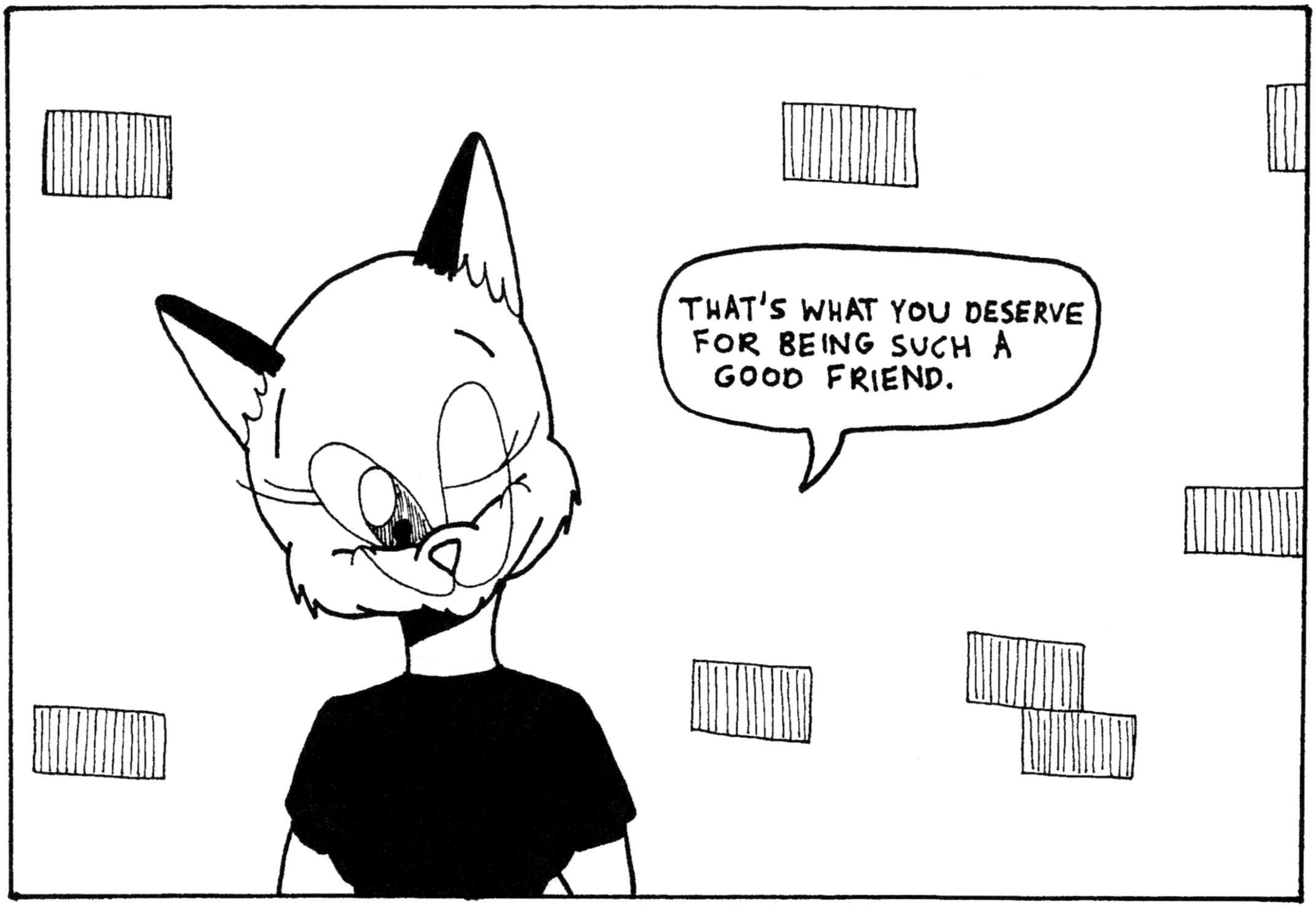
THAT'S WHAT YOU DESERVE FOR BEING SUCH A GOOD FRIEND.

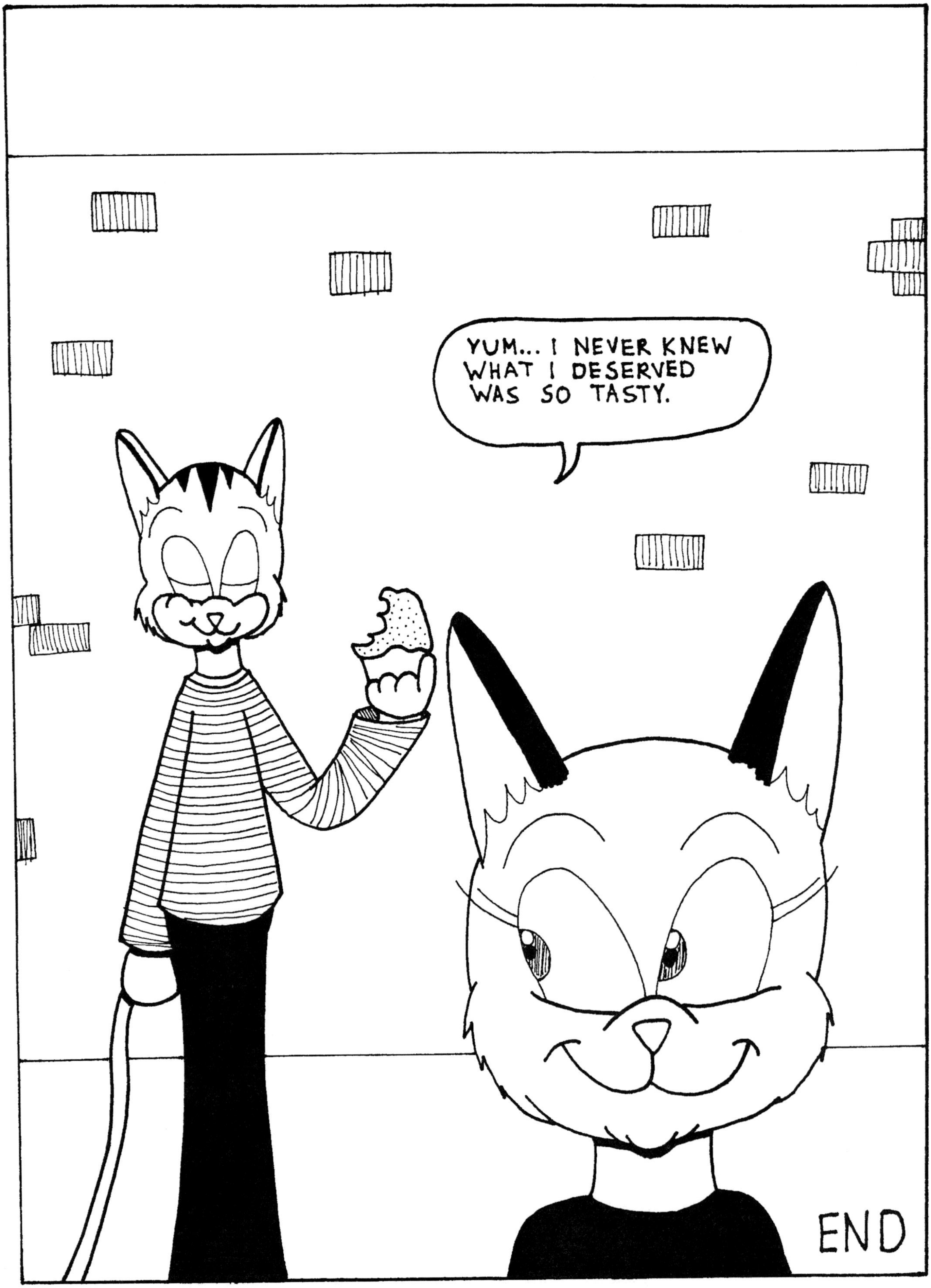
YUM... I NEVER KNEW WHAT I DESERVED WAS SO TASTY.
END

Be sure to visit the **OFFICIAL** blog at **sunnyvillestories.com** and visit the Facebook fan page at **facebook.com/sunnyvillestories**

Comments? Questions? Send them via email to **maxwestart@gmail.com**

Or write to us at:

Different Mousetrap Press LLC
PO Box 1321
Greensboro, NC 27403

ABOUT THE AUTHOR

Max West (born Jan. 4, 1980) grew up reading comics and travelling extensively.

He is a g   'ew York City
and hone   YA   West, Max.   isses at the
School o   Sunnyville Stories Volume
                    1.

He prese   ed States.